PENGUIN BOOKS

CURRY CURRY CURRY

Ranjit Rai was born in 1923 and was educated in England and Lahore. He qualified as a Commercial Accountant from the Hailey College of Commerce. After Partition in 1947 his family moved from Lahore to Delhi.

Ranjit Rai has travelled extensively through Europe, North and South America, China, Tibet, Afghanistan and Central Asia. During his travels he trained with many of the world's great chefs and as a result has mastered the intricacies of several types of international cuisine.

Ranjit Rai owns and manages an energy engineering firm in New Delhi.

RANJIT RAI

Curry Curry Curry

The Heart of Indian Cooking

PENGUIN BOOKS

Penguin Books India (P) Ltd., 210, Chiranjiv Towers, 43, Nehru Place, New Delhi-110 019. India
Penguin Books Ltd., 27 Wrights Lane, London W8 5TZ, UK
Penguin Books USA Inc., 375 Hudson Street, New York, N.Y. 10014, USA
Penguin Books Australia Ltd., Ringwood, Victoria, Australia
Penguin Books Canada Ltd., 10 Alcorn Avenue, Suite 300, Toronto, Ontario M4V 3B2. Canada
Penguin Books (NZ) Ltd., 182-190 Wairau Road, Auckland 10, New Zealand

First published by Penguin Books (India) Limited, 1990

10 9 8 7 6 5 4 3

Copyright © Ranjit Rai, 1990

Made and printed in India by Ananda Offset Private Ltd., Calcutta

*This book is dedicated to my
late father, Aftab Rai—
a perfect gentleman
and a perfect cook.*

CONTENTS

CONTENTS

ACKNOWLEDGEMENTS

In order to write a cookery book, one must share the text and the recipes with both friends and critics. Their advice has been of the utmost value.

My foremost acknowledgement is to my friend, Durga Prasad Mohlay, who has been associated with the book from the beginning. He has painstakingly checked and verified facts and figures, and monitored the typing of the manuscript, its assembly and structure. His sons, Rajiv and Sanjeev, professional five star cooks helped in testing the recipes.

Enough cannot be said for the help from my own family. My wife, Kamla helped to 'murder my darlings' and constantly watched my progress with anxiety and expectation. My daughter, Anuradha and my daughter-in-law, Purnima regularly cooked recipes from the book to see whether they worked!

I am really grateful to my sister, Baroness Shreela Flather and her family — her husband Gary Flather and their son Paul Flather. Gary chastened the language and put on the dictaphone forty pages of comments which proved invaluable. Paul who is a journalist, read the book from the point of view of the buyer and gave original suggestions about the new techniques used in the book.

I am indebted to the faculty, the Director, Dr Amla, the former Director, Dr Parpia and the Area Coordinator, Dr Rajalakshmi at the Food and Technology Research Institute, Mysore. The late Dr V.S. Govindaraja (a world authority on spices) also connected with the Institute, gave me valuable background on the origin of curry and its evolution and gifted me many papers on spices. I was extremely upset when he passed away before the book could be published.

Then there are friends who willingly contributed to special recipes in the book. Mrs Mariam Bilgrami contributed traditional Hyderabadi recipes and Mrs Shikha Misra who contributed recipes from Bengal.

There are others to whom I am grateful. Dr F. Konrad, a gourmet, was one of those who insisted that I write a cookery book — else it would mean that I was being lazy. Vivika Abraham, who was with the BBC, read the book and corrected errors and omissions.

My reverence to Dr D.D. Swami of the Jamia Millia University, who gave of his invaluable time to explain original meanings of Arabic and Persian words currently used in Indian cooking.

Special thanks to M.M. Chopra who often sat up all night to type and re-type on the word processor in order to correct and re-correct manuscripts.

9

Finally, I am most grateful to my friend R.K. Laxman who was one of the first to read the manuscript. He said reading curry books was strange to him, but after having read the manuscript, suggested that I publish it and introduced me to Penguin India.

PREFACE

The idea of writing a book on Indian cooking with international appeal has haunted me for many years.

My friends in India and abroad who have seen me in their kitchen and in my own have persuaded me to set out the techniques that I follow and to write down the recipes that have come down to me from the past generations of my family.

Foremost in my thoughts must be my father, Aftab Rai, whose culinary imagination and remarkable improvising skills were legendary within our family. His name will appear on several of the recipes, since he was their originator. Through him I have felt the strong influence of not only Indian, but Persian and Arabic cooking that he in turn received from his forebears. Entwined amongst these were other influences from Italian, French and Imperial kitchens that were often found at the table of Sir Ganga Ram, his grandfather.

The recipes that I now offer the reader derive their appeal and elegance from the exquisite blend of spices and many other selective ingredients.

The generic term 'spices' includes herbs and condiments which have from time immemorial grown on Indian soil and these have been readily available to the cooks of this land. It is no wonder that they have been put to such excellent use.

There are recipes handed down within the family, from friends, and some which are creations of my own. All of them embody the history and the romance of diverse flavours.

I do hope that this book will help in the understanding of the principal components and assembly of curry.

BON APPETIT!

April 1990   *Ranjit Rai*
New Delhi

11

INTRODUCTION

India is a home to many religions, cultures, castes and creeds, where the climates vary from temperate to tropical to near equatorial, where a variety of vegetables and lentils are found in abundance. All kinds of meat, fish and fowl are available. Naturally, the eating habits of the people vary greatly. Some eat meat, others do not. For some pork is forbidden, for others eating beef is a sacrilege. Some eat fish and no meat. Many forgo tubers, while some avoid roots. Yet the concept of curry is common to all these people, and the variety is absolutely amazing.

The word curry is universally used for any recipe consisting of vegetables, fish, chicken and/or meat, seasoned with various herbs and condiments which give the characteristic flavour and taste and enhance the texture. It probably originated from the Tamil *kari* meaning a blend of spices cooked with vegetables. It is believed that the 18th century British General Clive, when in South India, added meat and water to the kari, thus making a sauce of turmeric and other strong spices. This apparently was the genesis of the Madras curry.

To some the title *Curry Curry Curry* may conjure up images of red, hot chillies and curry powders. It is a mistaken notion that the curry is necessarily hot and corrosive. It is not, though an addition of extra hot peppers does make a curry hot. Traditionally, at home and at regular catering places curries are only marginally seasoned with chillies. Enterprising newcomers to the world of curry need not fear the pungent or hot curry, and neither should they be misled by the common belief that curries are difficult to make.

The spices and herbs that go into the making of the curry masalas are several, but there are 4 to 5 basic ones that form an essential ingredient of the masalas. These are turmeric, coriander, cumin, chilli and ginger. In the recipes the measures of every spice or herb used is given. A mixture of 2 or more of the herbs makes the masala, which is the primary ingredient that endows the curry with a unique flavour. The correct balance is the primary factor in the preparation of curries; mixing of the spices and the use of the masalas. It is very essential to achieve the right balance in the mixing proportions of spices and herbs used in the masalas. The ingredients and the cooking time should be carefully controlled.

The use of spices, herbs and masalas has been explained in every recipe along with the cooking stages where these should be used in the curry.

Some recipes do not have any cooking stages. These are mostly composite recipes like biryani, etc. Some recipes are based on European cooking techniques, such as the egg curries and batter fried dishes. But all these have curry spices. The curry mixtures, while unique to each family, differ in their formulation, because of the availability of different types of spices and the innovations introduced by each cook.

The herbs and spices have been widely used in the traditional methods of Indian medicine. Turmeric prevents ulceration. Nutmeg is excellent for mitigating diarrhoea if taken freshly ground with a little milk. Chillies contain vitamin K which assists blood coagulation. They are also a rich source of vitamins A and C. Cinnamon, mint and ginger have essential oils which aid digestion and can at times prevent diorrhoea. They are used in carminative mixtures. Clove oil for toothache and dental asepscis is still used all over the world.

It should be noted that apart from some exceptional brands, ready-made curry powders are never acceptable to serious cooks. Most brands are usually fortified with flour, food colours, indifferent qualities of spices—all of which are then over-powdered with chillies. Not only is it cheaper to combine the herbs and spices oneself, it also enables one to control the quality of ingredients and the proportions of the herbs and spices in the masala. By and large, spices are now available all over the world in reliable, special stores and come with standard specifications that can be conveniently followed.

It is not known yet as to where, why and how spices and herbs came to be added to the various dishes. But from all available sources it appears that most of them grew as cultigens and were first identified in India. This is supported by the fact that many spices and herbs were well-known in India for their therapeutic value. A detailed account of their importance is discussed in the chapter on spices. Ayurveda, the Indian school of medicine, deals in detail with their extensive use.

Most of the curries given are traditional, with some variation. Some recipes have been innovated from other kitchens of the world, embellished with the spices that constitute the curry. As the titles and the introductions to some recipes will indicate, they were made on the spot in various places of the world during my travels.

For convenience the weights and measures are given in the Metric, British and the American systems. The heating grades are given for the gas and electric stoves. Though a separate chapter discusses the utensils in the Indian kitchen, these are not quite necessary — a good heavy-bottomed pan and a ladle of any kind for stirring is sufficient to prepare these curries. For the curries, primarily it is the control of the heat and the application of the masalas that matter. An interesting observation is that the Kalibangan civilization of 6000 BC, prior to the Harrappan culture, used every kind of cooking vessel in use today the world over.

Each and every recipe in this book has been tried and tested by professional cooks and also by my friends and relatives. Yet these could be improvised upon and further refined to personal taste.

The sequence of the cooking stages used here has always existed in the preparation of the curries, but has never been expicitely stated in recipes. I find that these stages make it much easier to follow the method and simplify greatly the making of the recipe.

On Spices

It has been established by many authorities that the flavour of food constitutes the sense of taste and the sense of smell. Whereas the taste buds are sensors on the tongue the smell, or aromas and odours have sensors at the root of the nose. Their combined effect produces flavour.

The basic tastes have been defined as salty, sweet, bitter and pungent. As for aromas there are no basic ones. Each is distinctly different from the other. In the ancient times people did not differentiate between food and medicine. They believed that food was both diet and medicine. Because of the therapeutic value of the major spices, curry in itself is a protection against spoilage and contamination while aiding digestion. In the Indian medical system, it was widely acknowledged that spices and herbs when added selectively to certain meats and vegetables reduced the formation of gas while promoting digestion. We now tend to use spices and herbs for curries as a matter of course without knowing their significance in the Indian cuisine. Commenting on the therapeutic value of spices and herbs it is recognized that ginger prevents dyspepsia, garlic controls cholesterol and hypertension (this is the reason why the Mughal or red meat oriental kitchen is full of garlic), onions, fenugreek, mint and pepper are germifuges and often act as anti-histamines.

Spices optimize both taste and aroma, and for this reason are the essential alchemy for generating flavours in cooking. Spices have there-

15

fore played a very important role in our national history and economy and it has sometimes created havoc for the spice trading nations. There appears to be no other commodity which brings in so much money for so little in weight and volume. Imagine its value in terms of 'shipping space'. Empires have been settled and unsettled by the spice trade. Maritime wars have been fought between the European nations to keep the spice sea lanes open. Taxes have been demanded by payment in spices. Ships had to be loaded with pepper for the 'King' for fear of death. Today, spices means curry as far as the Indians are concerned. Nevertheless the history of spices has a frightening record of imperialism, avarice and shameless naval rivalry.

Loewenfed and Back in their book on *Herbs and Spices* very aptly say:

> How did the Phoenicians suddenly become so powerful, and how could even a small city like Venice employ an army with such a strategist as Othello? What made it possible for the Dutch people, being a small nation, to develop at one time a great empire? Why were Vasco da Gama and Christopher Colombus so interested to find a new sea route to India? How could it happen that the British East India Company became a political power? The answer is spices, spices and again spices.

From the London Times the magazine *Punch* reproduces the following:

THE THING FROM OUTER SPICE

> What first led Europeans to spread all over the globe? Was it religion and the rise of capitalism? Or was it more to do with pepper, which was essential to mask the flavour of salted meat, stinking fish and boring vegetables?

Despite all the multi-dimensional importance of spices to the world it is only now that their culinary importance is growing in acceptance outside its original home.

The glossary on spices at the end of the book deals briefly with the history, properties and use of spices in food and medicine.

Another glossary, included at the end, which gives the food values including energy balance, calories and mineral and vitamin content of spices, will surprise many with their energy resources.

16

On Masalas

The word *masala* is thought to have been derived from the Hindi word *masalna* meaning to rub between two surfaces: if green herbs are used it becomes a paste, while the use of dry spices makes a powder. No two cooks agree on the proportions and constituents of any *masala* but the essential spices used for *masala* are distinctly identified. There might be another derivation from the Arabic word *asal* meaning real, and *masal* meaning the real thing.

The word *garam masala* appears in every Indian cookery book and perhaps also on every page. The literal translation means hot masala, The translation is literal and ends there. In fact the word *garam* means hot as used in the therapeutic sense as capable of catalysing heat in the stomach to promote digestion. It is not to be confused with pungency as that of chillies or thermal heat. In fact some of the spices in the *garam masala* have a sweet after-taste and at best many are highly aromatic, astringent, slightly bitter and above all palatable.

Of all the masalas the *garam masala* is the most common and omnipresent at the finishing stage. It contains a lot of aromatic spices which gives the characteristic aroma and flavour to the dish.

Other masalas include the *khara masala* which consists of whole or coarsely pounded spices as against powdered spices and herbs.

HOW TO USE THE BOOK

Masalas Used in the Various Stages of Cooking

The basic ingredients responsible for giving that unique flavour to curries are the masalas used in it, which consist mainly of spices including herbs and condiments.

Different masalas are used at the various stages of cooking curries. First there is the masala for the marinade. After that is the masala used for the singe-fry. Then there is the masala for the follow-up stage, after which is the masala used for the cooking stage. At the finishing stage there is another masala. Then, finally, at the end is the garnish masala.

These various stages of adding the different masalas have been formulated after many years of cooking and observation. To a great extent this system makes it easier to understand the technique of making Indian curries. The curries may have one or more these stages of adding the masalas, and not necessarily all of them. The more complete and exotic dishes will have at least four or five of these stages.

It may be observed in the recipes that the spices, herbs and other ingredients in the masalas used in different stages are interchangeable. Thus, the masalas used for the follow-up in one recipe may be used for the singe-fry in another.

The quantities of spices and herbs used varies with each recipe.

The masalas may be in dry, roasted, or ground form (either finely or coarsely powdered); or may be in the paste form. The paste form of the masala generally includes garlic, ginger, onions, fresh coriander leaves and green chillies.

The masala for the MARINADE includes a tenderizer such as yoghurt, and flavouring and colouring spices or herbs such as turmeric, garlic or onions.

SINGE-FRYING is coined in this book for the first time. It is an apt description of the process that is vital for cooking Indian curries. In India this process is called *tadaka* or *bagaar*. To singe-fry, the masala is sprinkled into hot ghee or oil, and it produces a hissing and spluttering sound for a few seconds. The masalas used here are usually finely or coarsely pounded spices or herbs. Also, it is to be noted that singe-frying is always done on high heat.

In the FOLLOW-UP stage, the masala used is usually a paste made up of onion, ginger, garlic, coriander and green chillies, or dry spices. As a rule

19

this is followed by adding the main ingredient of the dish.

The DURING-COOKING masala is added while the main ingredient is being cooked. It normally consists of aromatic spices such as cardamoms, bay leaves, and some ground mace or nutmeg.

The FINISHING masala is added after the curry is nearly done, and normally consists of garam masala.

GARNISH masala is sprinkled on the curry after it is completely ready for serving in a serving bowl. It normally consists of green coriander leaves, green chillies, chopped onions and grated coconut.

No two cooks agree on the proportions and the constituents of any masala but the essential spices used for the masala are distinctly identified.

All masalas have 5 to 6 ingredients common to them. The more complex of the masalas may have upto 20 ingredients.

The fixing of masalas, their proportions and timing are solely at the discretion of the person making the dish. But it is absolutely essential that the curry is not over-spiced, because this will obliterate the taste of the main ingredient of the curry.

The proportions of the masalas used and the method of preparation have been discussed for every dish separately, but normally the constituents of the masalas for the stages are:

Masala for the MARINADE

yoghurt	garlic paste
lemon juice	salt
turmeric	pepper
ginger paste	

Masala for the SINGE-FRY: Freshly ground spices are preferred, but standard ground spice powder may be used.

cumin: powdered & whole	curry leaves, green
coriander powder	asafoetida
turmeric powder	carum
chilli powder	nigella
fenugreek: powdered & whole	mustard seed
dry red chillies: whole	

20

Masala for the FOLLOW-UP stage (pastes following singe-fry): These pastes are freshly prepared either by the traditional method or in the food-processor.

garlic, cloved	poppy seed
ginger root	pinenut
onions	almonds
green chillies, whole	hazelnut
green coriander leaves	coconut

Masala for the DURING-COOKING stage

bay leaves	*amchoor*
cardamom, large brown	saffron
cardamom, regular	

Masala for the FINISHING stage: The *garam masala* used has the following ingredients depending on the kind required.

normal black peppercorns

cumin	cloves
cardamoms	cinnamon

aromatic cinnamon

nutmeg	cloves
cardamoms	

special black peppercorns

cumin	nutmeg
cardamoms	mace
cloves	black cumin (shah zeera)
cinnamon	

Masala for GARNISH:

green coriander, scissor-cut	garlic, through press
spring onions, finely-cut	ginger, grated
green chillies, scissor-cut	nuts & peels

The sequence of the curries in the book has been such that, every sub-section of the book begins with the recipe having the least number of cooking stages followed by more and more elaborate recipes with more stages of cooking. Thus one may easily select the recipe depending on the time and the availability of herbs and spices. It is best to have the various masalas ready at hand in separate vessels before starting to prepare the curry, so that they are easily accessible at the respective stages of preparation as defined by the system used.

Cooking Time and Other Variants

Anyone having a fair knowledge of cooking will appreciate the need for flexibility with regard to the timing, use of salt and water, and the use of basic ingredients and herbs and spices.

It is very natural to expect a dish to turn out exactly as described in the recipe. This might not happen due to various reasons. The hardness of water varies from one place to another, and the more the hardness the longer the main ingredient takes to soften.

Cooking time of the dish also depends on the atmospheric pressure of a place. In low pressure areas, as high altitudes, the boiling point of water is lower consequently increasing the cooking time.

Sometimes the cooking appliances are not caliberated for degrees of heat. In such cases guaging the cooking time becomes even more difficult.

The approximate cooking time has been mentioned for each recipe. This may be adjusted according to experience.

The salinity of water, because of impurities and additives, also affects the dish. In the recipes therefore, the approximate measures of salt and water have been stated. These may be increased or decreased depending on the dish.

It is always better to under-salt the curry than to over-salt it. The same goes for pepper and chillies. More of them may be added later to the dish if required.

The main ingredient of the curry—eggs, vegetables, fish, meat, chicken—could be different, depending on the source. Gourds and marrows in India take longer to soften than in Europe.

A skewer or toothpick may be used to check if the meat or vegetables are done. This is more important for the meat as it should never be over-done or under-done in the oriental recipes.

22

The pungency index of chillies varies greatly though a particular type of chilli may be specified.

One should not hesitate to improvise, innovate, add to or take away from the given recipes to 're-mould' it nearer to the hearts' desire.

Care should be taken while handling the chillies and hot masalas—hands should be properly washed and wiped after handling them.

Kitchen paper is used to soak oil. Newspapers can be used for the purpose, but they should not be glazed.

Abbreviations

C	Centigrade	lb	pound
cm	centimetre	ml	millilitre
F	Fahrenheit	mm	millimetre
fl oz	fluid ounce	oz	ounce
g	gram	pt	pint
"	inch	tbsp	tablespoon
kg	kilogram	tsp	teaspoon
l	litre		

System and Conversion of Measures

In this book the measures are given in the British, Metric and American systems. All measures are level unless otherwise specified.

A British cup is a tea cup measuring 5 fl oz or 150 ml. An American (US) cup is 8 fl oz or 225 ml.

All spoon measures are flat. One tablespoon (tbsp) is 15 ml, and one teaspoon (tsp) is 5 ml. One salt spoon is about 2 ml.

The various quantities indicated in the recipes on spices and ingredients need not be taken as pharmacy measures. In Indian cooking a little more or a little less will not alter the dish.

Though the approximate quantity of salt, chillies and water proportions have been indicated, these can be increased or lessened according to discretion.

Terms Requiring Explanation

al dente:
literally 'to the tooth' in Italian. It means cooked until almost tender but still has resistance to the bite.

julienne cut:
cutting meat or vegetables like fine matchsticks of thickness approximately 3 mm and length 4-5 cm.

marinade:
a combination of tenderizer, yoghurt, lemon juice, salt and seasonings (ginger, garlic, pepper), to which turmeric may be added,

parboil:
means to partly boil. To boil until almost cooked but not completely.

purée:
means to make a smooth consistency by mashing or blending.

Curry Soups
and Sauces

Curry Soup: Mulligatawny

This is a lentil soup appearing in menus the world over. It uses the Madras curry (*rasam*) as the flavouring, and lentils as the main ingredient. Mulligatawny gets its name from the Tamil *mullagu* meaning pepper and *tanni* meaning water—literally 'pepper water soup'. This is my version.

Serves 8–10 soup bowls
Cooking Time: 60–70 minutes

British	Metric	Ingredients	American
14 oz (3 cups)	400 g	lentils (*masur ki dal*)	1¾ cups
4	4	onions, medium, cut in half	4
1 tbsp	15 g	salt, to taste	1 tbsp
2⅝ pt (10 cups)	1.5 l	water	6½ cups
11 oz	300 g	roast meat, cut in ⅓" cube pieces	11 oz
during-cooking masala			
8 oz	200 g	butter	1 cup
⅓ oz	10 g	curry leaves (*kari patta*)	⅓ cup
1 tbsp	6 g	coriander powder	1 tbsp
1 tsp	2 g	ginger powder	1 tsp
1 tsp	2 g	chilli powder	1 tsp
6	6	green chillies, whole, slit at the ends	6
1 tbsp	10 g	turmeric powder	1 tbsp
finishing masala			
1 fl oz (5 tsps)	25 g	garlic purée	⅛ cup
garnish masala			
as per taste		fresh lime juice	as per taste
as per taste		Tabasco sauce	as per taste

27

18 oz	500 g	boiled rice	18 oz

Method

Boil the lentils (*dal*) in the water together with the onions cut in half, for 30–45 minutes. Add water to keep the consistency as of a heavy gravy. Then, using blender, make a sauce of the lentils and onions. Add salt, keep on slow fire, adding butter and the *during-cooking masala*. Let the soup boil gently for about 30 minutes till the butter is released to the top.

The consistency should be even—not too thick, not too thin. Boil away water if thin, and add water if too thick—getting it close to the consistency of thick tomato soup. Add the *finishing masala* and stir.

Add roast meat cubes of any kind—lamb with a little fat preferred—dropping them with a ladle gently into the soup and keep stirring. Let it cook on low heat for about 10 minutes. Take soup bowls and put 2 or 3 tablespoons of boiled rice in each. If preferable serve the rice separately. Remove the curry leaves from the soup and pour the soup into the soup bowls.

It is better if the soup is served by the host/hostess, so that each bowl has an even distribution of meat and soup. Self service is fine as well.

For *garnishing*, squeeze lemon and add a few drops of Tabasco sauce for the ultimate flavour.

NOTE: For the roast meat use the leftover roasts or roast a leg of lamb, cool it, and cube it as indicated.

This is a meal in itself. Some of my friends have used fish instead of meat or chicken leftovers, the soup then takes on the description of mutton-fish-chicken Mulligatawny.

Mushrooms and/or home-made cottage cheese (*panir*) (pg 281), lightly sautéd, may be used for vegetarians.

Mixed Bean Curry Soup

A bean soup of great antiquity. It is served in India, Morocco, Egypt, Turkey and parts of old Armenia. The Indian version has the curry spices. It makes a hearty meal in itself.

Serves 6–8
Preparation Time: 6–8 hours
Cooking Time: 55–60 minutes

British	Metric	Ingredients	American
9 oz	250 g	dried mixed beans	9 oz
2	2	lemons, juice of	2
4 oz	100 g	butter	½ cup
7 oz	200 g	lamb or veal cubes, cut in cubes of ⅘"(2 cm)	7 oz
2⅝ pt (10 cups)	1.5 l	water(to be used several times as indicated)	6½ cups
singe-fry masala			
1 tsp	2 g	coriander powder	1 tsp
1 tsp	2.75 g	cumin powder	1 tsp
½ tsp	1 g	chilli powder	½ tsp
follow-up masala			
½ tsp	1.5 g	black pepper powder	½ tsp
1 tsp	3.5 g	turmeric powder	1 tsp
during-cooking masala			
2 tsps	10 g	salt, to taste	2 tsps
8	8	onions, quartered	8
		strained water—leftover from boiled beans	
4	4	tomatoes, large, puréed	4
6	6	bouillon consomme cubes	6

5 fl oz (1 cup)	150 ml	water	$\frac{5}{8}$ cup
		finishing masala	
1 tbsp(heaped)	15 g	white flour (*maida*)	1 tbsp (heaped)
5 fl oz (1 cup)	150 ml	water	$\frac{5}{8}$ cup
		garnish masala	
1	1	saffron powder, sachet of	1

Method

Soak beans in 9 cups ($3\frac{1}{2}$ pt/2 l) of water, preferably for 6–8 hours.

Boil tomatoes. Purée, strain and keep aside.

Strain soaked beans and add $4\frac{1}{2}$ cups ($1\frac{3}{4}$ pt /1 l) of water and cook for 30 minutes or till tender. Do not throw away the water—keep aside for the during-cooking masala. Drain again, add lemon juice and keep aside. Bring butter to foaming in a large cooking pan. Add the *singe-fry masala* followed a few seconds later by the *follow-up masala*. Immediately after the turmeric splutters add the meat cubes and the quartered onion, and all the beans. Stir fry for 3–5 minutes. Add the *during-cooking masala* and the leftover water of the beans. Let it simmer for 10–15 minutes.

After simmering, check consistency of soup—do not worry if it appears thin. Add the *finishing masala* and stir till the soup thickens.

Before serving, add the *garnish masala* and stir gently.

Serve in preheated soup bowls, preferably white.

NOTE:　The beans used may be of any kind—the more multicoloured they are the more interesting the dish is likely to be.

　　　　It is best to crush the soup cubes with the hands before adding.

Madras Curry Sauce

There are basically three flavours in curry sauces—Persian, Moghul and Madras. The evolution has been from the earliest sauce, which is the Madras curry sauce. The advantage of these sauces is that they can be kept in air-tight bottles in the fridge and used whenever required. This dish thus makes an 'instant curry'!

Serves 3
Cooking Time: 15–20 minutes
plus about 30 minutes to parboil the vegetables, meat takes 45 minutes to parboil, fish and poultry take lesser time

British	Metric	Ingredients	American
3 fl oz ($\frac{1}{2}$ cup)	75–80 ml	ghee or peanut oil	$\frac{3}{8}$ cup
singe-fry masala			
2 tbsps	12 g	coriander powder	2 tbsps
1 tbsp	8.25 g	fenugreek (*methi*) powder	1 tbsp
1 tbsp	8 g	cumin (*zeera*) powder	1 tbsp
1 tbsp	6 g	chilli powder	1 tbsp
1 tsp	3.25 g	black pepper powder	1 tsp
1 tbsp	10 g	turmeric powder	1 tbsp
follow-up masala (as paste)			
1 tsp	5 g	ginger	1 tsp
1 tsp	5 g	curry leaves	1 tsp
1 tbsp	2 g	green coriander, leaves only	1 tbsp
during-cooking masala			
$\frac{1}{2}$ pt (2 cups)	300 ml	coconut milk (pg 283)	$1\frac{1}{4}$ cups
3 fl oz ($\frac{1}{2}$ cup)	75 ml	tamarind, soaked and pulped (pg 282)	$\frac{3}{8}$ cup

2 tsps	10 g	salt, to taste	2 tsps
5 fl oz (1 cup)	150 ml	water	$\frac{5}{8}$ cup
1 tbsp	7 g	cornflour	1 tbsp

Method

Take a deep saucepan, and pour the ghee or oil into it. Keep on high heat and add all the *singe-fry masala* with the turmeric added last. When it stops sizzling, immediately add the *follow-up masala*.

Stir fry for 3–5 minutes till ghee or oil is released. Now mix the *during-cooking masala* to make a smooth sauce and add gently into the saucepan. Simmer for 10 minutes—stirring once or twice—on medium heat. Do not boil. When the fat is released take off the fire.

NOTE: If required to add any uncooked vegetable or meat, do so after the follow-up masala and cook till the vegetable or meat is done. Increase salt in the ratio of 1 teaspoon for $\frac{1}{2}$ kg of vegetables or meat. Follow the masala sequences as given. This quantity is adequate for $\frac{1}{2}$ kg (18 oz) of the main ingredient.

If stored in the fridge this curry sauce may be served by adding parboiled vegetables, meat, fish or poultry and keeping in the oven on medium heat.

Moghul Curry Sauce

This curry sauce is amongst the most commonly used in the staple 'home curries' in India. The origin of the sauce dates back to around the time of the Moghul Emperor Jehangir (1605–27 AD). Up until that time, tomatoes had not arrived in the Indian kitchen. They were brought by the Portuguese to Jehangir's court along with the pumalo (the forerunners of the grapefruit) tomatoes and sapota (*chickoo*).

Those who know of Moghul history will remember that Jehangir had a Rajput Hindu mother and that his father was the famous Emperor Akbar (1556–1603 AD). The creation of a curry sauce had much to do with the fact that a Muslim Emperor was the son of a Hindu mother, and the husband of Nur Jehan, the creator of many Indian perfumes (including *ittar*). The flavour created for this curry sauce was so unique and popular that no further innovation or improvement has been necessary.

The Indian spices, both aromatic and others, used by Jehangir's mother, were combined with the tomato and browned onions—and as the saying goes 'when mustard met the sausage history was made', history was made 'when mutton met the Moghul curry sauce'!

Serves 3
Cooking Time: 30–40 minutes
*   plus 15—20 minutes for meat to parboil*

British	Metric	Ingredients	American
5 oz (1 cup)	150 g	ghee, melted	$\frac{5}{8}$ cup
9 oz	250 g	onion rings, cut in medium	9 oz
1	1	garlic, large bulb, cloved	1
singe-fry masala			
1 tbsp	6 g	coriander powder	1 tbsp
1 tsp	2.75 g	cumin powder	1 tsp
1 tbsp	6 g	chilli powder	1 tbsp
1 tsp	3g	turmeric powder	1 tsp
follow-up masala			
2"	5 cm/2 g	cinnamon stick, whole	2"
5	5	cardamoms, large brown	5
3	3	bay leaves (*tejpat*)	3
during-cooking masala			
5 fl oz (1 cup)	150 ml	tomatoes, puréed & strained	$\frac{5}{8}$ cup
8 fl oz (1½ cups)	225 ml	water	1 cup
1 tsp	5 g	salt, to taste	1 tsp
finishing masala			

6	6	cardamoms, small green, finely ground	6
10	10	cloves, finely ground	10
$\frac{1}{2}$ tsp	1.25 g	garam masala	$\frac{1}{2}$ tsp

Method

Purée the tomatoes and strain them through a medium-sized mesh to get rid of the seeds and skin, and keep to one side.

Set aside 5 tablespoons (3 fl oz/75 ml/$\frac{3}{8}$ cup) of ghee for the singe-fry masala.

Pour the remaining ghee in a deep heavy-bottomed saucepan and cook on high heat. Add the onions and brown them. Add garlic cloves after smashing them with the blunt end of a cooking knife. Stir fry for a few minutes and keep the saucepan aside.

In another saucepan take the remaining ghee and bring to high heat. Add all the ingredients of the singe-fry masala, and singe for 30–40 seconds. Add this *singe-fried masala* to the saucepan containing the onion and garlic mixture. Add the *follow-up masala* and stir fry for a minute or two. Then add the *during-cooking masala* and simmer on medium heat for 10–15 minutes, or till ghee is released. Remove from fire, transfer to a serving dish and add the *finishing masala*.

NOTE: If you wish to use vegetables, meat or poultry (no fish goes well with this sauce), add $\frac{1}{2}$ kg (18 oz) of the main ingredient after the follow-up masala and increase salt by 1 tsp (5 g). Cook until the main ingredient is done. Follow the masala sequence as given.

If on the other hand you wish to have sauce handy in the fridge, parboil the main ingredient and increase salt by 1 tsp (5 g). Add to the ready sauce and bake in the oven for 15–25 minutes.

When Babar (1526–30 AD) made a similar sauce he used *ratanjyot* from Kashmir for the reddish colour and *amchoor* souring.

In Europe some strains/varieties of onions do not brown

easily. It is best to strain the chopped or quartered onions half way through fine muslin. Put the strained onion water to one side. The onions will then brown much faster. Add the onion water with during-cooking masala so that the onion flavour is not lost.

Bay leaves are removed before serving.

Persian Curry Sauce

This is amongst the most elegant curry sauces. It uses all the exotic spices, nuts and yoghurt. I am not quite sure why it has come to be known as Persian, since it was certainly the work of Indian cooks. It can be used for any kind of meat, fish or fowl and select vegetables. Since it is a sauce there is no main ingredient such as meat or vegetable.

Serves 3
Cooking Time: 20–30 minutes
          plus 10–20 minutes to cook the vegetables or meat

British	Metric	Ingredients	American
5 oz (1 cup)	150 g	ghee	$\frac{5}{8}$ cup
2 tsps	10 g	salt, to taste	2 tsps
singe-fry masala			
1 tsp	2 g	chilli powder	1 tsp
1 tsp	4g	turmeric powder	1 tsp
follow-up masala 1			
1 tbsp	15 g	ginger paste	1 tbsp
1 tbsp	15 g	garlic paste	1 tbsp
1 tbsp	10 g	poppy seed (*khas khas*) paste	1 tbsp
1 tsp	4.25 g	fenugreek (*methi*) powder	1 tsp
follow-up masala 2			

35

10	10	cardamoms, regular	10
2 tbsps	40 g	almond (I)/hazelnut paste	2 tbsps
		follow-up masala 3	
5 fl oz	150 ml	water	$\frac{5}{8}$ cup
7 oz (1$\frac{1}{3}$ cups)	200 g	yoghurt	$\frac{3}{4}$ cup
1 tsp	2.25 g	cornflour	1 tsp
		finishing masala 3	
2 tbsps	30 ml	cream	2 tbsps
$\frac{1}{2}$ tsp	0.25 g	saffron, soaked in milk	$\frac{1}{2}$ tsp
2 tbsps	30 ml	milk	2 tbsps
		garnish masala	
20		almonds (II), roasted & chopped lengthwise	20

Method

Soak the saffron in 2 tablespoons of milk and keep aside.

Soak and skin almonds (I). Grind to paste and keep aside. If using hazelnuts, grind unroasted into a paste.

Roast almonds (II), and cut in thin slivers lengthwise and keep aside.

Cream yoghurt along with cornflour in a blender for 5–10 seconds and keep aside.

Finely grind all the ingredients in the follow-up masala 1 in a food processor and keep aside.

Bring ghee to high heat in a heavy-bottomed, deep pan. Add the *singe-fry masala* and fry for 10–15 seconds. Add the *follow-up masala 1* immediately and stir fry for 3–4 minutes. Reduce heat. Add the *follow-up masala 2*, and cook on moderate heat for 5–10 minutes till ghee is released. Add the *follow-up masala 3* and salt. Stir gently and simmer for 5–8 minutes.

Before serving add cream to the soaked saffron and mix this gently in the sauce.

Finally, sprinkle the *garnish masala* and serve.

NOTE: This sauce can be used for any pre-cooked meat, fish or chicken by baking in an oven for 5–8 minutes at moderate heat. For a classical curry with Persian sauce, the meat (18 oz/ $\frac{1}{2}$ kg) should be added after the follow-up masala 3. Increase salt by 1 teaspoon and let simmer for 10–20 minutes till meat is done, then follow the recipe.

Hazelnuts can be substituted for almonds. I have tried this and it has proved to be an exciting innovation! However, since almonds are the traditional ingredient, chopped roasted almonds must go on top, even when using hazelnut paste.

Rice Dishes

Rice Dishes

Curried Meat with Rice (*Meat Biryani*): Hyderabad

This is the most popular pulao and the king among meat and rice dishes. Almost certainly it was created in Hyderabad. This recipe is from a friend who is renowned for her biryani. If any family had its way they would have this combination of dry-meat-curry-and-rice pulao every day. It is of utmost importance to use the best quality spices, especially the aromatic ones like saffron, cardamoms and cinnamon.

It is to be noted that this rice and meat composite dish does not conform to the cooking stages as others.

Serves 4–6
Preparation Time: 1 hour
Cooking Time: 60–70 minutes

British	Metric	Ingredients	American
2 lb 13 oz	1¼ kg	pulao meat, cleaned & cut into large pieces	2 lb 13 oz
2¼ lb	1 kg	basmati rice, best quality (washed & soaked in cold water 1 hour before cooking)	5 cups
9 oz (1⅔ cups)	250 g	ghee	1⅛ cups
masala for marinade			
1 tbsp	15 g	ginger paste	1 tbsp
1 tbsp	15 g	garlic paste	1 tbsp
1 tsp	2 g	chilli powder	1 tsp
1 tsp	5 g	salt (I), to taste	1 tsp
9 oz (1½ cups)	250 g	yoghurt, creamed & strained	1 cup
masala for meat			
2	2	green cardamoms, whole	2
½"		12 mm cinnamon(*dalchini*),whole (0.5 g)	½"

41

11 oz	300 g	onions, finely sliced	11 oz
1 pt (4 cups)	600 ml	water	$2\frac{5}{8}$ cups

garam masala (powdered)

4	4	green cardamoms	4
$\frac{1}{2}$"	$1\frac{1}{4}$ cm	cinnamon stick (0.5 g)	$\frac{1}{2}$"
1 tsp	2.5 g	black cumin (*shah zeera*)	1 tsp
2 tsps	10 g	salt (II), to taste	2 tsps

masala for rice

4	4	green cardamoms, whole	4
1 tsp	2.5 g	black cumin (*shah zeera*), whole	1 tsp
2 tsps	10 g	salt (III), to taste	2 tsps

masala for finishing

1 oz ($1\frac{1}{2}$ cups)	30 g	green coriander, leaves only	1 cup
4	4	green chillies, whole	4
3	3	lemons, large, juice of	3
$\frac{1}{2}$ tsp	0.25 g	saffron, soaked in milk	$\frac{1}{2}$ tsp
3 fl oz ($\frac{1}{2}$ cup)	75 ml	milk	$\frac{3}{8}$ cup

Method

Marinate the meat well with ginger and garlic pastes, chilly powder, salt(I) and creamed yoghurt. Let it stand for 1 hour, stirring every now and then.

Wash the rice well and soak it in cold water—cover and leave for about 1 hour.

Grind the saffron in a mortar and pestle, soak it in milk, and set aside.

Heat the ghee in a heavy saucepan. Add a couple of whole green cardamoms and a small piece of cinnamon. Then add onions and brown well. Now to this add the well-marinated meat. Cover lightly and let it simmer for about 10 minutes. Add salt(II).

Uncover, stir and cook till well-browned. Skim off the 2 tablespoons (30 ml) of ghee which will come to the top and keep aside in a cup. Add water and the powdered garam masala to the saucepan and simmer till the meat is tender and the gravy thick.

Meanwhile, in a large cooking pan pour about 9 cups ($3\frac{1}{2}$ pt/2 l) of water. To this add 4 green cardamoms, 1 teaspoon of black cumin (*shah zeera*) and salt (III). Cover and put on high heat to boil. When the water starts boiling, add the soaked rice and parboil on high heat for about 5 minutes or till the rice is almost cooked but remains *al dente*. Test a few grains by squeezing them between the two fingers—they should not mash completely.

When ready, remove from the heat and drain the rice in a colander. Keep a bowl underneath the colander to catch the water for later use.

Clean and oil the now empty cooking pan with a little ghee, and put half the parboiled rice into it and spread evenly. Spread the cooked meat curry *(korma)* over the rice. Put some green coriander leaves and whole green chillies on the meat curry, and spread the rest of the parboiled rice evenly on top.

Take 5 fl oz/150 ml/$\frac{5}{8}$ cups of the water, strained from the parboiled rice and pour evenly on top. Add the juice of 3 lemons and the ground saffron in milk. Finally spread evenly the 2 tablespoons of the meat curry ghee which was collected earlier. Cover the cooking pan with an aluminium foil and fit the lid firmly on top. Keep on medium heat and cook till you hear a hissing sound and can see steam when the cover and the foil are lifted. Turn off the heat, but leave the cooking pan covered for 5–6 minutes as this completes the cooking process. Lightly mix the rice and meat.

Serve in a large preheated platter, preferably white, silver or EPNS.

NOTE: To cream the yoghurt, pour it in a mixie or a blender and mix for 10–15 seconds and strain.

Pulao meat is mutton with some fat and bone pieces larger than those used for curries.

43

Yoghurt Curried Rice
(*Dahi Bhat*): Version A

A delicious and judicious combination of therapeutic spices and herbs, rice and yoghurt. An excellent dietetic recipe for upset stomachs.

Serves 3
Cooking Time: 5–7

British	Metric	Ingredients	American
9 oz (1½ cups)	250 g	yoghurt	1 cup
9 oz	250 g	boiled rice, may be used from leftovers	9 oz
2 tbsps	30 ml	groundnut oil	2 tbsps
singe-fry masala			
1 tbsp	11 g	mustard seed	1 tbsp
follow-up masala			
10	10	curry leaves	10
2	2	green chillies, chopped	2
1 tbsp	7.5 g	onions, finely chopped	1 tbsp
1 tsp	1 g	green coriander, scissor-cut	1 tsp
1 tsp	5 g	salt, to taste	1 tsp

Method

Take a wok or a deep frying pan, add oil and heat until it starts smoking. Add the *singe-fry masala*, and as soon as it splutters (after about 30 seconds), add the *follow-up masala*. Stir fry for 2–3 minutes. Add the rice and turn off the heat and mix well. Whisk the yoghurt in a blender for about 10 seconds and transfer to a glass serving bowl. Add the rice to the masalas. Mix and chill.

This is a meal in itself.

NOTE: In the singe-fry masala, cumin whole (*zeera*) and chopped dry red chillies may be added for a better flavour.

Yoghurt Curried Rice
(*Dahi Bhat*): Version B

This version is more original. It entails preparing the yoghurt yourself and therefore takes longer to prepare.

Serves 3
Preparation Time: over night
Cooking Time: 5–7 minutes

British	Metric	Ingredients	American
½ pt (2 cups)	300 ml	milk	1¼ cups
6 oz	175 g	boiled rice, large, fluffy	1¼ cups
2 tbsps	30 ml	groundnut oil	2 tbsps
2 fl oz	50 ml	yoghurt, culture	¼ cup
		singe-fry masala	
1 tbsp	11 g	mustard seed	1 tbsp
1 tbsp	8.5 g	cumin, whole	1 tbsp
2	2	red chillies, cut in 3, deseeded	2
		follow-up masala	
15	15	curry leaves	15
2	2	green chillies, chopped	2
1 tbsp	7.5 g	onions, finely chopped	1 tbsp
1 tbsp	2 g	green coriander, leaves only, scissor-cut	1 tbsp
1 tsp	5 g	salt, to taste	1 tsp

Method

Heat 2 tablespoons of oil in a saucepan until it begins to smoke. Add the mustard seeds, and after they stop spluttering add the rest of the *singe-fry masala*. Stir fry for 2 minutes and then add the *follow-up masala* and stir fry for 2–3 minutes.

45

Add the boiled rice and take off the fire. Mix well and set aside to cool.

Take an attractive glass or silver-plated bowl, put the rice with masalas in it.

Warm the milk to body temperature and put 3 tablespoons of yoghurt culture and mix well. Pour the milk into the rice and let it sit in a warm draft-free place for 4–6 hours or until the cultured yoghurt matures and sets.

Chill till ready to eat.

Vegetable Curried Rice
(*Vegetable Biryani*)

A light meal of rice with vegetables and spices. Vegetarians love it and non-vegetarians are palatably surprised.

Serves 4
Cooking Time: 40–45 minutes

British	Metric	Ingredients	American
11 oz	300 g	vegetables, diced or chopped	11 oz
2 oz (1 cup)	50 g	croûtons	$\frac{2}{3}$ cup
5 oz	150 g	cottage cheese (*panir*)	5 oz
$\frac{1}{2}$ pt (2 cups)	300 ml	water (I)	$1\frac{1}{4}$ cups
2	2	onions, finely sliced	2
3 fl oz (5 tbsps)	75 ml	cooking oil	$\frac{3}{8}$ cup
11 oz	300 g	basmati rice	11 oz
2 oz	50 g	ghee	$\frac{1}{4}$ cup
1 pt (4 cups)	600 ml	water (II)	$2\frac{5}{8}$ cups
		singe-fry masala	
1 tsp	3 g	cumin, whole	1 tsp

1 tsp	3.5 g	turmeric powder	1 tsp
1 tsp	2 g	chilli powder	1 tsp
		follow-up masala	
5	5	cloves	5
2	2	cinnamon pieces 1" (2.5 cm)	2
6	6	cardamoms, green, regular	6
10	10	black pepper corns	10
3	3	bay leaves (*tejpat*)	3
5 fl oz (1 cup)	150 ml	water (III)	$\frac{5}{8}$ cup
2 tsps	10 g	salt, to taste	2 tsps
		finishing masala	
$\frac{1}{2}$ tsp	0.25 g	saffron, soaked in milk	$\frac{1}{2}$ tsp
2 tbsps	30 ml	milk	2 tbsps
		garnish masala	
$\frac{1}{2}$ tsp	1.25 g	garam masala	$\frac{1}{2}$ tsp

Method

Soak saffron in milk and keep aside.

Dice the cottage cheese into pieces of 1"x1"x $\frac{1}{2}$" or smaller and keep aside.

Bring oil to smoking in a saucepan and sauté fry the diced cottage cheese (*panir*) until light brown. Remove and soak in hot water (I) and keep aside.

Take another heavy-bottomed, fairly large, cooking pot. Add ghee and bring to high heat and sauté fry the rice till glazed. Immediately add water (II) and bring to boil. Depending on the quality of rice, the boiling, till the rice is done, may take 10–20 minutes. Uncover and let the steam vapourize. Keep aside.

In the remaining oil, brown the onions. Then add the *single-fry masala* and stir fry for a minute or two. Add the vegetables, and the soaked *panir*, after draining through a colander. Mix together for 3–5 minutes, add the *follow-up masala* and the croûtons and again stir fry for 2–3 minutes till the contents are well coated with the spices. Add water (III) and simmer on low heat for 10 minutes to soften the vegetables. Turn off the heat and let it settle.

Take an oven-proof casserole or a baking dish. Layer the rice and vegetables with croûtons, starting with the rice then the vegetables, again rice then vegetables, and finally only rice. You can have one layer or two layers depending on the size of the dish and the oven.

Make sure the rice is cooked and not wet, like normal rice. In a pulao the rice grains should be separate and *al dente*.

Finally, spread the saffron with the milk over the rice and cover with foil. Bake in the oven at moderate heat for 10 minutes or so. Remove foil and sprinkle *garnish masala* just before serving.

NOTE: This dish may be eaten by itself, or with chutney or yoghurt.

Vegetables used here can be of any kind—carrots, potatoes, beans, cauliflower flowerettes (small), peas, gourds, squashes.

Egg Curries

Curry Omelette

This omelette recipe is very popular both in India and abroad. It was first made by my father, Aftab Rai, in the late thirties.

Serves 1 or 2
Cooking Time: 3–5 minutes

British	Metric	Ingredients	American
3	3	eggs	3
2 fl oz (3 tbsps)	50 ml	cooking oil	$\frac{1}{4}$ cup
1	1	onion, large, finely chopped	1
1	1	green chilli, sliced	1
3 tbsps	6 g	green coriander, leaves only	3 tbsps
1	1	tomato, peeled & chopped	1
$\frac{1}{2}$ tsp	2.5 g	salt, to taste	$\frac{1}{2}$ tsp
		curry spices	
1 tsp	3.5 g	turmeric powder	1 tsp
$\frac{1}{2}$ tsp	1.25 g	cumin powder	$\frac{1}{2}$ tsp
1 tsp	1 g	chilli powder	1 tsp
$\frac{1}{2}$ tsp	1.5 g	black pepper powder	$\frac{1}{2}$ tsp
$\frac{1}{2}$ tsp	1.5 g	fenugreek seed powder	$\frac{1}{2}$ tsp

Method

Beat the eggs as for an ordinary omelette. Pour oil in a frying pan and heat until it begins to smoke. Add the curry spices. Stir and add the eggs. Remove from heat and swirl the mixture in the pan. Spread all other ingredients, i.e., onions, green chillies, green coriander, tomatoes, on the eggs. Sprinkle salt.

Return to fire and let the eggs cook as for an omelette—when one side is done, turn it over and cook for a few minutes, or roll it as for the regular omelette.

Serve on a preheated plate sliced into four triangles.

NOTE: This recipe may be adapted for scrambled eggs, i.e., instead of omeletting the eggs, simply scramble them.

May be eaten by itself or with white bread.

Double Fry Egg Curry

Another egg curry, seldom made, but unique in itself. I first ate it with a school contemporary from the Nizam's family. The curry here is simple and made in a single process. It undoubtedly has an occidental touch in the use of sauces.

Serves 3–5
Cooking Time: 30–35 minutes

British	Metric	Ingredients	American
9	9	eggs	9
2 fl oz	50 ml	cooking oil (I), enough to fry the eggs in 3 to 4 manageable lots	$\frac{1}{4}$ cup
$3\frac{1}{2}$ fl oz	100 ml	cooking oil (II)	$\frac{1}{2}$ cup
3	3	onions, finely sliced	3
1 tsp	5 g	garlic paste	1 tsp
1 tsp	5 g	ginger paste	1 tsp
$1\frac{1}{2}$ tsps	7.5 g	salt, to taste	$1\frac{1}{2}$ tsps
		following to be mixed in a bowl	
$\frac{1}{2}$ oz	15 g	white bread crumbs, roasted	3 tbsps
1 tsp	3.5 g	turmeric powder	1 tsp
1 tsp	2 g	chilli powder	1 tsp
1 tsp	2.5 g	*amchoor*	1 tsp
5 fl oz (1 cup)	150 ml	water	$\frac{5}{8}$ cup

52

1 tsp	5 ml	Worcestershire sauce	1 tsp
1 fl oz	30 ml	tomato ketchup	2 tbsps
		garnish	
$\frac{1}{3}$ oz	10 g	green coriander, leaves only	$\frac{1}{3}$ cup
15	15	green curry leaves	15
3	3	green chillies, evenly cut	3

Method

Fry the eggs in oil (I) on both sides, making sure the yolks are well cooked and the whites are brownish. Take any glass or cup with a circumference that just covers the egg yolks plus a little of the whites and carefully punch cut all the yolks. Set aside on kitchen paper. When cold, lightly score the centre once like a plus (+) sign. The scoring should be just skin deep, and done with the tip of a very sharp knife.

Heat oil (II) until it smokes. Put onions and brown them. Then add the garlic and ginger pastes. Stir fry till the oil is released. Add the mixture of the various ingredients in the bowl. Spinkle salt and simmer on medium heat, stirring now and then. When the oil is released to the top and the bread crumbs are fully 'resolved', slip the punched out yolks into the sauce. Transfer to a baking dish and keep in an oven on low heat for about 10 minutes.

Finally, take the oil left over from the fried eggs. Heat until it smokes, and fry all the garnish greens till crisp. Take them out and drain on kitchen paper.

When ready to serve take the egg curry out of the oven and sprinkle the fried garnish greens on top. The curry should not be watery but like a thick sauce.

Serve with boiled rice.

NOTE: Although Worcestershire sauce is considered British, it is flavoured with Indian spices, vinegar and soya sauce. All these ingredients are oriental.

Along with tomato ketchup the addition of these sauces is a great convenience.

Maharaja Egg Curry

This was probably invented in the old Kingdom of Jaipur by the Rajas of Rajasthan. It is a very tasty dish and goes to show the many ways in which eggs can be curried.

Serves 3
Cooking Time: 15–20 minutes

British	Metric	Ingredients	American
6	6	eggs	6
2	2	onions, finely chopped	2
2 fl oz (3 tbsps)	50 ml	cooking oil	¼ cup
singe-fry masala			
1 tbsp	8 g	cumin powder	1 tbsp
1 tsp	2 g	chilli powder	1 tsp
1 tsp	3.5 g	turmeric powder	1 tsp
1 tsp	5 g	salt, to taste	1tsp
follow-up masala			
1 tsp	5 g	garlic paste	1 tsp

Method

Break the eggs and keep aside—do not beat them. Bring the oil to smoking point, add onions and brown them lightly. When the oil is released, add the *singe-fry masala* and stir fry for about 30 seconds. Add the *follow-up masala* and stir fry for another minute.

Take off the fire and gently add the six whole eggs—return to fire and stir slowly breaking the yolks. Keep stir frying till eggs are cooked. Eggs broken in this manner will resemble something in between scrambled and omelette eggs. Do not cook for too long as they will dry and lose the special characteristic of this dish.

NOTE: The dish may be garnished with chopped green chillies and scissor-cut coriander.

Best eaten with white bread or with parathas, or rice.

54

Eggs in Tomato Curry

A very popular dish of Hyderabadi origin. The sauce is basic and can also be used for such things as prawns (pg 71) or even mushrooms. The sauce is piquant and resembles, to some extent, the Hungarian Letcho.

Serves 6
Cooking Time: 40–50 minutes

British	Metric	Ingredients	American
6	6	eggs, large	6
7 fl oz (1⅓ cups)	200 ml	oil, preferably groundnut	⅞ cup
1 tbsp	15 g	salt, to taste	1 tbsp
singe-fry masala			
1 tsp	3 g	cumin seed, whole	1 tsp
⅓ oz	10 g	green curry leaves	⅓ cup
follow-up masala 1			
2	2	onions, large, finely sliced	2
1 tsp	5 g	ginger paste	1 tsp
1 tbsp	15 g	garlic paste	1 tbsp
1 tsp	2 g	chilli powder	1 tsp
2 tsps	5.5 g	cumin powder	2 tsps
follow-up masala 2			
3 lb 6 oz	1½ kg	tomatoes, large, red, skinned & strained	3 lb 6 oz
follow-up masala 3			
⅓ oz	10 g	green coriander, leaves only	⅓ cup
2	2	green chillies, sliced	2
garnish masala			
⅓ oz (½ cup)	10 g	green coriander, leaves only	⅓ cup

55

Method

Wash the tomatoes. Steam or boil for 8–10 minutes. Purée in a blender and strain. Keep the pulp to one side.

Heat oil until it is almost smoking, add the *singe-fry masala* and brown for about 2 minutes. Add the *follow-up masala 1*, starting with the onions until they are brown and follow it immediately with the remaining masala and salt. Stir fry for about 3 minutes, then add the *follow-up masala 2* of tomato pulp and cook on moderate heat for 15–20 minutes till the oil is released. Now add the *follow-up masala 3*. By now the consistency will be like thick tomato soup.

Transfer to a baking dish and add the eggs one by one (see note at the end). Have the oven preheated to 180 deg C and bake for 5–8 minutes or till the eggs have set. Remove from oven and add the *garnish masala*, and serve.

NOTE: Best eaten by itself. May also be had with any bread or boiled rice.

Do not put all the eggs together in one bowl. They should be broken one by one into a cup or a wine glass before being put together in a larger dish. There are two reasons for this. Firstly, it helps avoid a bad egg, secondly the yolk may break. If bad, throw it away and clean the cup. Should the yolk break keep it for scrambled eggs or omlette. Also, the egg from a cup or wine glass pours evenly onto the sauce.

Egg Curry in Tamarind Masala

An everyday fare for the masala and egg-loving gentry of the southern peninsula. A unique combination of an indigenous sauce and eggs.

Serves 3
Cooking Time: 25–30 minutes

British	Metric	Ingredients	American
6	6	eggs	6
3 fl oz ($\frac{1}{2}$ cup)	75 ml	cooking oil, preferably groundnut	$\frac{3}{8}$ cup
		singe-fry masala	
$\frac{1}{4}$ tsp	1 g	cumin (*zeera*), whole	$\frac{1}{4}$ tsp
$\frac{1}{2}$ oz ($\frac{3}{4}$ cup)	15 g	green curry leaves	$\frac{1}{2}$ cup
		singe-fry masala 2	
4	4	onions, medium finely sliced	4
		follow-up masala	
1 tsp	5 g	ginger paste	1 tsp
$1\frac{1}{2}$ tsps	7.5 g	garlic paste	$1\frac{1}{2}$ tsps
		during-cooking masala 1	
$\frac{1}{4}$ tsp	1 g	turmeric powder	$\frac{1}{4}$ tsp
$\frac{1}{2}$ tsp	1 g	chilli powder	$\frac{1}{2}$ tsp
1 tbsp	8 g	cumin (*zeera*) powder	1 tbsp
$\frac{1}{2}$ tsp	2.5 g	salt, to taste	$\frac{1}{2}$ tsp
		during-cooking masala 2	
3 fl oz ($\frac{1}{2}$ cup)	75 ml	tamarind pulp, thick (pg 282)	$\frac{3}{8}$ cup
		finishing masala	
4	4	green chillies	4
1 oz ($1\frac{1}{2}$ cups)	30 g	green coriander, leaves only	1 cup

Method

All the stages of the masala are used for the tamarind curry sauce.

Take a heavy-bottomed saucepan and heat the oil until it nearly smokes. Add the *singe-fry masala 1* and stir till dark brown or nearly blackish. Then add the *singe-fry masala 2* and stir till the onions are lightly browned. Then quickly add the *follow-up masala* and stir fry for 2–4 minutes. When a homogeneous consistency is obtained add the *during-cooking masala 1*, mix well and cook for 5–6 minutes. Follow by adding the *during-cooking masala 2*. Mix well and leave on low heat for 8–10 minutes. Now, add the *finishing masala* of the greens.

Transfer the contents into a baking dish. Make a depression in the mixture for each egg, using the back of a tablespoon. Then carefully break the eggs into the depression. Now cook on slow fire or bake in oven till eggs are set.

Serve in the baking dish.

NOTE: May be eaten by itself or with ordinary bread.

Egg Curry: Shredded Egg

Another variation of the egg curries. Many of these egg curries were innovated by strict 'eggatarians' (egg-eating vegetarians). They tried to use eggs in many forms and at any time of the night or day.

Serves 3–4
Cooking Time: 15–20 minutes

British	Metric	Ingredients	American
8	8	eggs	8
5 oz (1cup)	150 g	ghee	$\frac{5}{8}$ cup
		singe-fry masala	
5	5	red chillies, broken in 2 or 3 pieces & deveined	5

58

1 tsp	2.75 g	cumin powder	1 tsp
1 tsp	2 g	coriander powder	1 tsp
1 tsp	3.5 g	turmeric powder	1 tsp
		follow-up masala	
4	4	tomatoes, fresh, skinned & finely chopped	4
3	3	onions, finely sliced as rings, which are cut at one end to make shreds	3
1½ tsps	7.5 g	salt, to taste	1½ tsps
		during-cooking masala	
1 tsp	3 g	ginger, roughly grated	1 tsp
1 tsp	1.5 g	lemon peel, grated	1 tsp
1 tsp	5 ml	lemon juice	5 ml
		garnish masala	
½ tsp	1.5 g	black pepper, coarse, freshly ground	½ tsp
4	4	onions, finely sliced	4

Method

Make a thin single layer of plain omelettes from the eggs in the conventional manner. Eight eggs should make 16 pancake-type omelettes. When made, roll each pancake and slice the rolls about one-fifth inch wide like flat noodles. Put them together lengthwise and cut through the centre so as to reduce the length by half, and keep aside.

In a saucepan, bring ghee to high heat and brown the garnish masala onions in it. Remove and let sit on kitchen paper. Bring the remaining ghee to high heat and add the *singe-fry masala*. Stir fry for a few seconds. Add the *follow-up masala* and stir fry again till the onions are glazed and the tomatoes are soft. Add the 'egg noodles' and stir fry for a few minutes—the consistency of the sauce should be thickish. 3 fl oz/ 75 ml/⅜ cup of water may be added to get the right consistency. Now add the *during-cooking masala*. Continue to cook on medium plus heat

59

till ghee is released.

When ready to serve, transfer to a serving dish. Sprinkle the *garnish masala* on top.

NOTE: Serve with rice or any oriental bread. For many it tastes best with white bread or rolls or toast. This is of course a colonial development—so, for that matter are eggs !

Egg Kofta Curry

The traditional egg curry of boiled eggs in a curry sauce is often called a 'consolation curry' for eggatarians, i.e., vegetarians who eat eggs! There are more elegant preparations, but this particular curry has proved very popular with överseas friends and relatives.

Serves 3–5
Preparation Time: 15–20 minutes
Cooking Time: 25–30 minutes

British	Metric	Ingredients	American
12	12	eggs	12
1 tsp	2.5 g	chick pea flour	1 tsp
1 tsp	1.5 g	lemon peel, finely grated	1 tsp
3½ fl oz	100 ml	cooking oil(I), any kind	½ cup
3½ fl oz	100 ml	cooking oil(II)	½ cup
½ pt	300 ml	water	1¼ cups
½ tsp	1.75 g	black pepper powder	½ tsp
½ tsp	2.5 g	salt (I), to taste	½ tsp
for the curry sauce			
singe-fry masala			
1 tsp	2.5 g	caraway seed (not cumin)	1 tsp

60

4	4	red chilli, whole, crushed by hand	4
1½ tsps	5 g	turmeric powder	1½ tsps
1 tsp	5 g	salt (II), to taste	1 tsp
follow-up masala			
2	2	onions, finely sliced	2
3	3	tomatoes, skinned, finely chopped	3
during-cooking masala			
1 tsp	5 g	garlic paste	1 tsp
½ tsp	2.5 g	sugar	½ tsp
finishing masala			
1 tsp	2.75 g	garam masala	1 tsp
garnish masala			
1 tsp	1 g	green coriander, leaves only, scissor-cut	1 tsp
1 tsp	3 g	green chillies, scissor-cut	1 tsp
2	2	green spring onions, finely chopped with greens	2

Method

Hard boil 11 of the eggs and immediately put them in cold water. Leave them to cool for 10–15 minutes. Remove the shells and place the eggs in the refrigerator for about 30 minutes.

Meanwhile prepare the curry sauce. Heat the oil in a saucepan until it smokes. Add the *singe-fry masala*, with the turmeric powder coming last. Then immediately add the *follow-up masala*, starting with the onions which should be stir fried until they are soft but not brown. Add the tomatoes and stir fry till the oil is released. Add the *during-cooking masala*. Stir fry for a few minutes and set aside.

Take the shelled eggs out of the fridge and gently grate them into a mixing bowl. Add black pepper, half teaspoon salt, lemon peel and chick pea flour. (If chick pea flour is not readily available use cornflour.) Whisk the remaining uncooked egg and add it into the mix. With your hands make a smooth dough. It should now be possible to make *koftas* like meat-balls. There should be enough egg dough to make about 16–18 balls. Stir fry in oil (I) till light brown and keep aside on kitchen paper.

Reheat the curry sauce and carefully add the 'egg-balls'. Stir gently for 3–5 minutes, making sure the egg balls do not break.

Finally, add 300 ml water and simmer for 5–8 minutes. Add the *finishing masala*. Stir and transfer to a serving dish and sprinkle the *garnish masala*.

Serve immediately with boiled rice. If there is any delay in serving, place the curry in a moderately heated oven.

FISH
CURRIES

FISH
CURRIES

Curry Masala Fried Fish

A fish curry that has no end of admirers. It is one dish that never fails, and to my amazement has been relished by people from all ethnic groups. Some Bavarians who had it with us even learnt how to make it, and went as far as to say that a kiosk in a park in Munich serving this fish could make one a millionaire in no time!

For the preparation of this very special dish the selection of the type of fish is very important. In India pomfret, a fairly delicate fish is used. Otherwise, small brill, may be used. These are so-called flat fish but vertical swimmers with eyes on either side and not on the same side.

However, flat fish swimming horizontally could be used, but since their underskin does not have the same texture as their upperskin, the flavour is not uniform. Fishes used with success are rainbow trout, red mullet, small brill, flounder and herring or sprat. Ideally, fishes alongwith their head should not exceed 400 g per fish. A 500 g fish will also do.

Serves 1 or 2
Preparation: 30 minutes
Cooking Time: 5–8 minutes

British	Metric	Ingredients	American
14 oz–1 lb	400–500 g	flat fish (1)	14 oz–1 lb
		cooking oil, enough to deep fry	
marinade			
1 large or 2 medium		lemon, juice of	1 large or 2 medium
1 tbsp	15 g	salt, to taste	1 tbsp
masala			
2 tsps	5.5 g	cumin powder	2 tsps
3 tbsps	18 g	coriander, freshly ground from whole seed	3 tbsps
$\frac{1}{2}$ tsp	1 g	carum seed	$\frac{1}{2}$ tsp

1 tbsp	15 ml	ginger juice	1 tbsp
½ tsp	2.5 g	salt, to taste	½ tsp
		garnish	
as per taste		*amchoor* OR lemon juice	as per taste
1 tsp	2 g	chilli powder	1 tsp

Method

The fish should be gutted, not skinned. The head should be chopped off, but the tail retained. Remove any scales and cut off the fins (see illustration).

Using a sharp knife, score the fish twice on both sides starting an inch from the tail and ending at the head. The cuts should be about $1\frac{1}{2}$" apart (less for smaller fish). Make sure you do not score too deep and cut through the bones.

Apply lemon juice and salt evenly into the scored fish and marinate for 30–60 minutes.

In a wet grinder, grind the masala into a paste—add a little water if the mixture seems too dry. After the fish has been properly marinated, wash and pat dry.

Rub in the masala liberally and place on a rack for about half an hour before frying.

Heat some oil, preferably olive, peanut or sunflower oil, in a deep frying pan and, when really hot, deep fry the fish one at a time for 3–5 minutes (depending on weight) pushing it down in the oil once or twice with a wooden spatula. The fish is perfectly done when the skin is crisp.

Remove and drain on kitchen paper for 2–3 minutes. Serve right away, sprinkling chillies and *amchoor* or lemon juice according to taste.

To serve, carve along the centre bone as you would a dover sole.

This makes an excellent snack. It may be eaten by itself.

Some of the masala will come off during deep frying—do not worry as there is enough left in the fish.

To prepare the ginger juice, grate the ginger and squeeze through a fine cloth or a clean handkerchief.

Whole fish for masala fry fish.

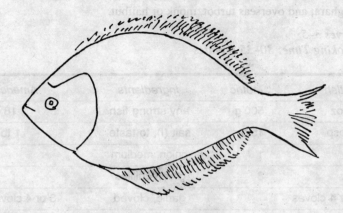

Fish after dressing and making incision for masala.

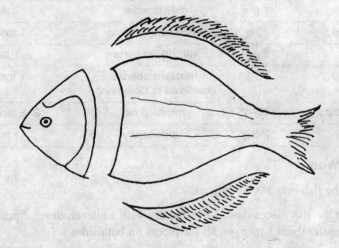

Curried Fish Bits (*Masala Fish Tukra*)

A recipe in the tradition of foil baking which is excellent as a snack or finger food. A strongly flavoured fish should be used to give the dish 'bite'. No masala stages apply here.

In this recipe fishes which have strong muscle (*machli*) should be used. In India the best would be betki, (beckti or begti), surmai or singhara; and overseas turbot, monk or halibut.

Serves 3–5
Cooking Time: 30–35 minutes

British	Metric	Ingredients	American
18 oz	500 g	any strong fish	18 oz
1 tbsp	15 g	salt (I), to taste	1 tbsp
1	1	onion, medium	1
3	3	green chillies	3
3 or 4 cloves		garlic, cloved	3 or 4 cloves
2"	5 cm	ginger	2"
1 tsp	3.5 g	turmeric powder	1 tsp
$\frac{1}{2}$ tsp	1 g	chilli powder	$\frac{1}{2}$ tsp
1 tbsp	10 g	white flour (*maida*)	1 tbsp
1 tsp	5 g	salt (II), to taste	1 tsp
1 tbsp	10 g	mustard seeds, powdered or Colemans	1 tbsp
2–3 tsps	10–15 ml	mustard oil	2–3 tsps
1 tsp	2.5 g	*amchoor*	1 tsp

Method

Cut the fish into 3"x 11" pieces.

Wash the fish pieces thoroughly and dry with a kitchen towel. Sprinkle some salt (about 1 tbsp) on all the pieces on both sides.

Grind the onions, green chillies, garlic and ginger root into a paste. Mix in the powdered spices, namely turmeric, chilli, salt, mustard seed powder and flour. To this mixture, add about 2 teaspoons of mustard oil (substitute rapeseed oil if not available) to make a homogeneous batter. Use more oil if the batter appears too dry. Coat the fish pieces with the batter.

Wrap each piece of fish securely in an aluminium foil which is brushed with mustard oil.

Put in an oven-proof baking dish and cook for 20–25 minutes on medium heat.

Remove from the oven, open the foil and set aside for 5 minutes. Sprinkle dry raw mango powder (*amchoor*) or lemon juice on top and serve the fish in the opened foil packages.

NOTE: This is basically a finger food, but may also be had with plain boiled or fried rice.

Fish Fry With Batter

A popular finger food or a cocktail snack that you will run short of, no matter how much you make.

In India singhara, mali or surmai may be used. Otherwise halibut, plaice or any similar type of fish will do.

Serves 4 or 5
Preparation Time: 30 minutes
Cooking Time: 4–5 minutes

British	Metric	Ingredients	American
2¼ lb	1 kg	fish, medium, fillet	2¼ lb
1 tbsp	15 ml	lemon juice	1 tbsp
1 tsp	5 g	salt (I), to taste	1 tsp
1 tsp	5 g	garlic paste	1 tsp

18 fl oz	$\frac{1}{2}$ l	cooking oil, preferably groundnut or sunflower seed oil	$2\frac{1}{4}$ cups

		batter	
$3\frac{1}{2}$ oz	100 g	chick pea flour (*besan*)	$\frac{7}{8}$ cup
1 oz	30 g	plain flour (*maida*)	3 tbsps
$\frac{1}{2}$ tsp	1 g	carum seed (*ajwain*), whole	$\frac{1}{2}$ tsp
$\frac{1}{2}$ tsp	1 g	chilli powder	$\frac{1}{2}$ tsp
$\frac{1}{2}$ tsp	1.75 g	turmeric powder	$\frac{1}{2}$ tsp
$\frac{1}{2}$ oz	15 g	green coriander, leaves only	$\frac{1}{2}$ cup
$\frac{1}{2}$ tsp	2.5 g	salt (II), to taste	$\frac{1}{2}$ tsp
$\frac{1}{2}$ tsp	1.75 g	cuttle-bone powder (*samunder jhag*) or baking powder	$\frac{1}{2}$ tsp
5–8 fl oz ($1-1\frac{1}{2}$ cups)	150–225 ml	water	$\frac{5}{8}$–1 cup

		garnish	
$\frac{1}{2}$ tsp	1.25 g	aromatic garam masala	$\frac{1}{2}$ tsp
1 tsp	2.5 g	*amchoor*	1 tsp
$\frac{1}{2}$ tsp	2.5 g	salt (III), to taste	$\frac{1}{2}$ tsp

Method

Wash the fish and dry with a kitchen towel. Mix salt (I) and lemon juice and garlic paste. Rub the paste into the fish and leave for 30 minutes.

Mix all the ingredients for the batter with water. The batter should be well beaten for 5 minutes and allowed to stand for 15 minutes.

Put the cooking oil into a deep frying pan and bring to high heat. Dip each fillet into the batter and deep fry in 2 lots. Then drain on kitchen paper. When all the fish has been fried, transfer to a preheated platter and sprinkle with the garnish mixture of garam masala, amchoor and salt (III) and serve immediately.

NOTE: May be eaten by itself, and also with home-made bread.

If the batter turns out a bit soggy after frying the first piece, add an extra half teaspoon of baking powder.

Cream Cheese Batter Prawns with Curry Mustard Sauce

This special batter is incredibly simple and very satisfying. The batter is made from yoghurt which has been hung overnight to drain out the water and mixed with herbs and spices.

The prawns used here should not be less than medium-sized.

Serves 4–6, depending on prawn lovers
Preparation Time: 1 hour
Cooking Time: 25–30 minutes

British	Metric	Ingredients	American
20	20	prawns, shelled and de-veined	20
		marinade	
1 tbsp	15 ml	ginger, grated and pressed through a muslin cloth	1 tbsp
1 tsp	5 g	garlic paste	1 tsp
1 tsp	3.25 g	black pepper powder	1 tsp
1 tbsp	15 ml	lemon juice	1 tbsp
		batter	
18 oz (1½ cups)	500 g	yoghurt (hung in muslin overnight)	2¼ cups
3½ oz (1 cup)	100 g	plain flour	⅔ cup
2 tbsps	12 g	green chillies, finely sliced without seeds	⅛ cup
2	2	eggs	2

71

1 tsp	2.5 g	caraway seeds, roasted	1 tsp
1 tsp	5 g	salt, to taste	1 tsp
1 tbsp	4.5 g	lemon peel rind, very finely chopped or grated from full lemons	1 tbsp

mustard curry sauce

1 tbsp	10 g	mustard powder, from freshly ground mustard seeds or Coleman's	1 tbsp
1 tsp	3.5 g	turmeric powder	1 tsp
1 tsp	2 g	chilli powder	1 tsp
2 tbsps	30 ml	lemon juice	$\frac{1}{8}$ cup
5 fl oz (1 cup)	150 ml	water	$\frac{5}{8}$ cup
$\frac{1}{2}$ tsp	2.5 g	salt, to taste	$\frac{1}{2}$ tsp
$\frac{1}{2}$ tsp	2.5 g	sugar	$\frac{1}{2}$ tsp
3 fl oz ($\frac{1}{2}$ cup)	75 ml	mustard or rapeseed or olive oil	$\frac{3}{8}$ cup

Method

Shell and de-vein prawns—wash and blot dry and set aside.

Mix all the marinade ingredients together. Put the prawns into the marinade making sure each prawn is properly coated and leave for 1 hour.

Meanwhile, place all the ingredients for batter in a bowl and mix by hand into a thickish mixture.

Also prepare the sauce while the prawns are marinating. For this, mix the mustard powder with water and make a smooth emulsion. Then mix in the other ingredients, whisking all the time as if 'you are making mayonnaise. Finally add the oil slowly till it is all absorbed. The sauce should be served at room temperature.

Remove the prawns from the marinade and pat dry with a kitchen towel. Dip each one in the batter and put them in a steamer. Steam for 20–25 minutes till done and serve with the sauce as a dip.

NOTE: May be eaten by itself or with soft boiled rice, which should
be plain fluffy rice, rather than basmati.

The sauce mixture may be made according to taste with more
chilli, more or less souring, and so on.

This is not a curry dish of the conventional form, but the
herbs and spices are the same.

1 cup (9 oz/250 g) of yoghurt hung in muslin overnight will
require about 2¼ cups (18 oz/500 g) of regular yoghurt.

Fried Fish in Curry Batter
(*Amritsari Fish*)

Made famous as the Amritsari fish it gets its name from the city of its
origin—Amritsar in Punjab. It is a tasty snack for all seasons and for
any time of the day or night.

For this curry the best fish in India would be singhara, mali or river
salmon. Otherwise carp or cod may be used.

Serves 3–5
Preparation Time: 30 minutes
Cooking Time: 5–8 minutes

British	Metric	Ingredients	American
2¼ lb	1 kg	fish	2¼ lb
1 pt (4 cups)	600 ml	cooking oil, any kind, enough for deep frying	2⅝ cups
marinade			
3 fl oz	75 ml	lemon juice	⅜ cup
1 tsp	5 g	salt, to taste	1 tsp
1 tsp	3 g	ginger, grated	1 tsp
1 tsp	3.25 g	black pepper powder	1 tsp
batter			

4½ oz (1⅔ cups)	125 g	chick pea flour	1 cup
2 tbsps	30 g	ginger paste	⅛ cup
2 tbsps	30 g	garlic paste	⅛ cup
2 tsps	4 g	chilli powder	2 tsps
2 tbsps	12.5 g	carum seeds (ajwain)	2 tbsps
4	4	red chillies, whole, scissor-cut	4
1 tbsp	10 g	turmeric powder	1 tbsp
1 tbsp	7 g	red colour cochineal or Hungarian red paprika	1 tbsp
1 tsp	3.5 g	baking powder	1 tsp
1 tsp	5 g	salt, to taste	1 tsp
3 – 3½ fl oz	75 – 100 ml	water	⅜ – ½ cup
		garnish	
1 tsp	2.75 g	garam masala	1 tsp
1 tsp	5 g	salt, to taste	1 tsp
6	6	lemons, wedges of	6

Method

The fish may be cut in any way you like (with skin or without) in thick rectangles about 2"x 3"x 1" or the thickness of the fillet.

Wash fish and blot dry with a kitchen towel.

Dissolve salt in the lemon juice and mix the grated ginger and black pepper. Put in a large bowl and marinate the fish for about half an hour. Take the fish out of the marinade and once again blot with a kitchen towel (do not wash), and keep aside.

Now prepare the batter. Mix the chick pea flour with 75–100 ml water as you would for an ordinary flour batter. Add all the other ingredients of the batter into the chick pea batter and mix well with hand or a wooden spoon. Remember the batter should be quite thick and of such a consistency that it will stick easily to the fish. If it seems too thin add more chick pea flour to it.

74

Coat each piece of fish with the batter. When coated, take out and arrange on a kitchen paper—if preferable dip the fish in the batter piece by piece. Leave the fish thus coated with the batter for about 15 minutes before deep frying.

Heat oil to smoking point and deep fry the fish in batches until it is crisp and light brown. Remove from the oil with a slotted spoon to kitchen paper for a few minutes to let the excess oil drain off.

Transfer to a serving platter. Sprinkle garam masala and salt, and place lemon wedges on the side.

NOTE: It is generally better not to use expensive fish for this dish because of the spicy batter.

Baked Curry Fish

This dish is adapted from European cooking methods, but has an oriental flavour. Similar dishes are made in Latin and Adriatic countries as well. The herbs and spices combine well and it is simple to prepare.

Beckti or sole may be used in India. Overseas, sole, flounder or baby sea bass have been successfully used.

Serves 3–5
Preparation Time: 30 minutes
Cooking Time: 40 minutes

British	Metric	Ingredients	American
1 lb 6 oz–1¾ lb	600 –800 g	fish, 6–8 pieces, fillet	1 lb 6 oz–1¾ lb
		marinade	
1 tsp	3.5 g	turmeric powder	1 tsp
1 tsp	2 g	chilli powder	1 tsp
1 tsp	3 g	mustard seed, ground, black or yellow	1 tsp
½ tbsp	4 g	cumin powder	½ tbsp

½ tsp	1.25 g	carum seed powder	½ tsp
2 tbsps	30 g	onion paste	2 tbsps
1 tsp	5 g	garlic paste	1 tsp
7 oz	200 g	yoghurt	¾ cup
1 tsp	5 g	salt, to taste	1 tsp
during-cooking masala			
4	4	cardamoms, shelled	4
6	6	cloves	6
1 tsp	3.25 g	black pepper	1 tsp
1 tbsp	7 g	Hungarian red sweet paprika	1 tbsp
finishing masala			
½ tsp	2.5 ml	lemon juice	½ tsp
½ tsp	2.5 g	sugar	½ tsp

Method

Combine the turmeric, chilli, mustard, cumin and carum or thyme powder with garlic and onion paste and mix with creamed yoghurt. Add salt and marinate the fish fillets with this mixture for half an hour.

Grind the shelled cardamoms, cloves and black pepper in a clean pepper mill—the resultant mixture will be about 1 flat tablespoon. If the spices prove too coarse for the pepper mill use a mortar and pestle.

Once the fish is marinated, spread half the marinade onto a piece of aluminium foil large enough to wrap the fish. Sprinkle half the Hungarian paprika on it and half the during-cooking masala which is kept aside. Lay the fish fillets on the foil and sprinkle with the other half of the marinade, paprika and the *during-cooking masala*. Wrap the fish securely without disturbing the fillets. Bake in an oven on medium heat for 30 minutes. Turn the heat to high for 3 minutes.

Keeping the fish in a foil, place in an attractive serving dish—open the foil from the top (do not remove completely). Sprinkle the *finishing masala* on top and serve.

NOTE: A snack that may be eaten by itself or with bread of any choice or boiled rice.

This was originally an Indian tandoori dish. But it adapts very well for European homes. Hungarian paprika imparts the red colour so essential for Indian tandoori recipes, instead of the traditional Kashmir red chilli which is now rarely available—even in India. It also enhances the flavour. You can adapt the same recipe for white veal fillet or chicken breasts—but increase the time for marinating by an hour.

Shrimp Cocktail (Bengal Curry Mayonnaise)

This used to be served by the Chittagong cook of my father's best friend, Mr Moosa. It is a cold dish and is an ingenious combination of the East and the West. If you like mustard you will love this version of the shrimp cocktail.

Serves 5
Cooking Time: 20 minutes

British	Metric	Ingredients	American
18 oz	$\frac{1}{2}$ kg	shrimps, medium or small, shelled and de-veined	18 oz
		for the sauce	
1 tbsp	9 g	mustard seed powder or Coleman's	1 tbsp
1 tsp	3.5 g	turmeric powder	1 tsp
2	2	egg yolks	2
$\frac{1}{2}$ tsp	1 g	chilli powder	$\frac{1}{2}$ tsp
2 tsps	10 ml	lemon juice	2 tsps
7 oz (1$\frac{1}{3}$ cups)	200 g	yoghurt	$\frac{3}{4}$ cup
1 tsp	5 g	salt, to taste	1 tsp
1 tsp	5 g	sugar	1 tsp
4 tsps	20 ml	olive oil	4 tsps

Method

Wash shrimps and pat dry with a kitchen towel. Steam cook for 10–12 minutes. Keep aside in the fridge.

Prepare the sauce. Whisk the yoghurt and add all the ingredients, except the oil and continue whisking. Add a little oil at a time, stirring continuously as you would for a mayonnaise and making sure you do not whisk too hard as this would release butter from the yoghurt.

Stop when the sauce is smooth and emulsified. Taste for tartness and sugar and adjust accordingly.

Put the shrimps in the sauce and leave in the refrigerator till serving time.

Serve in cocktail cups accompanied by Tabasco sauce.

NOTE: It is important that the shrimps are at room temperature before they are steamed.

Madras Curry Shrimp Cocktail

This may be termed a colonial dish, obviously invented during the Raj.

Serves 4
Cooking Time: 18–20 minutes

British	Metric	Ingredients	American
18 oz	$\frac{1}{2}$ kg	small shrimps	18 oz
3 tbsps	45 ml	cooking oil, any	3 tbsps
2 tbsps	9 g	coconut, freshly grated	2 tbsps
		singe-fry masala	
15	15	green curry leaves	15

1 tsp	2 g	chilli powder	1 tsp
½ tsp	1.75 g	turmeric powder	½ tsp
½ tsp	1.5 g	pepper powder	½ tsp
1 tsp	5 g	sugar	1 tsp
1 tsp	5 g	salt, to taste	1 tsp
		garnish masala	
1 tbsp	2 g	green coriander, leaves only, scissor-cut	1 tbsp
1 tsp	2 g	green chilli, scissor-cut	1 tsp
2	2	lemons, juice of	2

Method

Bring oil to smoking in a saucepan. Add the singe-fry masala starting with the curry leaves and when they are crisp add the other ingredients. When the spices start spluttering, remove from heat. Put the mixture on kitchen paper to drain the oil.

Mix the shrimps with the grated coconut and the *singe-fry masala* and leave to cool for 10 minutes. Take a fresh saucepan and put the shrimps with all the above ingredients. Stir fry without any more oil till all the water has evaporated. This takes 8–10 minutes.

Transfer to a serving dish and add the *garnish masala* adding the lemon juice first and then the other greens.

NOTE: Serve in glass or ceramic bowls. May be eaten by itself or with any kind of bread or with fluffy rice.

             The dish like all dishes from Madras tends to be hot. Reduce chillies to taste.

Prawns in Tomato Curry Sauce

This curry is very popular with prawn lovers. Seldom have tomatoes been used to such effect with prawns. A bit of tact is required to handle the prawns, but otherwise the method is the same as for eggs in tomato curry.

Serves 6
Cooking Time: 45–50 minutes

British	Metric	Ingredients	American
18 oz	500 g	prawns, medium-size, shelled, de-veined and washed	18 oz
3½ oz (1 cup)	100 g	white flour (*maida*)	$\frac{7}{8}$ cup
5 fl oz (1 cup)	150 ml	water	$\frac{5}{8}$ cup
		cooking oil (I), preferably groundnut, enough to deep fry prawns	
9 fl oz (1¾ cups)	250 ml	cooking oil (II), preferably peanut	1⅛ cups
1 tbsp	15 g	salt, to taste	1 tbsp
singe-fry masala			
1 tsp	3 g	cumin seed, whole	1 tsp
⅓ oz (½ cup)	10 g	green curry leaves	⅓ cup
follow-up masala 1			
2	2	onions, large, finely sliced	2
1 tsp	5 g	ginger paste	1 tsp
1 tbsp	15 g	garlic paste	1 tbsp
1 tsp	2 g	chilli powder	1 tsp
2 tsps	5.5 g	cumin powder	2 tsps
follow-up masala 2			
3 lb 6 oz	1½ kg	tomatoes, large, skinned and strained	3 lb 6 oz

follow-up masala 3

⅓ oz (½ cup)	10 g	green coriander, leaves only	⅓ cup
2	2	green chillies, sliced	2

garnish masala

⅔ oz (1 cup)	20 g	green coriander, leaves only	⅔ cup

Method

Make a medium batter with the flour and water.

Dry the washed prawns with a kitchen towel and put them into the batter.

Bring cooking oil (I) to high heat in a deep frying pan and deep fry the prawns making sure they are well coated with the batter. Fry 4–5 at a time. Take them out and put them on a paper to cool. The frying time should be anywhere between 3–4 minutes. Do not overcook the prawns.

Wash and strain, and boil the tomatoes for about 8–10 minutes. Purée in a blender and strain. Keep the pulp to one side.

Heat oil (II) to near smoking and add the *singe-fry masala*—brown for about 2 minutes. Add the *follow up masala 1*, browning the onions before adding the rest and salt. Stir fry for about 3 minutes and add the *follow-up masala 2* of tomato pulp. Cook on moderate heat for 15–20 minutes till all the oil is released. Now add the *follow-up masala 3*. By now the consistency will be like thick tomato soup.

Put the tomato curry into a baking dish. The fried prawns should have cooled by now. Carefully remove all the batter from the prawns—throw it away or give it to your pet cat. Put the prawns in the baking dish with the tomato curry. Mix gently till all the prawns are well coated with the tomato curry sauce. Place in a preheated oven on 180°C, and bake for 5–8 minutes. Do not over-bake the dish as the prawns are already cooked and could become hard. Remove from the oven, sprinkle the *garnish masala* and serve.

NOTE: Best eaten by itself, with bread of your choice or boiled rice.

Those not accustomed to even moderate chillies may reduce the proportions of red and green chillies by half.

Prawns once deep fried in batter are cooked in a manner which prevents them from becoming hard. When put in a thick sauce they remain succulent.

The removed batter might be given to a pet cat or used to feed birds.

Garlic Fish Curry

A very simple and quick preparation, it combines the Chinese Szechwanese hot cuisine with Indian spices and Indian cooking techniques.

This dish is very popular with those fond of garlic.

Serves 4
Cooking Time: 15–20 minutes

British	Metric	Ingredients	American
$2\frac{1}{4}$ lb	1 kg	fish, any white fillet	$2\frac{1}{4}$ lb
7 fl oz ($1\frac{1}{3}$ cups)	200 ml	cooking oil, any	$\frac{7}{8}$ cup
singe-fry masala			
1	1	onion, medium, coarsely chopped	1
6	6	red chillies, broken in 3 pieces each and deseeded	5
follow-up masala			
1 tbsp	15 g	garlic paste	1 tbsp
1 tbsp	5 g	coriander, roasted, whole	1 tbsp
1 tbsp	8.5 g	cumin, roasted, whole	1 tbsp
1 tbsp	6 g	chilli powder	1 tbsp
1 tbsp	10 g	turmeric powder	1 tbsp
during-cooking masala			

82

2 tsps	10 g	salt, to taste	2 tsps
1 tsp	5 g	sugar	1 tsp
2 tbsps	30 ml	vinegar	2 tbsps

Method

Wash the fish thoroughly, drain and blot dry with a kitchen towel. Roast coriander and cumin seeds on a *tawa* or griddle.

Roughly pound or grind in a blender the follow-up masala and keep aside.

Heat the oil to high heat and add the *singe-fry masala*. Fry till light brown. Then add the *follow-up masala* and stir fry for 4–5 minutes. Add the *during-cooking masala*, mix well and leave on low heat for 2 minutes. Remove the pan from heat and carefully add the fish fillets. Return to the fire and cook for 3–4 minutes on one side. Then turn over the fish fillets and cook for a further 2–3 minutes on low heat.

Check fish for salt, souring and sugar. Transfer to an attractive preheated China platter and serve.

NOTE: Reduce or increase the amount of chillies and garlic according to taste. May be eaten by itself, with fluffy boiled rice.

Spiced Mustard Fish Curry

This is a combination of the Bengal and traditional Oudh kitchens. The dish can be made as hot with chilli and as piquant with mustard as desired.

For this curry any strong white fish is required. In India surmai or rahu may be used; overseas turbot, red snapper, sturgon or monk can be used to prepare this curry.

Serves 4
Cooking Time: 15–20 minutes

British	Metric	Ingredients	American
$2\frac{1}{4}$ lb	1 kg	fish fillets	$2\frac{1}{4}$ lb
7 fl oz ($1\frac{1}{3}$ cups)	200 ml	cooking oil, any except olive oil	$\frac{7}{8}$ cup
1 tsp	3 g	ginger, grated	1 tsp
3	3	bay leaves (*tejpat*)	3
3	3	cardamoms, regular	3
6	6	cardamoms, large brown, seeds	6
1 tsp	2.75 g	black pepper corns	1 tsp
singe-fry masala			
1 tbsp	11 g	mustard seeds, (preferably Chinese mustard green seeds which are small and reddish, commonly called rye)	1 tbsp
5	5	red chillies, whole, broken into 3 pieces	5
1 tbsp	6 g	chilli powder	1 tbsp
1 tbsp	10 g	turmeric powder	1 tbsp
during-cooking masala			
1 tsp	3 g	mustard powder or Coleman's	1 tsp
12 oz (2 cups)	325 g	yoghurt	$1\frac{1}{4}$ cups
1 tsp	2.25 g	cornflour	1 tsp
2 tsps	10 g	salt, to taste	2 tsps
garnish masala			
1 tbsp	2 g	green coriander, scissor-cut	1 tbsp
2 tbsps	15 g	spring onions, finely chopped with the green stem	2 tbsps

Method

Take a large shallow pan and line it with muslin or any porous cloth, making sure some of the cloth hangs over the edges. Place the fish fillets gently in the pan over the muslin. Pour sufficient water to cover the fish—about $3\frac{1}{2}$ cups (18 fl oz/500 ml/$2\frac{1}{4}$ cups). Add ginger, bay leaves, cardamoms, pepper corns and cardamom brown seeds to the water and cook on low heat. Bring the water to boil. Poach on medium heat for about 3–5 minutes till the fish turns completely white.

Lift the muslin out of the pan and let all the water run out. Be careful not to break the fillets. If they are too large or long, slice them in 2 or 3 pieces.

Take a clean cooking pan and heat oil to smoking point. Add the *singe-fry masala* starting with the mustard seeds. When they splutter add the rest. Stir for a few seconds and again very gently place the fish in the singe-fry masala and fry for 3–4 minutes. Transfer the contents to a baking dish.

In a blender, cream the yoghurt with mustard powder, cornflour and salt. Pour the *during-cooking masala* on top of the fish in the baking dish and cook on medium heat in an oven for 5–10 minutes till the oil is released from the fish and the masala. The mustard aroma will now be strongly evident.

Before serving, sprinkle the *garnish masala* evenly on top.

Serve in the baking dish with boiled rice.

NOTE: Squeeze a lemon on the fried fish, and add, if you prefer, a dash of Tabasco sauce.

This dish can only be accompanied with boiled rice.

This recipe can be adapted for 'veal meat balls'. Poaching time for veal meat balls is 3–5 minutes longer.

Mustard Fish Soup Curry

This recipe is from Bengal. It is highly piquant and takes very little time to prepare. Use any kind of strong fish. It should be de-boned or have a central bone which can be removed during eating.

Serves 3
Cooking Time: 15–18 minutes

British	Metric	Ingredients	American
18 oz	500 g	fish cuts, medium to large	18 oz
3½ fl oz (⅔ cup)	100 ml	cooking oil, preferably mustard or rapeseed	½ cup
½ pt (2 cups)	300 ml	water	1¼ cups
singe-fry masala			
1 tsp	3.75 g	mustard seed, whole	1 tsp
1 tsp	3.5 g	turmeric powder	1 tsp
follow-up masala			
1½ tbsps	15 g	mustard powder, freshly pounded or from grinder	1½ tbsps
1 tbsp	7.5 g	chick pea flour	1 tbsp
1 tsp	2 g	chilli powder	1 tsp
½ tbsp	7.5 g	salt, to taste	½ tbsp
garnish masala			
1 tsp	1 g	green coriander, scissor-cut	1 tsp
1 tsp	2 g	green chilli, scissor-cut	1 tsp
2	2	lemons, juice of	2

Method

Wash the fish and dry on kitchen paper. Take a shallow cooking pan, bring oil to smoking and sauté fry the fish in it for 2–3 minutes. Remove the fish from the oil and keep aside on a newspaper.

Bring the remaining oil to near smoking, add the *singe-fry masala*—first the mustard seeds, and as soon as they stop spluttering, the turmeric. Then, immediately, add the *follow up masala*. Stir fry for 2–3 minutes.

Return the fish to the pan and stir fry for another 2–3 minutes. Add the water and mix gently. Simmer on medium heat for 6–8 minutes or till the fish is done.

Remove to a serving dish and sprinkle the *garnish masala*.

Serve with boiled rice.

NOTE: Increase or decrease water and salt depending on the amount of soup preferred. Chillies may also be increased or decreased depending on individual taste.

It is not necessary to use expensive fish or oil.

Easily adapted for any vegetable—aubergine diced with potatoes is an ideal combination.

Dry Prawn Curry

A North Indian version of a daily South Indian preparation. Some of the flavours are from the South, but other masalas are typical of North Indian curries.

Serves 3
Cooking Time: 25–30 minutes

British	Metric	Ingredients	American
18 oz	500 g	prawns, medium-size, shelled de-veined and washed	18 oz
5 fl oz (1 cup)	150 ml	cooking oil (not olive) preferably groundnut or sunflower seed oil	$\frac{5}{8}$ cup
5 fl oz (1 cup)	150 ml	water	$\frac{5}{8}$ cup

		singe-fry masala 1	
4	4	Szechwan or Indian red pepper, whole	4

		singe-fry masala 2	
1 tsp	3.5 g	turmeric powder	1 tsp
2 tsps	4 g	coriander powder	2 tsps
1 tsp	2.75 g	cinnamon powder	1 tsp
1 tsp	2 g	chilli powder	1 tsp
$\frac{1}{2}$ tsp	1.5 g	black pepper powder	$\frac{1}{2}$ tsp
$\frac{1}{2}$ tsp	1 g	ginger powder	$\frac{1}{2}$ tsp

		during-cooking masala	
2	2	onions, medium	2
3	3	tomatoes, medium	3
2 tsps	10 g	salt, to taste	2 tsps

		finishing masala	
6 rims	6 rims	lime, thinly sliced along with rind	6 rims

		garnish masala	
1 tbsp	4.5 g	coconut, freshly grated or copra grated	1 tbsp
$\frac{2}{3}$ oz (1 cup)	20 g	green coriander, leaves only	$\frac{2}{3}$ cup

Method

Peel the onions, slice finely and keep aside.

Put the tomatoes in boiling water for a few minutes—skin and slice and keep aside. Scissor-cut the green coriander.

Pour oil in a heavy saucepan and heat till it smokes. Add the *singe-fry masala 1*. Stir for a minute. Then add the *singe-fry masala 2* and quickly stir fry for another half a minute.

Add the prawns and stir fry for 2–3 minutes till well coated with masala, and the prawns turn pinkish white.

88

Add the *during-cooking masala* and keep stir frying for 2–3 minutes making sure the prawns are well mixed with all the masalas.

Now add water, cover the pan and simmer for 15–20 minutes till oil is released. Uncover and check liquid—if too liquidy, stir fry on high heat till moist (not too dry or too wet).

Add the *finishing masala* and mix by turning over the prawns gently in the curry—by this time the masalas should be sticking to the prawns.

Transfer to a serving dish and sprinkle with the *garnish masala*.

Serve with boiled rice or eat plain as a snack or on pizza bread.

Spicy Curry Prawns

A very early curry creation, unusually made. If prepared carefully this dish is both wholesome and conveys the importance of Indian herbs and spices for flavour.

Serves 4–6
Cooking Time: 40–50 minutes

British	Metric	Ingredients	American
2¼ lb	1.25 kg	prawns, king size or medium, shelled & de-veined	2¼ lb
5 fl oz (1 cup)	150 ml	cooking oil, preferably groundnut	⅝ cup
singe-fry masala			
20	20	green curry leaves	20
1 tsp	2.5 g	black cumin (*shah zeera*) powder	1 tsp
1 tsp	3.5 g	turmeric powder	1 tsp
1 tsp	2 g	chilli powder	1 tsp
1 tsp	2 g	ginger powder	1 tsp

follow-up masala

6	6	onions, finely sliced	6
1 lb 6 oz	600 g	tomatoes, finely sliced, preferably after peeling	1 lb 6 oz
$\frac{1}{2}$ tbsp	7.5 g	salt, to taste	$\frac{1}{2}$ tbsp

finishing masala

4	4	green chillies, medium-size scissor-cut, without seeds	4
2 tbsps	30 ml	lemon juice, freshly squeezed	2 tbsps

garnish masala

1 tbsp	15 ml	garlic, through press	1 tbsp
2 tbsps	4 g	green coriander, leaves only, scissor-cut	2 tbsps

Method

Wash prawns well and drain on kitchen paper.

Bring oil to smoking in a wok or a deep heavy-bottomed saucepan and quickly fry the prawns, 4–5 at a time, for a minute or so. When they become pinkish and curl they are done. Remove from oil and drain on kitchen paper.

Reheat the oil in a saucepan and add the curry leaves of the singe-fry masala. As soon as they are crisp (this takes about 15–20 seconds) add the remaining ingredients of the *singe-fry masala*. When it stops spluttering, add the finely sliced onions of the follow-up masala and cook until the onions glaze and soften. Now add the remaining *follow-up masala*. Stir fry for 3–5 minutes and then cook uncovered on high heat for 10–15 minutes, till the water from the onions and tomatoes evaporates and the sauce becomes homogenous and thick.

Remove the saucepan from heat and gently place the sauté fried prawns in the sauce. Return to the fire and cook on moderate heat for 10 minutes or so. Turn off the heat, add the *finishing masala* and mix gently.

Transfer to a wide white serving dish and sprinkle the *garnish masala* on top.

Serve hot with fluffy boiled rice.

NOTE: After the prawns have been put in the sauce the dish can be heated in an oven for 10–12 minutes on moderate heat and then the same steps followed.

Fish Curry: Bengal

No book on curries is complete without the famous fish curry of Bengal. A piquant mustard based curry made according to the same recipe for several centuries.

Use preferably a strong fish with only a centre bone. In India rahu or, surmai could be used; overseas red snapper, carp, cod is popular.

Serves 6–7
Preparation Time: 10–15 minutes
Cooking Time: 35–40 minutes

British	Metric	Ingredients	American
4½ lb	2 kg	fish	4½ lb
½ pt (2 cups)	300 ml	mustard or rapeseed oil (if not readily available any cooking oil with the addition of 1 tsp Coleman's mustard powder)	1¼ cups
		marinade masala	
2 tbsps	20 g	turmeric powder	2 tbsps
1 tbsp	15 g	salt, to taste	1 tbsp
1½ tbsps	9 g	chilli powder	1½ tbsps
2tbs	30g	Garlic paste	2tbs
		singe-fry masala	
1 tsp	2.75 g	nigella (*kalonji*) seed	1 tsp
1 tsp	3 g	cumin seeds, whole	1 tsp

		follow-up masala	
4 tbsps	40 g	mustard, finely ground	4 tbsps
1 tbsp	10 g	turmeric powder	1 tbsp
16 fl oz (3 cups)	450 ml	water	2 cups
1 tbsp	15 g	salt, to taste	1 tbsp
1 tsp	5 ml	mustard oil	1 tsp
		garnish masala	
1 tbsp	5 g	green chillies, scissor-cut	1 tbsp

Method

Cut the fish into rectangle of about 2"x1" with the thickness being 1".

Wash fish under running water in a colander and dry with a kitchen towel. Sprinkle the *marinade masala*, and leave for 10–15 minutes.

Heat oil to smoking point and sauté the fish in 2 or 3 lots till partly crisp. Drain on kitchen paper.

Mix together the follow-up masala, starting with the mustard powder and water and whisk till milky. Add the rest of the follow-up masala and again whisk till smooth and set aside.

Drain three quarters of the oil from the pan in which you have fried the fish and heat the rest to smoking point. Add the *singe-fry masala* and cook for about 30 seconds till it starts spluttering. Reduce the heat and add the *follow-up masala* prepared earlier. Simmer on medium heat for 15–20 minutes. Remove from heat and carefully add the sauté fried fish. Cover and cook on moderate heat for 5 minutes. Remove the lid and cook for another 10 minutes.

Transfer to a serving dish, preferably white, and sprinkle the *garnish masala*.

Serve with boiled fluffy rice. This curry does not go with breads.

Yoghurt Fish Curry (*Dahi Mean*): Bengal

A delicate tasting dish which no Bengali home can do without. It needs a light touch while preparation. This version comes from a home renowned for its family recipes.

Strong fish with centre bone, preferably rahu, surmai or beckti in India, and carp, monk fish overseas, can be used.

Serves 6–8
Preparation Time: 15–20 minutes
Cooking Time: 40–45 minutes

British	Metric	Ingredients	American
$4\frac{1}{2}$ lb	2 kg	fish	$4\frac{1}{2}$ lb
7 fl oz ($1\frac{1}{3}$ cups)	200 ml	cooking oil, definitely mustard or rapeseed	$\frac{7}{8}$ cup
marinade masala			
2 tsps	10 g	salt, to taste	2 tsps
1 tbsp	10 g	turmeric powder	1 tbsp
1 tbsp	6 g	chilli powder	1 tbsp
singe-fry masala			
4 tbsps	60 g	onion paste	4 tbsps
1 tbsp	15 g	ginger paste	1 tbsp
2 tbsps	30 g	garlic paste	2 tbsps
follow-up masala			
1 tbsp	15 g	salt, to taste	1 tbsp
1 tbsp	10 g	turmeric powder	1 tbsp
$1\frac{1}{2}$ tbsps	9 g	chilli powder	$1\frac{1}{2}$ tbsps
1 tsp	2 g	coriander powder	1 tsp
4	4	cloves coarsely powdered	4

$1\frac{1}{2}$"	4 cm	cinnamon	$1\frac{1}{2}$"
5	5	cardamoms, regular powdered	5
during-cooking masala			
$5\frac{1}{2}$ oz	165 g	yoghurt, whisked	$\frac{5}{8}$ cup
1 tbsp	12 g	raisins	1 tbsp
$\frac{1}{2}$ pt	300 ml	water	$1\frac{1}{4}$ cups

Method

Soak the raisins in 1 cup of water and set aside.

Cut the fish in to 2"x 2" pieces and wash in running water. Dry with a kitchen towel, smear with the marinade masala and set aside for 15–20 minutes.

Take a deep frying pan and bring oil to smoking point. Shallow fry the fish until it is golden brown. Lift the fish out of the oil with a slotted spoon and drain on kitchen paper.

Remove almost all the oil from the frying pan, leaving about 3 tablespoons (50 ml) behind. Bring to smoking point and add the *singe-fry masala* and cook till light brown. Add the *follow-up masala* and stir fry mixing the ingredients thoroughly. This should take 2–3 minutes. Then add the *during-cooking masala*. Simmer on medium heat for about 5 minutes. Add the fish and cook uncovered on moderate heat for 15–20 minutes.

Goes well with fluffy boiled rice.

Fish Curry With Yoghurt

An everyday dish for fish lovers. It is especially good when prawn or lobster are used. But has also been made with white veal with excellent results.

Any large, strong fish is used such as rahu, beckti or surma in India and monk overseas.

Serves 3, or may be 4
Cooking Time: 25–30 minutes

British	Metric	Ingredients	American
2¼ lb	1 kg	fish	2¼ lb
4 fl oz	120 ml	cooking oil, any	½ cup
2 tsp	10 g	salt, to taste	2 tsp
		singe-fry masala	
⅔ oz (1 cup)	20 g	green curry leaves	⅔ cup
1 tsp	4.25 g	fenugreek, whole	1 tsp
		follow-up masala 1	
7 oz	200 g	yoghurt, creamed and strained	¾ cup
1 tbsp	15 g	garlic paste	1 tbsp
1 tbsp	15 g	ginger paste	1 tbsp
1 tsp	3.5 g	turmeric powder	1 tsp
1 tsp	2 g	chilli powder	1 tsp
		follow-up masala 2	
⅔ oz (1 cup)	20 g	green coriander, leaves only	⅔ cup
6	6	green chillies, medium, scissor-cut	6
1 tbsp	8 g	cumin powder	1 tbsp

Method

Cut the fish into chunks of 2"x1"x1" and keep aside.

Blend all the ingredients of the follow-up masala 1 for 1–2 minutes and keep aside.

Heat oil in a large heavy-bottomed pan until it starts smoking. Add the *singe-fry masala* and as soon as the curry leaves become crisp, which takes about 1 minute, add the blended *follow-up masala 1*. Stir and simmer on medium heat till the water is reduced by half. This takes 6–8 minutes. Add salt and the *follow up masala 2* and stir fry for another 3–4 minutes. Take off the fire, add the fish chunks, and mix well.

95

Return the cooking pan to the fire and cook on medium to low heat for 15–20 minutes.

Transfer to any attractive preheated white dish and serve with fluffy boiled rice.

CHICKEN CURRIES

Rampur Chicken Casserole Curry

A Rampur dish made from breasts of chicken, pheasant, partridge or turkey. A genuine casserole since no 'transfers' or stir frying is necessary.

Seven tried and tested curry casseroles have been included in this book.

Serves 3–4
Preparation Time: 30 minutes
Cooking Time: 45–50 minutes

British	Metric	Ingredients	American
6	6	breast of chicken	6
$\frac{1}{2}$ tsp	0.25 g	saffron, soaked in milk	$\frac{1}{2}$ tsp
2 tsps	30 ml	milk	2 tsps
		Rampur sauce	
12 oz (2 cups)	325 g	yoghurt, whisked	$1\frac{1}{4}$ cups
5 fl oz (1 cup)	150 ml	cream	$\frac{5}{8}$ cup
4 oz ($\frac{2}{3}$ cup)	100 g	butter, melted	$\frac{1}{2}$ cup
$\frac{1}{2}$ tbsp	7.5 g	salt, to taste	$\frac{1}{2}$ tbsp
$\frac{1}{2}$ tsp	2.5 g	garlic paste	$\frac{1}{2}$ tsp
1 tsp	3.5 g	turmeric powder	1 tsp
1 tsp	2 g	chilli powder	1 tsp
1 tsp	2.25 g	cornflour	1 tsp
2 tbsps	40 g	almond paste, fine	2 tbsps
2	2	onions, medium, whole, boiled	2

Method

Blend all the Rampur sauce ingredients in a food processor and keep aside.

Place the chicken breasts in a casserole, preferably in a single layer. Cover with the sauce and mix well by hand. Leave to marinate for half an hour.

Cover the casserole and place in an oven on medium heat for 30–40 minutes till the chicken is done. Check with a skewer. Butter will appear on top.

Before serving, add the saffron and mix gently. Be careful not to break the chicken breasts.

Serve with rice.

Saffron   Curry   Chicken   Casserole
(*Zafrani   Murgi*)

I am not quite sure if this dish went to Spain or came from Spain. The Spanish have a dish which resembles this in many ways. Here the saffron is predominant and other spices are minimal.

Serves 2–3
Cooking Time: 45–50 minutes

British	Metric	Ingredients	American
1	1	chicken, large, jointed	1
3 fl oz ($\frac{1}{2}$ cup)	75 ml	ghee or cooking oil	$\frac{3}{8}$ cup
$\frac{1}{2}$ tsp	0.25 g	saffron	$\frac{1}{2}$ tsp
2 tbsps	30 ml	milk	2 tbsps
for the blender			
$\frac{1}{2}$ pt	300 ml	coconut milk	1$\frac{1}{4}$ cups
5$\frac{1}{2}$ oz (1 cup)	165 g	yoghurt	$\frac{5}{8}$ cup
3	3	onions, boiled	3
1$\frac{1}{2}$ tsp	7g	turmeric powder	1$\frac{1}{2}$ tsp
$\frac{1}{2}$ tsp	1 g	ginger powder	$\frac{1}{2}$ tsp

½ tbsp	7.5 g	salt, to taste	½ tbsp
1 tbsp	20 g	almond paste	1 tbsp
1 tsp	2 g	chilli powder	1 tsp

Method

Soak the saffron in warm milk and set aside.

Put all the remaining ingredients, except the chicken and ghee, in a blender and liquidize.

Heat the ghee in a heavy saucepan and stir fry the chicken on high heat until light brown.

Transfer to a heavy casserole and pour the liquidized masala on top. Cover and place in an oven on moderate heat for 30–40 minutes. Then add saffron and milk. Cover and return to the oven for another 10 minutes or until the chicken is done.

Do not remove the cover until you are ready to serve the casserole, because the saffron aroma will escape.

Should only be eaten with fluffy large-grained rice.

NOTE: Hand-crushed whole red chillies as garnish go very well.

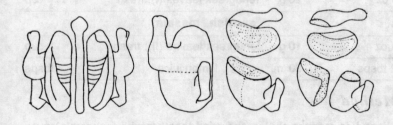

Normal chicken cut in 8 pieces for curry or casseroles.

Boneless Chicken Curry in Fenugreek

Another dish made resplendent by the Nizam's cooks. Simplified for greater delicacy of flavour.

Serves 4
Cooking Time: 10–15 minutes

British	Metric	Ingredient	American
2¾ lb	1¼ kg	broiler chicken, de-boned, cut into medium size pieces	2¾ lb
2¾ oz (4 tbsps)	60 g	ghee	¼ cup
5 oz	150 g	butter	⅝ cup
½ tbsp	7.5 g	salt, to taste	½ tbsp
½ tsp	2.5 g	sugar	½ tsp
singe-fry masala			
2 tsps	5.5 g	nigella (*kalonji*) seed	2 tsps
1 tbsp	10 g	turmeric powder	1 tbsp
follow-up masala			
3	3	green chillies, medium	3
⅔ oz	20 g	fenugreek leaves (I), fresh	⅔ cup
garnish masala			
⅓ oz	10 g	fenugreek leaves (II), fresh	⅓ cup
2 tbsps	30 ml	lemon juice	2 tbsps

Method

Slit and de-seed the chilles, and grind together with fenugreek leaves (I) and keep aside.

Put the ghee in a wok or a heavy-bottomed saucepan, and bring to high heat. Fry the green fenugreek (II) till the light green leaves become dark and crisp. Remove the fried leaves and leave them to drain on kitchen paper.

Return the saucepan to fire and heat the remaining ghee. Add the *singe-fry masala*—first the nigella, which will crackle in a few seconds, followed by turmeric. Then add the *follow-up masala* of green chillies and green fenugreek paste and stir fry the mixture for a few minutes till a thickish emulsion is formed and all the ingredients are properly mixed. Now add the butter and let it foam, but not boil. Add the chicken and stir fry until it becomes whitish. Be careful not to over-cook the chicken, for if this happens, all the juices will be released and the chicken is likely to become tough. (Always remember that only broilers should be used here.)

The chicken will take anything between 5–10 minutes to cook.

Test the chicken with a toothpick and if done, add sugar and salt and mix well. Transfer to an attractive serving dish.

Sprinkle the *garnish masala* on top and serve.

NOTE: May be eaten with plain boiled rice or any oriental bread. Even plain white bread will do. It also makes a good snack by itself. The chicken used should be broiler chicken only.

Fenugreek greens have a slightly bitter after-taste. But they are available only in season. If fenugreek greens are not available, green coriander leaves may be used. Each has its own distinctive flavour.

Curried Chicken With Fenugreek Greens (*Murgah Methi*): Hyderabad

This is a typical Hyderabadi dish, which I have not seen cooked anywhere else. This version was made specially for me by a very eminent cook from the Nizam's kitchen.

Serves 3–4
Cooking Time: 35–40 minutes

British	Metric	Ingredients	American
$2\frac{3}{4}$ lb	$1\frac{1}{4}$ kg	chicken, broiler, made into 8–10 pieces	$2\frac{3}{4}$ lb
5 fl oz (1 cup)	150 ml	cooking oil	$\frac{5}{8}$ cup
3	3	onions, medium, finely chopped	3
16 fl oz (3 cups)	450 ml	water, enough to make chicken tender	2 cups
$3\frac{1}{2}$ oz	160 g	fenugreek, green & tender leaves only	$3\frac{1}{2}$ cups
$\frac{1}{2}$ tsp	2.5 g	salt (I), to taste	$\frac{1}{2}$ tsp
singe-fry masala			
1 tbsp	15 g	garlic paste	1 tbsp
1 tbsp	15 g	ginger paste	1 tbsp
1 tsp	3.5 g	turmeric powder	1 tsp
follow-up masala			
$5\frac{1}{2}$ oz (1 cup)	165 g	yoghurt, creamed	$\frac{5}{8}$ cup
$\frac{1}{2}$ tbsp	7.5 g	salt (II), to taste	$\frac{1}{2}$ tbsp
during-cooking masala			
6	6	green chillies, finely ground	6
1 oz	30 g	green coriander, leaves only, finely ground	1 cup

Method

Heat the oil until it is very hot, then lightly brown the onions. Add the *singe-fry masala* and fry for about 2 minutes till all of it is light brown. Add the *follow-up masala* of yoghurt and salt, and simmer on medium heat till most of the water from the yoghurt evaporates. Add the chicken pieces and fry in the masala on medium to high heat till it is brown. Take care not to let it stick to the pan. Pour water, cover pan and cook on low heat for 10–12 minutes until the chicken is tender. At this time about half a cup (3 fl oz /75 ml /$\frac{1}{3}$ cup) water will remain. Add the *during-cooking masala* plus fenugreek leaves and salt (I). Stir briskly and cook for another 5–6 minutes.

Remove from fire—do not over-cook or the fenugreek will become bitter.

Transfer the chicken to a pre-heated white China bowl and serve with rice or Indian bread. Squeeze a little lime juice if preferred.

NOTE: Green fenugreek is available round the year in Hyderabad. This may be the reason why this dish is predominant in that region.

Coconut Chicken Curry: Madras

A South Indian non-vegetarian dish. Fairly simple and made for daily fare. This recipe is less spicy than it is actually made in the South.

Serves 3
Cooking Time: 35–40 minutes

British	Metric	Ingredients	American
2¼ lb	1 kg	broiler chicken, skinned & cut into 4–6 pieces	2¼ lb
3½ fl oz (⅔ cup)	100 ml	cooking oil, preferably ghee	½ cup
2 tsps	10 g	salt, to taste	2 tsps
3	3	onions, finely sliced	3
singe-fry masala			
½ tsp	1 g	chilli powder	½ tsp
1 tsp	3.5 g	turmeric	1 tsp
follow-up masala			
½ tsp	2.5 g	garlic paste	½ tsp
½ tbsp	7.5 g	ginger paste	½ tbsp
1 tsp	3.25 g	black pepper powder	1 tsp

½ pt (2 cups)	300 ml	coconut milk	1¼ cups
18 oz	500 g	tomatoes	18 oz
		garnish masala	
⅓ oz (½ cup)	10 g	green coriander, leaves only	⅓ cup

Method

Lightly steam or single boil the tomatoes. Purée and strain. Keep aside.

Heat the oil or ghee. Fry the onions till light brown, then add the *singe-fry masala* and fry for half a minute. Add the *follow-up masala* and salt and stir fry for about 5 minutes. Add the pieces of chicken, stir fry and simmer for another 10 minutes, or until the water from the chicken evaporates. Add the *during-cooking masala* of coconut milk and the tomato purée. Cook on slow fire until the chicken is tender. The consistency should be of a thick sauce.

Transfer to a serving bowl and sprinkle with the *garnish masala*.

NOTE: Serve with boiled rice or any oriental bread. Tortillas go well with this dish.

Only broiler chicken should be used to prepare this curry.

'Five Greens' Chicken Curry

Each of the greens used in this recipe has its own singular flavour and texture. Their blending with chicken makes for such a natural combination that it seems as if they always belonged together. A very healthy and complete food.

Serves 4–6
Preparation Time: 30 minutes
Cooking Time: 45 minutes

British	Metric	Ingredients	American
2	2	broiler chicken, cut into 8–10 pieces per bird, about $2\frac{1}{4}$ lb (1 kg)	2
9 oz	250 g	spinach	9 oz
9 oz	250 g	mustard greens	9 oz
$3\frac{1}{2}$ oz	100 g	coriander greens	$3\frac{1}{2}$ oz
$3\frac{1}{2}$ oz	160 g	fenugreek greens	$3\frac{1}{2}$ oz
2 oz	50 g	dill greens	2 oz
5 oz (1 cup)	150 g	ghee	$\frac{5}{8}$ cup
8 fl oz ($1\frac{1}{2}$ cups)	225 ml	milk	1 cup
2 oz	50 g	butter	$\frac{1}{4}$ cup
		marinade masala	
9 oz ($1\frac{1}{2}$ cups)	250 g	yoghurt	1 cup
1 tbsp	15 g	salt, to taste	1 tbsp
2 tsps	10 g	garlic paste	2 tsps
		singe-fry masala	
1 tbsp	8 g	cumin powder	1 tbsp
1 tbsp	6 g	coriander powder	1 tbsp
1 tbsp	10 g	turmeric powder	1 tbsp
		during-cooking masala 1	
1 tbsp	15 g	ginger paste	1 tbsp
1 tsp	5 g	garlic paste	1 tsp
1 tsp	5 g	green chilli paste	1 tsp
		during-cooking masala 2	
3	3	bay leaves (*tejpat*)	3
5	5	brown cardamoms	5
1"	2.5 cm (1 g)	cinnamon	1"

1 tbsp	15 g	salt, to taste	1 tbsp
		finishing masala	
		leftover marinade	
1 tsp	2.25 g	cornflour	1 tsp
		garnish masala	
2	2	green chillies, chopped	2
8	8	green spring onions, chopped	8
3	3	garlic, cloves, through press	3

Method

Cut each chicken into 8–10 pieces and steep in the marinade masala for half-an-hour. Wash and clean the greens in water several times. Put in a colander and pour boiling water over them till all the greens are limp and turn dark green. When cool, medium chop or cut the greens into 1–2 cm pieces.

Heat the ghee in a wok or pan, add the *singe-fry masala* and then the chicken. Stir fry for about 5 minutes until light brown and ghee is released. Add the *during-cooking masala 1* followed by the milk plus the *during-cooking masala 2*. Simmer till done. Transfer to a baking dish.

Take the leftover marinade and add 1 teaspoon cornflour and cream it in a blender. Add the blended marinade and the chopped greens to the baking dish. Put 50 g of butter on top and bake on medium heat for 15 minutes.

Sprinkle the *garnish masala* evenly on top and serve in the baking dish with rice or bread.

NOTE: The greens should not be over-cooked.

Only broiler chickens should be used for preparation.

Chicken Curry Do Piazza

There is a historical anecdote of 'Do Piazza' relating to the famous Mullah Do Piazza who was at Akbar's court. He is supposed to have cooked all his dishes with but two onions—hence *do piaza*. Somehow the dish acquired its present form with another interpretation—that of 'onions twice'.

Serves 3
Cooking Time: 45–50 minutes

British	Metric	Ingredients	American
$2\frac{1}{4}$ lb	1 kg	chicken, one large curry-cut 6–8 pieces	$2\frac{1}{4}$ lb
5 oz (1 cup)	150 g	ghee	$\frac{5}{8}$ cup
11 oz	300 g	onions(l), finely sliced	11 oz
$\frac{1}{2}$ pt (2 cups)	300 ml	water	$1\frac{1}{4}$ cups
singe-fry masala			
$\frac{1}{2}$ tsp	5 g	cumin whole	$\frac{1}{2}$ tsp
$\frac{1}{2}$ tsp	1.25 g	cumin powder	$\frac{1}{2}$ tsp
1 tsp	2 g	coriander powder	1 tsp
1 tbsp	10 g	turmeric powder	1 tbsp
1 tsp	2 g	chilli powder	1 tsp
follow-up masala			
1 tsp	5 g	ginger paste	1 tsp
1 tbsp	15 g	garlic paste	1 tbsp
during-cooking masala			
2 tsps	10 g	salt, to taste	2 tsps
3	3	bay leaves (*tejpat*)	3
5	5	green chillies, slit lengthwise	5

4	4	cardamoms, large, brown	4
1"	2.5 cm	cinnamon (1 g)	1"
1 tsp	2.5 g	amchoor	1 tsp
6	6	onions(II), quartered	6
		finishing masala	
1 tsp	2.5 g	garam masala	1 tsp
		garnish masala	
1 tbsp	2 g	green coriander, scissor-cut	1 tbsp

Method

Heat the ghee in a heavy-bottomed saucepan and brown the first lot of onions—remove on paper and keep aside.

Bring the remaining ghee to high heat and mix in the *singe-fry masala* adding turmeric last. As soon as it splutters, add the *follow-up masala* and the browned onions. Stir fry for 5–6 minutes. Add the chicken and stir fry till reddish brown, then add salt and the *during-cooking masala* including the second lot of onions. Mix well and stir fry for a few minutes. Add water, cover and cook on low heat till the chicken is soft (this takes about 20 minutes for a broiler and 40 minutes for a regular chicken).

Transfer to a white serving bowl and sprinkle with the *finishing masala* and then the *garnish masala*.

Serve with boiled rice.

NOTE: Onions are used twice—when they are browned and when they are added quartered, the latter remain soft and glazed. On special occasions, saffron, soaked in milk, is added before the garam masala.

Bouquet Chicken Curry With Spiced Yoghurt

An elegant dish which combines all the spices of South India with ingredients of the North. A unique blend of spices and yoghurt. This is a dish for special occasions.

Serves 2–3
Cooking Time: 50–55 minutes

British	Metric	Ingredients	American
1	1	broiler chicken, medium-size, cut into about 8 pieces	1
3½ fl oz (⅔ cup)	100 ml	cooking oil	½ cup
18 fl oz (3½ cups)	500 ml	water	2¼ cups
½ tbsp	7.5 g	salt, to taste	½ tbsp
singe-fry masala			
½ tsp	2.75 g	cumin powder	½ tsp
1 tsp	3.5 g	turmeric powder	1 tsp
½ tsp	1 g	coriander powder	½ tsp
1 tsp	2 g	chilli powder	1 tsp
follow-up masala			
1 tsp	5 g	ginger paste	1 tsp
1 tsp	5 g	garlic paste	1 tsp
during-cooking masala			
5½ oz (1 cup)	165 g	yoghurt	⅝ cup
1 tbsp	2 g	green coriander, scissor-cut	1 tbsp
1 tsp	0.5 g	green mint, scissor-cut	1 tsp
5	5	curry leaves	5
1 tsp	2.75 g	garam masala	1 tsp
2 tbsps	20 g	poppy seed, roasted & ground	2 tbsps

1 tbsp	10 g	pinenuts (*chironji* seed)	1 tbsp
1 tbsp	7.5 g	onions, finely chopped	1 tbsp
finishing masala			
½ tsp	1.25 g	cardamoms, small, seeded, coarsely ground	½ tsp
garnish masala			
1 tbsp	2 g	green coriander, scissor-cut	1 tbsp
½ tbsp	3 g	green chilli, scissor-cut, de-seeded	½ tbsp
1 tbsp	7.5 g	spring onions, green, finely chopped	1 tbsp

Method

Take a saucepan, bring the oil to smoking point and cook the onions until they are golden brown. Remove the onions from the oil with a slotted spoon and set aside on kitchen paper to drain.

Put the during-cooking masala, including the fried onions, in a liquidizer and blend with about half cup of water until smooth. Set aside.

Heat the remaining oil from the saucepan in a heavy flame-proof pan and bring to smoking. Add the *singe-fry masala* and stir fry for 10–20 seconds. Add the *follow-up masala* and again stir fry for a minute or two. Now add the jointed chicken and stir fry on high heat for 5 minutes till light brown. Add salt. Add the blended *during-cooking masala* and the remaining water. Cover and cook in a moderate oven for 30–40 minutes depending on the size and type of chicken. Check to make sure the sauce has become viscous.

Remove from the oven, sprinkle the *finishing masala* first and then the *garnish masala*.

Serve with rice or any oriental bread.

NOTE: This is one of the few dishes which makes use of practically every aromatic spice and herb in the Indian kitchen. If well made with good quality spices, the aromas and flavour will linger in your memory.

Butter Chicken Curry

Currently a much fancied dish. Perhaps this dish has something of goulash, curry and tomato cream soup—all occidental flavours.

Serves 2
Cooking Time: 40–45 minutes

British	Metric	Ingredients	American
2¼ lb	1 kg	chicken	2¼ lb
6 oz (1 cup)	150 g	butter, melted	¾ cup
singe-fry masala			
½ tbsp	4 g	cumin powder	½ tbsp
1 tsp	2 g	coriander powder	½ tsp
follow-up masala 1			
1 tsp	5 g	ginger paste	1 tsp
2 tbsps	20 g	poppy seed paste	2 tbsps
1 tsp	2 g	chilli powder	1 tsp
follow-up masala 2 (boiled & puréed)			
6–8 cloves	6–8 cloves	garlic	6–8 cloves
2	2	onions, medium	2
during-cooking masala 1			
5 fl oz (1 cup)	150 ml	coconut milk	⅝ cup
2 tsps	10 g	salt, to taste	2 tsps
during-cooking masala 2			
6	6	tomatoes, medium, skinned & deseeded	6
3 oz (½ cup)	85 g	yoghurt	⅜ cup
1 tbsp	7 g	Hungarian sweet red paprika	1 tbsp
3 fl oz (½ cup)	75 ml	cream	⅜ cup

½ tsp	2.5 g	sugar	½ tsp
1 tbsp	7 g	cornflour	1 tbsp
		finishing masala	
1 tbsp	8.25 g	garam masala	1 tbsp
		garnish masala	
4	4	red chillies, whole, dried, cut into 3 pieces & deseeded	4

Method

Soft boil the garlic and onions of the follow-up masala 2. Then purée and keep aside.

Put the during-cooking masala 2 in a blender and liquidize for about 2 minutes till smooth and keep aside.

Cut the chicken into 6–8 pieces, wash and dry with a kitchen towel and keep aside.

Heat the butter in a deep cooking pan until it is bubbling but not burning, add the *singe-fry masala* and stir fry for 2–3 minutes. Add the *follow-up masala 1* and stir fry for another 3–5 minutes. Add the *follow up masala 2* and mix well for a few minutes till onions glaze. Now add the chicken and fry on moderate heat making sure the chicken is well coated with the masala in the pan. Add the *during-cooking masala 1* and simmer for 5–8 minutes till the chicken is almost done. While the chicken is simmering add the *during-cooking masala 2* and simmer till oil is released. This takes about 20 minutes.

The chicken will by now be really tender. Check and taste for salt and chilli. Reduce heat to minimum add the *finishing masala*, and stir.

Transfer to a white serving bowl and top it with the *garnish masala*.

Serve with rice or any oriental bread.

MEAT CURRIES

Sealed-Pot Curries: Sindhi

This is an extraordinary dish in the best traditions of a casserole. Only a single stage of cooking is required since all the other masala stages are within the single stage. It keeps all the aromas intact and renders the meat soft but palpable.

These sealed-pot curries are extremely easy to make and have a bewildering texture and flavour.

Serves 4
Cooking Time: 70-80 minutes

British	Metric	Ingredients	American
2¼ lb	1 kg	mutton or lamb goulash (cut preferably with some fat)	2¼ lb
4½ oz	125 g	ghee	½ cup
7 oz (1⅓ cups)	200 g	yoghurt	¾ cup
1 tsp	2.25 g	cornflour	1 tsp
7 oz	200 g	tomatoes	7 oz
9 oz	250 g	onions	9 oz
1	1	garlic, bulb	1
10	10	cardamoms, regular	10
3	3	bay leaves (*tejpat*)	3
1 tbsp	10 g	turmeric powder	1 tbsp
2 tbsps	12 g	coriander powder	2 tbsps
2 tsps	10 g	salt, to taste	2 tsps
1 tbsp	7 g	Hungarian sweet red paprika	1 tbsp
1 tsp	2 g	chilli powder	1 tsp

Method

Wash the meat and dry with a kitchen towel.

Clove and skin the garlic, smash with a knife handle.

117

Cream the yoghurt with cornflour in a blender, for just 5–10 seconds—otherwise butter will be released. Put the tomatoes in boiling water for a few minutes and peel. Slice the tomatoes,in thickness of $\frac{1}{5}$" ($\frac{1}{2}$cm), and the onions in medium thickness.

Now put everything including the rest of the ingredients into a pot with a flat lid. Seal the lid and pot with dough—made from flour. Put 2 lb (1 kg) weight on top.

Cook on slow fire for 70-80 minutes. Uncover and test the meat and salt. If the meat is not done, cook a little more.

Ladle the curry into a fancy dish and serve with boiled rice or any oriental bread.

NOTE: Mutton may be substituted with beef, pork or venison. Venison may take a little longer to cook, or 1 tsp (4 g) of meat tenderizer may be added to the curry and the salt reduced by half a teaspoon or 5 g.

One can use a heavy flame-proof casserole with a heavy lid instead of sealing with dough. It can also be baked in an oven instead of cooking on open fire.

Hungarian paprika is substituted for the Indian Kashmir red pepper because of its ready availability in Europe.

In India it is advisable to use lamb meat from shoulder 'Machhli', striped muscle with bone, some fatty breast pieces and 'Puth', never from the lower spinal column—the leg meat so-called 'Gol Boti' tends to be hard.

Big chunk of fatty lamb for goulash cut.

Note: Goulash comes from Hungarian *gulyas*. It is similar size as for 'curry cut'. All European butchers understand this term. In India curry meat is similar to goulash cut.

Beef Stroganoff: *a l'Indienne*

The Slav kitchen of Georgia is very famous. The stroganoff is one of their most prized national dishes. The Slav palate accepts spices to a considerable extent. At the instance of friends in Czechoslovakia this dish was made and has since been repeated many times.

Serves 2–4
Cooking Time: 25–30 minutes

British	Metric	Ingredients	American
18 oz	500 g	beef fillet	18 oz
4 oz	100 g	butter	$\frac{1}{2}$ cup
3	3	onions, large, finely sliced	3
$5\frac{1}{2}$ oz (1 cup)	165 g	yoghurt	$\frac{5}{8}$ cup
1 tsp	2.25 g	cornflour	1 tsp
1 tsp	3 g	mustard seed, freshly ground ground or Coleman's	1 tsp
2 oz	50 g	morel dry (*gucchi*)	2 oz
1 tsp	3.5 g	turmeric powder	1 tsp
1 tsp	2 g	coriander powder	1 tsp
1 tsp	5 g	salt, to taste	1 tsp
$\frac{1}{2}$ tsp	1.5 g	pepper, freshly ground in pepper mill	$\frac{1}{2}$ tsp
1 tsp	2 g	chilli powder	1 tsp

Method

Cut the beaf fillet into strips of $2" \times \frac{1}{2}"$. Keep aside.

Pour boiling water over the dry morel and keep aside for about 10 minutes.

Cream the yoghurt with mustard and cornflour, and keep aside. This is a substitute for the sour cream in the classical stroganoff. Gently fry the

119

onions in 2 tablespoons (30 g) of butter until they are golden brown. Add the morel after taking them out of the hot water and squeezing them partially. Stir fry for another 2 minutes.

Remove the onions and morel into another dish, and use a fresh large chafing-dish or saucepan and bring the remaining butter to high heat. Stir fry the beef very quickly without letting the juices run out. As you do this, sprinkle all the turmeric and coriander powder on top. Add the onion and morel to the meat and cook slowly for 2–3 minutes. Add the salt, chilli powder and yoghurt with mustard and stir till creamy and near boiling. Top it with black pepper and serve with boiled rice, gnocci or boiled potatoes.

NOTE: Gnocci is European pasta. They are dumplings made of flour, corn meal, semolina or even potatoes, poached and then baked. Often topped with cheese and butter.

Because of the mustard, this dish has a piquant taste, not unlike the Georgian stroganoff.

Because of its nutty flavour a jigger of Kirsch can be added.

The classical sequence of the masala stages is not applicable to this dish because of its simplicity. In case morel are difficult to procure use any mushroom.

'Canteen' Mince Meat Curry

A staple dish on canteen menus, this curry meat sauce is easy to make and has a flavour which is universally popular.

Serves 3
Cooking Time: 35–40 minutes

British	Metric	Ingredients	American
18 oz	$\frac{1}{2}$ kg	any mince meat	$2\frac{1}{2}$ cups
2 oz	50 g	split chick pea lentil (*chana ki dal*)	$\frac{1}{4}$ cup

4	4	onions, finely chopped	4
1 tbsp	7.5 g	garlic, finely chopped	1 tbsp
5 oz	150 g	yoghurt, hung in muslin overnight to drain water	5 oz
1 tbsp	8.25 g	garam masala	1 tbsp
1 tsp	2 g	coriander powder	1 tsp
1 tsp	2 g	chilli powder	1 tsp
$\frac{1}{2}$ tbsp	7.5 g	salt, to taste	$\frac{1}{2}$ tbsp
5 fl oz	150 ml	cooking oil, any	$\frac{5}{8}$ cup
13 fl oz	375 ml	water	$1\frac{5}{8}$ cups

Method

Mix all the ingredients well by hand except for water and oil. Take a heavy-bottomed pan, bring oil to smoking point and add the mixture. Stir fry on high heat vigorously for 5–6 minutes. Add water, cover and simmer on moderate heat for half an hour or till the mince and dal are done.

Remove the cover and continue cooking, stirring now and then, till the excess water evaporates and the oil comes to the top. Stir fry till the meat is well browned and the aromas are distinct.

NOTE: Serve with anything—rice, potatoes, noodles, dumplings or any kind of bread—chapattis, naan, puri, plain bread, kulcha, paratha, pizza bread—along with chopped raw onions and green chillies.

This dish has only one stage of cooking, and most of the ingredients are usually available in the Indian kitchen. The 'cream cheese' of hung dried yoghurt is always available because leftover yoghurt which tends to sour is usually tied in a muslin and hung out in North India. All the spices are the standard masalas readily available in all homes and canteens.

If you have the Kashmir red colour chilli powder or Hungarian red paprika—add a tablespoon to make the dish more spicy.

The beauty of this dish extends further. If there is any leftover, it may be used as a samosa filling or paratha filling or made into burgers by shaping it and dipping it in whisked egg, after which it is crumbed and deep fried.

It can also be used as a filling for round or crook neck gourds, as well as for courgette (zuccini), tomatoes, aubergine or capsicum. After filling the vegetable baste with butter, bake for 10–15 minutes in a foil.

It can also be made into a European meat loaf. Bake it with a puff pastry crust or use it as a filling for Vol au Vent.

Do not worry if the chick pea lentil feels hard to bite as this lends 'bite' when the mince is stir fried at the end.

Roast Shoulder With Curry Masala Filling—Served With Curry Sauce

Traditionally it is *masala ran* or leg of lamb that is used. I tried the shoulder which was more pleasing—perhaps easier to make as well. This dish is credited to the Moghul and Rampur cooks.

Serves 3–4
Cooking Time: 90–100 minutes

British	Metric	Ingredients	American
1⅛–1½ lb	500–700 g	shoulder of lamb	1⅛–1½ lb
9 oz	250 g	butter, melted for basting	1¼ cups
stuffing			
1 oz	30 g	cottage cheese (*panir*), finely grated, (mozzarella cheese will also do)	¼ cup
1 tsp	2.75 g	garam masala	1 tsp
3½ oz	100 g	mince meat	½ cup
¼ tsp	0.5 g	nutmeg, grated	¼ tsp

122

½ tsp	1 g	chilli powder	½ tsp
1 tsp	2.5 g	garlic, finely chopped	1 tsp
1	1	egg, lightly beaten	1
½ tsp	1 g	ginger powder	½ tsp
20	20	black pepper corn, whole	20
1 tbsp	10 g	poppy seed, roasted, grounded	1 tbsp
1 oz	30 g	butter	2 tbsps
1 tsp	5 g	salt, to taste	1 tsp
2 oz	60 g	semolina, roasted light brown	⅓ cup
3 fl oz (½ cup)	75 ml	water	⅜ cup
		sauce	
4 oz	100 g	butter	½ cup
2	2	onions, finely sliced	2
1 tsp	3.5 g	turmeric powder	1 tsp
1 tsp	2 g	coriander powder	1 tsp
1 tsp	2.25 g	cornflour	1 tsp
2 tbsps	30 ml	water (I)	2 tbsps
5 fl oz	150 ml	water (II)	⅝ cup
½ tsp	1.5 g	black pepper powder	½ tsp
½ tsp	1.25 g	black cumin powder	½ tsp
½ tsp	1.25 g	garam masala	½ tsp
1 tsp	5 g	salt, to taste	1 tsp

Method

De-bone the shoulder—this is best done by the butcher.

After roasting to light brown, soak the semolina in half a cup of water for 15 minutes. Mix well by hand all the ingredients of the stuffing including the soaked semolina.

Fill the stuffing as for normal shoulder. Stitch the open ends securely.

Place the shoulder in a roasting tray and smear it with butter. Roast in medium heat of 180–200 deg C, for 60–75 minutes. If wanted well done, roast for another 15 minutes or so; but the best is medium done.

From time to time baste lamb with butter and turn sides. When lamb is done, remove from baking tray and pour all the liquid from the tray to another bowl. Return lamb to the roasting tray and let it stay in a warm oven with the heat turned off.

Mix the cornflour in water (I) and keep aside.

Now to make sauce, bring butter to bubbling and brown the onions—fairly dark brown—add all the ingredients except water (II) and stir fry for about 30 seconds. Add water (II) and the mixed cornflour and keep stirring till the sauce is medium thick and aromatic. Add the gravy left from the roasting and mix well.

Serve the shoulder sliced to your liking with gravy sauce. Do not slice when too hot. Let shoulder rest outside the oven for 15 minutes before slicing. The sauce should have the flavour of curry meat.

NOTE: Best eaten with boiled potatoes or dumplings. Also goes well with rice. Gravy sauce goes well with potatoes and dumplings as well.

Roast masala leg of lamb, which is a little more arduous, is given in another recipe.

Traditionally *khoya,* a form of unsweetened condensed milk, was used instead of *panir* or mozzarella cheese. If available do use it.

Shoulder.

Big chunks of fatty lamb from shoulder.

Curried Hamburgers: *a l' Indienne*

A very popular dish at cocktail parties. Basically these are mince cutlets from beef, pork or lamb shaped in a 'burger' mould or by hand. They are served in between mini naans, small round naans made to the diameter of the burger.

Serves 3–4
Preparation Time: 30 minutes
Cooking Time: 35– 40 minutes

British	Metric	Ingredients	American
		burger mix	
2¼ lb	1 kg	mince meat, semi-coarse to make about 10–12 burgers	5 cups
½ tbsp	4 g	garam masala	½ tbsp
1	1	egg	1
2 tbsps	15 g	onion, finely chopped	2 tbsps
2 oz (1 cup)	50 g	bread crumbs	½ cup
1½ tbsps	22 ml	Worcestorshire sauce	1½ tbsps
2 tsps	10 g	salt, to taste	2 tsps
1½ tbsps	3 g	green coriander, scissor-cut	1½ tbsps
1 tbsp	15 ml	cooking oil	1 tbsp
1 tsp	3.25 g	black pepper powder	1 tsp
1 tsp	2 g	chilli powder	1 tsp
5 fl oz	150 ml	melted butter, for basting	⅝ cup
		garnish (as for hamburger)	
		onion rings—to individual taste	
		amchoor— to individual taste	
		tomato, sliced—to individual taste	

Method

Mix all the ingredients, except butter, thoroughly and let sit it in a bowl for half-an-hour.

Take a burger mould and make 10–12 burgers. You can also do it by hand. The thickness should be of about half to one inch.

Put aluminium foil on a baking grill, and coat it with melted butter. Place the burgers on the foil and baste them with melted butter. Cover with another foil and fold over the tray.

Bake for half-an-hour in moderate heat. Open and test with a toothpick, it should come out clean—otherwise cover again and bake for another 5–10 minutes. When done remove both foils and place burgers on the grill on full heat (both upper and lower) for 2–3 minutes.

Serve between 'mini naans' (made to order or make yourself as per recipe on page 241), in hamburger buns or muffins alongwith the onion rings and tomato slices with a little *amchoor* on the onion rings.

NOTE: The same mix can be used for *seekh kabab* and barbecued meat. It can also made into koftas and put in various curry sauces.

Red Pepper Beef Curry

One of the most popular forms of cooking in Europe and elsewhere is the casserole. It is usually a single process dish which ensures aromas and flavour.

Serves 3
Cooking Time: 60–70 minutes

British	Metric	Ingredients	American
18 oz	½ kg	beef, preferably lean, cut for normal stew	18 oz
1 oz (2 tbsps)	30 ml	cooking oil	2 tbsps

2 oz	50 g	butter	$\frac{1}{4}$ cup
2	2	capsicums, red, quartered	2
8	8	red chillies, dry, whole	8
4	4	onions, finely chopped	4
3 or 4 cloves		garlic, through press	3 or 4 cloves
$1\frac{1}{2}$ fl oz	40 g	tomato purée	3 tbsps
$\frac{1}{2}$ tbsp	7.5 g	salt, to taste	$\frac{1}{2}$ tbsp
1 tsp	2.75 g	cumin powder	1 tsp
1 tsp	3.5 g	turmeric powder	1 tsp
$\frac{1}{2}$ tsp	1.5 g	black pepper powder	$\frac{1}{2}$ tsp
4	4	cloves	4
2	2	bay leaves (*tejpat*)	2
2	2	cardamons, brown, large	2
1 tsp	2 g	chilli powder	1 tsp
8 fl oz ($1\frac{1}{2}$ cups)	225 ml	boiling water	1 cup

Method

Chop the beef to cubes of one-and-a-half inch. Keep aside.

Take a heavy saucepan, pour oil and bring to smoking. Brown the onions, add tomato purée and stir fry till oil is released. Add meat and stir fry till brown.

Transfer to a casserole dish. Add all the other ingredients and mix. Then bake covered for 40–45 minutes till meat is done and the butter is released. Serve with rice or eat with bread as stew.

Goulash cut about $1\frac{1}{2}$ "
—may be irregular.

Roast Leg of Lamb with Masala Filling—Served with Curry Sauce

This is the traditional recipe for *masala ran* and comes from the plain 'spit' roast leg of lamb or other animals eaten by nomads and hunters.

A more sophisticated version was evolved. This was mainly due to the availability of herbs and spices. The stuffing is the same as for the shoulder of lamb.

Serves 3–4
Cooking Time: 90–100 minutes

British	Metric	Ingredients	American
$1\frac{1}{8}$–$1\frac{1}{2}$ lb	500–700 g	leg of lamb, de-boned	$1\frac{1}{8}$–$1\frac{1}{2}$ lb
9 fl oz	250 ml	butter, melted for basting	$1\frac{1}{4}$ cup
		stuffing	
1 oz	30 g	cottage cheese (*panir*), finely grated, (mozzarella cheese will also do)	$\frac{1}{4}$ cup
1 tsp	2.75 g	garam masala	1 tsp
$3\frac{1}{2}$ oz	100 g	mince meat	$\frac{1}{2}$ cup
$\frac{1}{4}$ tsp	0.5 g	nutmeg, grated	$\frac{1}{4}$ tsp
$\frac{1}{2}$ tsp	1 g	chilli powder	$\frac{1}{2}$ tsp
1 tsp	2.5 g	garlic, finely chopped	1 tsp
1	1	egg, lightly beaten	1
$\frac{1}{2}$ tsp	1 g	ginger powder	$\frac{1}{2}$ tsp
20	20	black pepper corns, whole	20
1 tbsp	10 g	poppy seed, roasted & ground	1 tbsp
1 oz	30 g	butter	2 tbsps
1 tsp	5 g	salt, to taste	1 tsp

2 oz ($\frac{1}{2}$ cup)	60 g	semolina, roasted light brown	$\frac{1}{3}$ cup
3 fl oz ($\frac{1}{2}$ cup)	75 ml	water	$\frac{3}{8}$ cup

sauce

4 oz	100 g	butter	$\frac{1}{2}$ cup
2	2	onions, finely sliced	2
1 tsp	3.5 g	turmeric powder	1 tsp
1 tsp	2 g	coriander powder	1 tsp
1 tsp	2.25 g	cornflour	1 tsp
2 tbsps	30 ml	water (I)	2 tbsps
5 fl oz (1 cup)	150 ml	water (II)	$\frac{5}{8}$ cup
$\frac{1}{2}$ tsp	1.5 g	black pepper powder	$\frac{1}{2}$ tsp
$\frac{1}{2}$ tsp	1.25 g	black cumin powder	$\frac{1}{2}$ tsp
$\frac{1}{2}$ tsp	1.25 g	garam masala	$\frac{1}{2}$ tsp
1 tsp	5 g	salt, to taste	1 tsp
		juices from roasting—collected from tray	

Method

After roasting the semolina to light brown, soak it in half a cup of water for 15 minutes. Mix well by hand all the ingredients of the stuffing, including the soaked semolina.

Mix the cornflour in water (I) and keep aside.

De-bone the leg of lamb—best done by the butcher. Make sure both the leg bone and the shank bone are removed. The leg is then cut open. Leave the outer membrane of the leg intact. Lay the open leg flat with the skin side down and fill it with stuffing by hand. Now roll the spread out meat to ensure the stuffing is totally enclosed. Tie the rolled leg 2" apart. Secure it by knotting the strings at the ends. This will hold the shape and prevent the stuffing from spilling out.

Preheat oven to very hot, about 340° C.

Place the leg in a roasting tray and smear it with butter. The roast is uncovered after reducing oven to medium heat of 180–200 deg C, for

129

$1-1\frac{1}{2}$ hours. If you want the lamb to be well done, roast for another 15 minutes or so. It is best when medium done.

From time to time baste lamb with butter and turn sides. When lamb is done remove from the baking tray and pour the liquid from the tray into another bowl. Return lamb to the roasting tray and place in the warm oven turning off the heat.

Now to make the sauce, bring butter to bubbling and brown the onions (fairly dark brown). Add all the ingredients, except water (II), and stir fry for about 30 seconds. Add water (II) and cornflour to water (I) and keep stirring till the sauce is medium thick and aromatic. Add the gravy left from the roasting and mix well.

After removing the strings serve the leg sliced to your liking with 'gravy sauce'. Do not slice when too hot. Let the rolled leg rest outside for 15 minutes before slicing. The sauce should have the curry meat flavour.

This dish is best eaten with boiled potatoes or dumplings, otherwise rice will do. Gravy sauce goes well with potatoes and dumplings as well.

NOTE: Traditionally *khoya,* a form of unsweetened condensed milk, was used instead of *panir* or mozzarella cheese. If available somehow, do use it.

Lamb with bone from leg.

Lamb with bone curry pieces.

Black Curry (*Jungle Gosht*)

This is basically a hunter's curry. The venison or wild boar or even wild pheasant is shot and cooked at site. The flavour can be described as a bit 'savage'—and the sauce in between a pickle and pepper soup. Very piquant.

Serves 4–6
Cooking Time: 45–50 minutes

British	Metric	Ingredients	American
2¼ lb	1 kg	venison, goulash cut	2¼ lb
3½ oz (⅔ cup)	100 g	ghee, or any cooking oil	½ cup
18 fl oz (3½ cups)	500 ml	water	2¼ cups
during-cooking masala			
1¾ oz	50 g	black pepper, ground	⅓ cup
1 tsp	5 g	salt, to taste	1 tsp
4	4	lemons, juice of	4

Method

Take any kind of cooking pan. Heat the ghee to high heat, put venison and stir fry till browned. Add the *during-cooking masala* and stir fry till well mixed. Add water and let simmer on medium fire for an hour (may be longer) till the venison is done.

Open the lid of the pan and cook a little while longer till most of the free water evaporates and ghee comes on top.

Serve with dry chappati or any bread, or with rice. Goes well with chopped raw onions.

The dish is incredibly simple and very piquant.

Lamb Curry (*Habshi Gosht*)

A great many Ethiopians were imported to India (probably as slaves) by the earlier Nizams of Hyderabad. Goat was plentiful and they created a dish with minimal spices with maximum effect and without the complex procedures of cooking.

Serves 4–6
Cooking Time: 75–80 minutes

British	Metric	Ingredients	American
2¼ lb	1 kg	goat/lamb/mutton, goulash cut	2¼ lb
2 fl oz (3 tbsps)	50 ml	cooking oil	¼ cup
18 fl oz (3½ cups)	500 ml	water	2¼ cups
2 tsps	10 g	salt, to taste	2 tsps
		masala	
5	5	chilli, whole, broken into 3 pieces	5
1 tbsp	7.5 g	garlic, finely chopped	1 tbsp
1 tbsp	5 g	allspice berries, powdered	1 tbsp
		other ingredients	
9 oz	250 g	potatoes, quartered	9 oz
9 oz	250 g	onions, quartered	9 oz
		finishing masala	
1 tbsp	10 g	turmeric powder	1 tbsp

Method

Heat oil in a deep heavy saucepan and add all the ingredients of the masala. Stir fry for 3–5 minutes. Add meat and stir fry for about 5 minutes. Add salt and mix. Then add water and let cook for 1½ hours till meat is almost done. Add the potatoes and onions, stir and let cook for another half an hour till the potatoes are done and the gravy is thick. Just before serving add the *finishing masala*.

Serve with rice or any bread or with saved up cold Indian breads.

NOTE: This is the authentic method for this curry. The simplicity of cooking speaks for its expediency. It is obvious that the particular consumers did not like the colour and added turmeric as an after thought, but it works very well. The dish has an invigorating flavour.

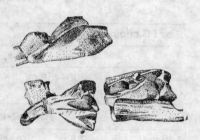

Goulash—medium cut—muscle from the leg

Machli cut — "stripe muscle' from the leg.

Korma Curry with Coarsely Ground Spices
(*Khade-Masale-Ka-Curried Lamb*)

This dish was introduced to me by a dear friend from Hyderabad. Originally founded in the royal kitchens of Rampur, Oudh and Murshidabad (now a part of Bengal), it is very wholesome and meaty. Although it has a normal curry format, it varies to the extent that there are only two stages and therefore is less complicated in preparation.

Serves 3–4
Cooking Time: 50–55 minutes

British	Metric	Ingredients	American
2¼ lb	1 kg	lamb, large pieces with bone	2¼ lb
9 oz (1⅔ cups)	250 g	ghee	1⅛ cups
3	3	onions, large, finely sliced	3
½–¾ pt (2–3 cups)	300–450 ml	water	1¼–2 cups
follow-up masala			
1 tbsp	7.5 g	garlic, finely sliced	1 tbsp
1 tbsp	6 g	ginger, matchstick slivers (irrespective of length)	1 tbsp
8	8	chillies, red, dry, whole	8
during-cooking masala			
2 tsps	10 g	salt, to taste	2 tsps
9 oz	250 g	yoghurt, creamed & strained	1 cup

Method

Break the red whole chillies to 3 pieces each and de-seed them. Keep aside.

Take a heavy copper-bottomed pan. Pour ghee, and bring to high heat, and fry onions to light brown. Add the *follow-up masala* and brown the whole mixture.

Add meat and stir fry till all the water released from meat evaporates. Then add salt.

Add the *during-cooking masala* and continue frying on slow fire for about 20–25 minutes stirring the meat, till yoghurt along with the mixture is well browned and the ghee is released to the surface.

Add water according to the amount of gravy required. Altogether the gravy should be approximately 5 cups($1\frac{1}{3}$ pt/750 ml/3 cups). Turn the heat to low and let simmer till the meat is tender. This takes 20–25 minutes.

The gravy should be fairly thick—evaporate water if too thin, add water if too thick.

Check meat with a toothpick or skewer. Taste to check salt.

Transfer into a white China serving bowl preheated with hot water and serve with rice or any of the Indian breads.

NOTE: *Khara masala* is coarsely ground masala in which the spices and herbs are neither ground to paste nor a powdered.

Creaming yoghurt means to put it in a mixer or blender for 10–15 seconds and then straining it.

Brain Curry with Fenugreek and Dill Greens

This is an unusual curry. It is best made in season when fresh fenugreek and dill greens are available—in North India from December to March and in South India throughout the year.

In Europe, where it may be difficult to get fenugreek greens, coriander greens can be substituted for fenugreek and 1 teaspoon of roasted and powdered fenugreek can be used in the singe-fry masala. Very flavourful and habit-forming though the taste is acquired.

135

Serves 2–3
Preparation Time: 15–20 minutes
Cooking Time: 35–40 minutes

British	Metric	Ingredients	American
4	4	sheep brains	4
5 fl oz	150 ml	cooking oil, preferably groundnut or sunflower	$\frac{5}{8}$ cup
2	2	onions, large, sliced	2
1 tsp	5 g	salt, to taste	1 tsp
singe-fry masala			
$\frac{1}{4}$ tsp	0.5 g	chilli powder	$\frac{1}{4}$ tsp
$\frac{1}{2}$ tsp	1.75 g	turmeric powder	$\frac{1}{2}$ tsp
1 tsp	3 g	fenugreek seed powder (if using coriander greens)	1 tsp
follow-up masala 1			
1 tsp	5 g	ginger paste	1 tsp
1 tsp	5 g	garlic paste	1 tsp
follow-up masala 2			
$4\frac{1}{2}$ oz ($\frac{3}{4}$ cup)	125 g	yoghurt	$\frac{5}{8}$ cup
follow-up masala 3			
$1\frac{1}{3}$ oz (2 cups)	40 g	fenugreek, green leaves only	$1\frac{1}{3}$ cups
$\frac{2}{3}$ oz	20 g	green coriander, leaves only (increase to double the quantity when fenugreek greens are unavailable)	$\frac{2}{3}$ cup
4	4	green chillies, sliced lengthwise & de-seeded	4
follow-up masala 4			
2 oz	50 g	dill greens, without stems	$\frac{5}{8}$ cup

Method

After cleaning the brains well, which is very important, soak them in cold water for 15 minutes. Then carefully remove the membrane surrounding each brain. Cut each in half and wash and let sit in water.

Bring oil in a deep frying pan to high heat. Add the onions and brown them. Remove and keep aside.

In the remaining oil add the *singe-fry masala* and fry for 30–40 seconds—immediately after which add the *follow-up masala 1* and the browned onions and stir fry for 2–3 minutes. Then add the *follow-up masala 2* and salt and let it simmer on low heat for 6–8 minutes. Now add the *follow-up masala 3* and again cook on slow fire for 10–15 minutes without stirring. After this add the *follow-up masala 4* and cook for another 3–5 minutes. Remove the pan from fire and after gently arranging the halved brain on top of the mixture in the pan return to the fire and let simmer for another 10 minutes on moderate heat. Do not stir. Shake the pan gently and turn the brains very carefully with a flat spatula to avoid breaking.

This is best served in the cooking pan or may be transferred very carefully with a flat spatula into a serving dish.

It is good by itself or with boiled buttered rice.

NOTE: This curry ends at the follow-up stage and all the masalas are used before the main ingredient because of the delicate nature of the brain which would be destroyed if cooked any further.

Red Curry (*Roghan Josh*): Kashmir

There are so many versions of *roghan josh* and so many interpretations of the words *roghen* and *josh* that one is always circumspect to say that this is the 'real thing'!

According to Persian cooks and scholars both words *roghan* and *josh* are pure Persian. *Roghan* means any kind of cooking fat, and *josh* means to augment by or accelerate or inspire.

Serves 3–5
Cooking Time: 40–45 minutes

British	Metric	Ingredients	American
2¼ lb	1 kg	meat, preferably mutton, goulash cut	2¼ lb
7 fl oz(1⅓ cups)	200 ml	ghee	⅞ cup
during-cooking masala 1			
3½ oz	100 g	yoghurt	½ cup
1 tbsp	7.5 g	ginger, finely chopped	1 tbsp
2½ tsps	12.5 g	salt, to taste	2½ tsps
2	2	cinnamon 1" (2.5 cm)	2
2	2	bay leaves (*tejpat*)	2
1 tbsp	6 g	chilli powder	1 tbsp
6	6	cloves	6
5	5	cardamoms, large brown	5
6	6	cardamoms, small green	6
during-cooking masala 2			
1 tsp	5 g	garlic paste	1 tsp
during-cooking masala 3			
1 tbsp	10 g	poppyseed, soaked & ground to a paste with a little water	1 tbsp
2 tsps	5.5 g	cumin powder	2 tsps
2 tsps	4 g	coriander powder	2 tsps
1 tbsp	7 g	Hungarian red paprika or *ratan jyot* (2 sticks)	1 tbsp
3 fl oz (½ cup)	75 ml	water	⅜ cup
finishing masala			
1 tbsp	8.25 g	garam masala	1 tbsp

Method

Put the meat alongwith the *during-cooking masala 1* in ghee. Cover and let cook on slow fire till the water from the meat evaporates. Turn the meat with a spatula or a large spoon and sprinkle a little of the garlic water, the *during-cooking masala 2* and keep stir frying. Repeatedly add the garlic water till meat is dry and reddish brown. The cooking pan should be heavy-bottomed to avoid sticking or burning during cooking. Now add the *during-cooking masala 3* and 3 fl oz (75 ml/⅜ cup) of water and again stir fry taking special care not to make the meat hard. This can be tested with a toothpick. By now the ghee which will be reddish, after adding *ratan jyot*, will have come to the top.

Transfer to a white serving bowl and add the *finishing masala*. Serve with rice or any Indian bread.

NOTE: Traditionally one uses asafoetida in water instead of garlic paste. Kashmiris will never use garlic. Asafoetida is very difficult to control, due to the fickle nature of the asafoetida gum which can vary from innocuous to the very strong. If one is not experienced in the organoleptic control of asafoetida, the dish can either become bland or inedible. If using *ratan jyot* remove the pieces before serving.

Sliced Liver Moghul Curry

A delectable dish which takes very little time. The Moghul curry sauce is incredibly simple. Supposedly a great favourite of Babar, the first Moghul emperor, this curry was invented in India.

Serves 3
Cooking Time: 18–20 minutes

British	Metric	Ingredients	American
18 oz	$\frac{1}{2}$ kg	lamb liver or calf liver	18 oz
$\frac{1}{2}$ tbsp	7.5 g	salt, to taste	$\frac{1}{2}$ tbsp
6 oz	150 g	butter, preferred over oil	$\frac{3}{4}$ cup
		follow-up masala	
1 fl oz (2 tbsps)	30 g	onions paste	$\frac{1}{8}$ cup
1 tsp	5 g	garlic paste	1 tsp
1 tsp	5 g	green chillies paste	1 tsp
1 tsp	5 g	green coriander paste	1 tsp
2	2	tomatoes, boiled, skinned & puréed	2
		finishing masala	
1 tsp	2.75 g	garam masala	1 tsp

Method

Wash the liver thoroughly several times in cold water. Wipe dry gently with a towel or kitchen cloth. Slice to slivers of $\frac{1}{2}$" and keep aside.

Bring $3\frac{1}{2}$ oz/100 g of butter (leaving 50 g for later use) to near boiling but not browning. Add the follow-up masala—first the onions and after frying them for 5–10 minutes, till golden brown, add the garlic paste and stir fry for 2–3 minutes and finally put in the rest of the *follow-up masala*. Cook till butter is released and the mixture is viscous. This is the curry sauce.

Take a fresh saucepan and bring $1\frac{1}{2}$ oz/50 g of butter to near boiling. Quickly sauté fry the liver for 2–3 minutes. If you take too long the liver tends to dry. Add the salt and pour the curry sauce. Stir fry for about half a minute. Mix the *finishing masala*.

Transfer to a white serving dish.

Goes well with crisp naan or pizza bread.

NOTE: The same recipe is used for meat ball curry except that a cup of water is added and after sauté frying the meat balls, they are

140

allowed to simmer on medium heat in the curry sauce for 10–15 minutes. Garnish with 1 tablespoon of scissor-cut green coriandor.

This recipe is also good for cottage cheese koftas.

Yakhni Kofta Curry: Kashmir

This particular recipe has come down from the Kashmiri cooks since God knows when. The spices and herbs are minimal and the meat is allowed to develop its own flavour.

Serves 3–4
Preparation Time: 4–6 hours
Cooking Time: 45 minutes

British	Metric	Ingredients	American
2½ oz	75 g	ghee (I)	5 tbsps
for the kofta			
18 oz	½ kg	mince meat	2½ cups
1	1	green chilli	1
1 tbsp	2 g	green coriander, scissor-cut	1 tbsp
1	1	egg	1
1 tbsp	12 g	semolina	1 tbsp
½ tsp	1.25 g	aniseed powder	½ tsp
½ tbsp	7.5 g	garlic paste	½ tbsp
1 tsp	5 g	salt, to taste	1 tsp
for the yakhni meat stock			
2¼ lb	1 kg	bones & trotters	2¼ lb
10	10	black pepper corns, whole	10
1 tbsp	15 ml	ghee (II)	1 tbsp

$1\frac{3}{4}$ pt (7 cups)	1 l	milk	$4\frac{1}{2}$ cups
		singe-fry masala	
1 tsp	2.5 g	black cumin (*shah zeera*)	1 tsp
1 tsp	3.25 g	black pepper powder	1 tsp
		follow-up masala	
$5\frac{1}{2}$ oz (1 cup)	165 g	yoghurt, whisked	$\frac{5}{8}$ cup
$\frac{1}{2}$ tsp	2.5 g	salt, to taste	$\frac{1}{2}$ tsp

Method

Blend all the ingredients for the kofta in a food processor and make a fine mince. Set aside in a refrigerator.

Put all the ingredients of the yakhni in a heavy-bottomed pot and let simmer for 3–4 hours (in the classical style it is 4–6 hours) adding 3 tablespoons (45 ml) of water every now and then. When there is a flavour of meat from the stock, strain through a colander, return to the pot and let it simmer on low heat.

Now, take the kofta mix from the fridge and make 20 meat balls. In another saucepan pour ghee (I) and bring to high heat. Add the *singe-fry masala* and stir for a few seconds. Sauté fry the meat balls on high heat in two lots till slightly brown.

Immediately add the yakhni and simmer without covering on medium heat. When the liquid is reduced by half take off the heat and let it cool for 15 minutes.

Whisk the yoghurt in a blender for 2–3 seconds and add to the *yakhni* and the meat balls. Also add the salt. Return to fire and let simmer (do not boil) for 10 minutes.

Transfer to serving dish—goes well with Kashmiri boiled rice similar to Hungarian round rice and romali roti.

White Meat Curry (*Safed Gosht*)

This dish was created by some remote Kashmiri Brahmin cook who was also a Tantrik. It is seldom made these days because it is a bit time consuming. Many friends from Europe have mistaken this white lamb for veal!

Serves 4
Cooking Time: 100–120 minutes

British	Metric	Ingredients	American
2¼ lb	1 kg	lamb chops, preferably fatty about 10–12 pieces	2¼ lb
1¾ pt (7 cups)	1 l	milk (I)	4½ cups
1¾ pt (7 cups)	1 l	milk (II)	4½ cups
3½ fl oz (⅔ cup)	100 g	ghee	½ cup
5½ oz (1 cup)	165 g	yoghurt, creamed	⅝ cup
1 tbsp	7.5 g	fennel or aniseed, whole	1 tbsp
		OR	
4	4	star anise	4
singe-fry masala			
1 tbsp	8.5 g	cumin, whole, roasted	1 tbsp
during-cooking masala			
20	20	black pepper corns	20
3	3	bay leaves (*tejpat*)	3
6	6	cardamoms, regular	6
½ tbsp	7.5 g	salt, to taste	½ tbsp
garnish masala			
2 tbsps	20 g	poppy seed, ground	2 tbsps

Method

Wash the chops in water and dry with a clean kitchen towel. Place the chops in a deep, **heavy**-bottomed saucepan and add milk (I) (which should cover the chops) alongwith the fennel. Let it parboil on medium heat for one hour. The milk should turn reddish. Remove and put in a colander and let it stand till all the milk has drained through. Place the chops in a clean pan and add milk (II). Let it simmer for another half an hour. When the chops are done they turn whitish.

Take a clean saucepan, pour the ghee into it, bring it to high heat, and add the *singe-fry masala*. When the spluttering stops put the chops alongwith the remaining milk. Stir fry for a few minutes. Add the *during-cooking masala*, and simmer for 5–6 minutes.

Cream the yoghurt and add to the chops, cook on very slow fire for about 5 minutes, never letting the yoghurt boil.

Transfer to a serving dish, top it with *garnish masala* and serve.

Tastes best with romali roti.

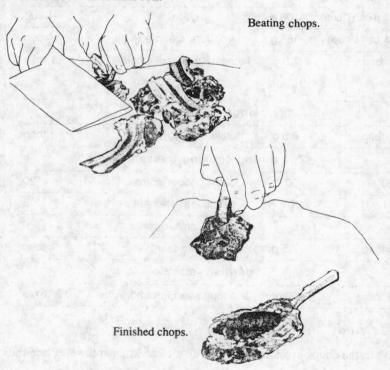

Beating chops.

Finished chops.

144

Kidney Dry Curry

This is actually an Indian 'finger food' or snack and may be eaten as a
sandwich with fresh hot rolls.

Serves 3–5
Preparation Time: 25–30 minutes
Cooking Time: 18–20 minutes

British	Metric	Ingredients	American
1⅓ lb	600 g	kidneys, about 10 of lamb, or 5 of calf or 6 of pork	1⅓ lb
1 tbsp	15 g	soda-bicarb	1 tbsp
1 tbsp	15 ml	vinegar, preferably cider	1 tbsp
½ tbsp	7.5 g	salt, to taste	½ tbsp
5 fl oz (1 cup)	150 ml	cooking oil	⅝ cup
dry curry sauce			
4	4	onions, finely sliced	4
4	4	tomatoes, finely sliced	4
1 tsp	2.5 g	garlic, finely chopped	1 tsp
1 tsp	2.5 g	ginger, finely chopped	1 tsp
singe-fry masala			
1 tbsp	8 g	cumin powder	1 tbsp
1 tsp	2 g	coriander powder	1 tsp
1 tsp	2 g	chilli powder	1 tsp
during-cooking masala			
1 tsp	2.5 g	*amchoor*	1 tsp
½ tbsp	7.5 g	salt, to taste	½ tbsp
finishing masala			
½ tsp	2.75 g	garam masala	½ tsp

Method

First prepare the kidney for cooking. Wash and blot with kitchen paper and cut off the outer thin membrane with a sharp knife. Slice the kidneys horizontally in half. Trim away the streaks of fat keeping the kidneys flat on a cutting board and score the surface both lengthwise and breadthwise, keeping the squares long or small according to the size of the kidney. For lamb kidney a small '+' plus score is enough. Never cut too deep or else they will split open during cooking.

Toss the kidney with the soda-bicarb and let them sit for 15–20 minutes. Remove and wash them well with cold water, preferably running cold water. Now toss the kidneys in a bowl containing salt and vinegar for 10 minutes.

To prepare sauce take a saucepan and bring (100 ml) of the oil to smoking. Put onions and brown them. Then add garlic and ginger, stir fry for a minute or two and add tomatoes. Keep cooking till it becomes a mild brown emulsion and the oil comes to the top. Keep aside.

Take another saucepan and put the remaining 50 g oil and bring to smoking, add the *singe-fry masala* and transfer to the first pan containing the onions and tomatoes emulsion. Bring to medium heat and add the kidneys (It is better to cut the larger kidneys such as pork's and calf's in halves.) and stir fry. Immediately add the *during-cooking masala* and continue stir frying till the kidneys are glazed, dry and dark brown with a reddish tinge of the tomatoes.

Transfer to a serving dish and add the *finishing masala*.

Serve with rice or with fresh hot rolls as a sandwich. Goes very well with any oriental bread.

NOTE: My late father who was a 'kidney fan' and according to me the best 'kidney cook' would serve this dish as a snack. He dried the kidneys and placed them on a quartered toast. Before serving 'kidney on toast' they were kept in a moderately heated oven.

It is to be noted that turmeric in some way is inimical to kidney meat. It spoils both the texture and flavour. For this reason kidney cooked with curry powder containing turmeric tastes flat. It is therefore best is to avoid using turmeric.

Sausage Kofta in Tomato Curry

An incredibly simple creation. My grand uncles were all educated in
England and despite their 'English' image they often got fed up with
eating English food. A conference took place in a suburb of London
(Lea) where they kept residence when away from London. And this is
the dish that was created.

Serves 4–6
Cooking Time: 40–45 minutes

British	Metric	Ingredients	American
6–8		long 'wurst type' sausages, preferably which have beef or veal meat alongwith pork	6–8
3 ½ fl oz	100 ml	cooking oil (I)	½ cup
2 fl oz	50 ml	cooking oil (II)	¼ cup
1 tbsp	7 g	cornflour	1 tbsp
1	1	egg	1
1 tbsp	6 g	green chilli, deseeded & finely chopped	1 tbsp
1 tbsp	2 g	green coriander, finely scissor-cut	1 tbsp
1 tsp	5 ml	garlic, through press	1 tsp
½ tsp	1.25 g	cardamom powder	½ tsp
½ tsp	1.25 g	garam masala	½ tsp
		tomato curry sauce	
		singe-fry masala	
½ tsp	1.5 g	cumin seed, whole	½ tsp

147

$\frac{1}{6}$ oz	5 g	curry leaves, green	$2\frac{1}{2}$ tbsps
		follow-up masala 1	
1	1	onion, large, finely sliced	1
$\frac{1}{2}$ tsp	2.5 g	ginger paste	$\frac{1}{2}$ tsp
$\frac{1}{2}$ tbsp	7.5 g	garlic paste	$\frac{1}{2}$ tbsp
$\frac{1}{2}$ tsp	1 g	chilli powder	$\frac{1}{2}$ tsp
1 tsp	2.75 g	cumin powder	1 tsp
1 tsp	5 g	salt, to taste	1 tsp
		follow-up masala 2	
1 lb 10 oz	750 g	tomatoes, large, red skinned & strained	1 lb 10 oz
		follow-up masala 3	
$\frac{1}{6}$ oz	5 g	green coriander, leaves only	$\frac{1}{4}$ cup
1	1	green chillies, sliced	1
		garnish masala	
$\frac{1}{3}$ oz	10 g	green coriander, leaves only	$\frac{1}{3}$ cup
4	4	spring onions, finely chopped	4

Method

To prepare the sausage meat balls cut one end of the sausage and squeeze out the meat. Mix by hand with cornflour and one egg (lightly beaten) and all the other ingredients. Test the consistency and elasticity. The basic sausage dough is now ready.

Make about 20–25 medium to small meat balls and set aside for half an hour.

To make the tomato curry sauce,wash and strain and boil tomatoes for 8–10 minutes. Purée in a blender and strain. Keep the pulp aside

Heat oil (I) to near smoking and add the *singe-fry masala*. Singe for about 2 minutes till curry leaves turn brown. Add the *follow up masala 1*, first the onions and then brown, follow immediately with the rest.

148

Stir fry for **about** 3 minutes, then add the *follow-up masala 2* and cook on moderate heat for 15–20 minutes till oil is released. Now add the *follow-up masala 3*. By now the consistency will be like thick tomato soup. Transfer to a baking dish.

Now take the sausage meat balls. Bring oil (II) to smoking and sauté fry the meat balls till the outside is brown. Because of the individual nature of each kind of sausage you may need to increase the cornflour as a 'binder'. When the meat balls have fried, spoon them gently in the sauce and bake in moderate heat for 8–10 minutes.

Sprinkle the *garnish masala*.

Serve in a baking dish. Goes very well with fluffy boiled rice.

Everyday Mutton Curry

This is the type of curry eaten everyday in most homes. It is a staple meat dish and does not require a complicated technique or too many spices.

Serves 4
Cooking Time: 60 minutes

British	Metric	Ingredients	American
2¼ lb	1 kg	lamb, mutton or beef, goulash cut	2¼ lb
5 oz	150 g •	onions, finely chopped	1¼ cups
5 oz	150 g	tomato purée	⅝ cup
½ pt	300 ml	water	1¼ cups
5 fl oz	150 ml	cooking oil, preferably ghee	⅝ cup
		singe-fry masala	
1 tbsp	15 g	ginger paste	1 tbsp
1 tbsp	15 g	garlic paste	1 tbsp

British	Metric	Ingredients	American
1 tbsp	6 g	chilli powder	1 tbsp
		during-cooking masala 1	
5	5	cardamoms, brown, large	5
4	4	bay leaves (*tejpat*)	4
2 tsps	10 g	salt, to taste	2 tsps
		during-cooking masala 2	
1 tbsp	8.25 g	garam masala	1 tbsp

Method

Bring oil to smoking in a deep heavy pan. Add onions, brown them and remove with a slotted spoon and keep aside.

Again over-heat oil and put the *singe-fry masala*. Sauté fry for 2–3 minutes, add the fried onions to the singe-fry masala, add meat and stir fry till well browned. Add *during-cooking masala 1*, and 2 cups water, and simmer on medium heat about half-an-hour. Add the tomato purée and cook for another 20 minutes till oil appears on top. Add the *during-cooking masala 2*, stir and let cook till meat is done.

Transfer to a serving dish, preferably white.

Serve with rice or any oriental bread.

Escalopes Saffrano in Curry Sauce

As the name suggests it is an innovation on a 'Latin dish'. The transformation to a curry seems natural, blending ideally the exotic spices with the main ingredients. Spinach is a natural accompaniment with this curry.

Serves 3
Cooking Time: 30–40 minutes

British	Metric	Ingredients	American
6–8	6–8	veal escalopes	6–8

4 oz	100 g	butter (I)	$\frac{1}{2}$ cup
2 oz	50 g	butter (II)	$\frac{1}{4}$ cup
		singe-fry masala	
$\frac{1}{2}$ tsp	1 g	coriander powder	$\frac{1}{2}$ tsp
$\frac{1}{2}$ tsp	1.25 g	cumin powder	$\frac{1}{2}$ tsp
1 tsp	2 g	chilli powder	1 tsp
$\frac{1}{2}$ tsp	1.75 g	turmeric powder	$\frac{1}{2}$ tsp
		follow-up masala	
2 tbsps	30 g	onion paste	2 tbsps
1 tsp	5 g	garlic paste	1 tsp
$\frac{1}{2}$ tbsp	7.5 g	salt, to taste	$\frac{1}{2}$ tbsp
		during-cooking masala	
$5\frac{1}{2}$ oz	165 g	yoghurt	$\frac{5}{8}$ cup
$\frac{1}{2}$ tsp	1 g	cornflour	$\frac{1}{2}$ cup
		garnish masala	
1	1	capsicum (sweet green), finely chopped	1
1	1	radish white, medium size, grated	1
1	1	saffron powder, sachet	1
		spinach preparation	
$2\frac{1}{4}$ lb	1 kg	spinach, fresh, tender,	$2\frac{1}{4}$ lb
		boiling water as required	
1 tsp	5 g	salt (II), to taste	1 tsp

Method

Cream the yoghurt in a blender alongwith the cornflour for 10–15 seconds and keep aside.

Take a large heavy saucepan, add butter (I) and bring to foaming. Add veal escalopes and sauté fry quickly for 3–4 minutes till golden brown.

This may be done in 2 lots—dividing the butter for sauté fry. Remove escalopes, cover and keep aside.

Add butter (II) and bring to high heat. Add the *singe-fry masala* of coriander, cumin, red chilli, followed by turmeric. Within half a minute of adding turmeric add the *follow-up masala* and cook for 4–5 minutes stirring the mixture.

Return the escalopes to the mixture, cover and let simmer for 5–10 minutes.

Add the *during-cooking masala* of creamed yoghurt and bring to near boiling (do not boil) till the sauce is creamy. Cover the pan and let simmer on medium heat for 5–10 minutes—check salt and escalopes.

Before serving, sprinkle the *garnish masala* adding powdered saffron first and then the rest.

Clean and wash the spinach, pour boiling water over it and set aside for 5 minutes. Strain in a colander. The spinach will turn soft and brilliant green—sprinkle salt (II) and a dollop of butter and serve with escalopes.

It is best eaten with bread of your choice. Also served with buttered rice.

Curry Meat Sauce (*Bolognese a l'Indienne*)

Not much different from the regular 'Bolognese sauce' except for the distinctive Indian spices and flavour. Cooked regularly during my overseas travels with repeated requests.

Serves 3
Cooking Time: 50–55 minutes

British	Metric	Ingredients	American
18 oz	500 g	mince beef or lamb, hand-chopped coarsely	2½ cups
4 oz	100 g	butter, ghee or sunflower	½ cup

		oil or olive oil	
1 tsp	5 g	salt, to taste	1 tsp

singe-fry masala

1½ tbsps	10 g	coriander powder	1½ tbsps
1 tbsp	7 g	cayenne pepper	1 tbsp
1 tsp	2 g	ginger powder	1 tsp
½ tbsp	5 g	turmeric powder	½ tbsp

follow-up masala (coarsely chopped)

1	1	capsicum, green large	1
1	1	capsicum red	1
1 bulb	1 bulb	garlic, cloved & smashed	1 bulb
5 oz	150 g	onions	5 oz
3½ oz	100 g	tomatoes	3½ oz

during-cooking masala

3	3	bay leaves (tejpat)	3
1 tbsp	7 g	Hungarian sweet red paprika	1 tbsp
8 fl oz	225 ml	water	1 cup
1 tsp	2.25 g	cornflour	1 tsp

garnish masala

½ tsp	0.75 g	nutmeg, grated	½ tsp
1 tsp	3.25 g	black pepper, freshly milled	1 tsp
1 tsp	2 g	green chilli, finely chopped	1 tsp
2 tbsps	4 g	green coriander, scissor-cut	2 tbsps

Method

Coarsely chop ingredients of the follow-up masala. Keep all these on the side.

Heat to near boiling the cooking oil, butter, ghee or any other oil. Add the *singe-fry masala*. As soon as they bubble and settle, add all the coarsely chopped *follow-up masala*. Stir fry for 5–6 minutes. Now add the meat, salt and *tejpat*.Cover and cook on a slow fire for about 20 minutes, stirring every few minutes so that the meat does not stick to the bottom. Add the Hungarian paprika.

Meanwhile mix the cornflour in 1½ cups.of water and add to the meat. Cook again on slow heat till meat is done. This takes about 30 minutes. Test the meat as you would test any other mince. When it is cooked the fat is released on top. Check the sauce. If too thick add a little more water but remember that it should not be liquidy and should be like the classical bolognese.

The sauce is now ready and after transferring it to the serving dish sprinkle grated nutmeg on top along with the milled black pepper and top it with the chopped green chillies and green coriander.

Goes well with noodles or any plain pasta or with boiled rice.

NOTE: Hungarian paprika is substituted for *ratan jyot*, an Indian colouring bark which is fat soluble. Besides, the paprika improves flavour.

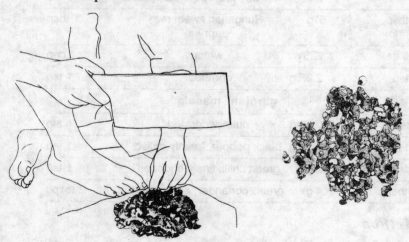

Coarse, hand-chopped mince.

154

Sausage Curry

I ate this delicious curry for the first time when I was studying in Prep school in a London suburb in 1930. To the best of my knowledge it was innovated by my late father as a quick means to satisfy our oriental tastes by using readily available pre-cooked English sausages.

Serves 4
Cooking Time: 20–25 minutes

British	Metric	Ingredients	American
12	12	fresh Oxford sausages, or any spiced sausage, wurst continental style	12
5 fl oz	150 ml	cooking oil, except olive (in this dish good lard will also work)	$\frac{5}{8}$ cup
5 fl oz	150 ml	water	$\frac{5}{8}$ cup
		singe-fry masala	
1 tsp	2.75 g	cumin powder	1 tsp
1 tsp	2 g	coriander powder	1 tsp
1 tbsp	6 g	chilli powder	1 tbsp
1 tsp	3.5 g	turmeric powder	1 tsp
		follow-up masala	
2	2	capsicums, finely chopped	2
4	4	onions, finely chopped	4
4	4	tomatoes, finely chopped	4
1 tsp	5 g	garlic paste	1 tsp
$1\frac{1}{3}$ oz	40 g	pearl onions	$\frac{1}{3}$ cup
1 tsp	5 g	salt, to taste	1 tsp
		during-cooking masala	
2	2	bay leaves (*tejpat*)	2

British	Metric	Ingredients	American
½ tsp	0.75 g	nutmeg, grated	½ tsp
1 tsp	2.5 g	amchoor	1 tsp
		garnish masala	
1 tbsp	2 g	green coriander, scissor-cut	1 tbsp
3	3	green chillies, scissor-cut	3

Method

Single boil sausages, drain through a colander and cut each into 3 pieces.

Take a saucepan and bring oil or lard to smoking. Add the *singe-fry masala,* adding turmeric last of all. When it stops spluttering add the *follow-up masala* and stir fry for 5–10 minutes till the ingredients are soft and brownish.

Add the sausages and stir fry. Mix them well with the ingredients in the pan. Add 1 cup of water and simmer for 5–7 minutes. Add the *during-cooking masala* and simmer for another 5 minutes. Transfer to a serving dish and top it with the *garnish masala.* Serve immediately. Goes well with noodles or plain boiled fluffy rice.

Yellow Meat Curry (*Zard Gosht*)

This dish could be Persian or even Armenian but in its present form it is strictly Indian.

This is what one might call 'down-the-line' curry—starting its process somewhere in Armenia or Central Asia and gathering spices and herbs down the line into the Indo-Gangetic plain.

Serves 4–6
Cooking Time: 50–55 minutes

British	Metric	Ingredients	American
2¼ lb	1 kg	meat, goulash cut	2¼ lb

$2\frac{1}{2}$ oz	75 g	chick pea flour	$\frac{5}{8}$ cup
12 oz	325 g	yoghurt	$1\frac{1}{4}$ cups
$1\frac{1}{3}$ pt	750 ml	water	$3\frac{1}{4}$ cups
5 fl oz	150 ml	ghee	$\frac{5}{8}$ cup
		singe-fry masala	
$\frac{1}{2}$ tsp	2 g	fenugreek seed	$\frac{1}{2}$ tsp
6	6	red chillies, whole, dry, broken in 2 pieces	6
2 tbsps	20 g	turmeric powder	2 tbsps
		follow-up masala	
1 tbsp	15 g	garlic paste	1 tbsp
1 tbsp	15 g	ginger paste	1 tbsp
2 tbsps	40 g	almond paste	2 tbsps
2 tsps	10 g	salt, to taste	2 tsps
		during-cooking masala	
2	2	bay leaves (tejpat)	2
6	6	cardamoms, regular	6
		garnish masala	
1 tbsp	6 g	green chillies, scissor-cut	1 tbsp
2 tbsps	4 g	green coriander, scissor-cut	2 tbsps

Method

Mix the yoghurt, chick pea flour and water in a blender and keep aside.

Take a heavy-bottomed cooking pan and bring ghee to high heat. Add the *singe-fry masala*. When spluttering stops add the *follow-up masala* and stir fry till ghee is released. Now add meat and stir fry till nearly brown. Add the blended mixture gently to the meat along with the *during-cooking masala*. Lower heat and let cook for 40 minutes till the meat is done.

157

Transfer to a serving oven-proof dish and keep in an oven on low heat.

Sprinkle the *garnish masala* on top of it and serve with boiled rice.

Double Grill Curry

An ideal dish to use leftovers. Every household roasts meat or chicken and often some is left over. This is one of the curries that it can be put to tasty use. And it hardly takes any time!

Serves 3
Cooking Time: 20–25 minutes

British	Metric	Ingredients	American
18 oz	½ kg	leftover roast mutton, beef or pork, sliced	18 oz
2 oz	50 g	butter	¼ cup
		singe-fry masala	
½ tsp	1.25 g	cumin powder	½ tsp
½ tsp	1 g	chilli powder	½ tsp
½ tsp	1 g	coriander powder	½ tsp
½ tsp	1.5 g	fenugreek seed powder	½ tsp
½ tsp	2.5 g	salt, to taste	½ tsp
		follow-up masala	
4	4	onions, sliced	4
4	4	tomatoes, sliced	4
½ tsp	1.25 g	garlic, finely chopped	½ tsp
½ tsp	1.5 g	ginger, grated	½ tsp
		during-cooking masala	
3	3	green chillies, slit lengthwise	3
		finishing masala	

158

½ tsp	0.75 g	nutmeg, grated	½ tsp
½ tsp	1.75 g	black pepper, from mill	½ tsp

Method

In a saucepan bring butter to bubbling, but do not brown. Add the *singe-fry masala* and let it splutter. Add the *follow-up masala*, stir fry till soft. Then add the *during-cooking masala* and stir. Finally add the meat, stir fry for a few minutes, transfer to a baking dish and leave in an oven for 10 minutes on medium heat.

Before serving add the *finishing masala* and serve in the baking dish.

Goes extremely well on pizza bread or rice.

NOTE: 'Double grill' probably means that the roasts *per se* are grills and when put back in the oven they become 'double grill'.

              Leftover meat already has salt in it. It is therefore necessary to taste for salt before adding any more.

Madras Curry

This can be termed as the 'entrepreneurs curry' and was the first curry to be eaten by Europeans of the East India Company. The spices and herbs are freshly pounded or ground and their regular use must have resulted in standardizing the ubiquitous curry powder.

Serves 4–6
Cooking Time: 55–60 minutes

British	Metric	Ingredients	American
2¼ lb	1 kg	meat, mutton, beef or veal, goulash cut	2¼ lb
3½ fl oz	100 ml	cooking oil, preferably groundnut	½ cup
2 oz	50 g	butter	¼ cup

2 tsps	10 g	salt, to taste	2 tsps
16 fl oz	450 ml	water	2 cups

singe-fry masala

1 tsp	2 g	chilli powder	1 tsp
3	3	red chillies, whole	3
5	5	garlic cloves	5
4 tsps	20 g	ginger, puréed	4 tsps
12	12	curry leaves	12
$\frac{1}{2}$ tsp	1.5 g	black pepper	$\frac{1}{2}$ tsp
1 tsp	2 g	coriander powder	1 tsp
1 tsp	2.75 g	cumin powder	1 tsp
1 tsp	4.25 g	fenugreek seed or powder	1 tsp
1 tbsp	10 g	turmeric powder	1 tbsp
$1\frac{2}{3}$ oz	45 g	coconut, freshly grated	$\frac{5}{8}$ cup

finishing masala

1 tsp	2.75 g	garam masala	1 tsp
2 tbsps	30 ml	ghee, melted	$\frac{1}{8}$ cup

garnish masala

2 tbsps	4 g	green coriander, scissor-cut	2 tbsps
2 tbsps	30 ml	lemon juice	$\frac{1}{8}$ cup

Method

Put all the ingredients of the singe-fry masala in a blender with a little water and liquidize.

Take a heavy-bottomed pan and bring oil to boiling point add the butter and continue to keep on high heat. Then add the liquidized *singe-fry masala* and stir fry till oil is released. Add meat and again stir fry again till all the water from the masalas and meat has evaporated. Keep stir frying the meat till brownish. Add salt and (3 cups) 450 ml water and let it cook on slow fire for 45 minutes or till the meat is **done**. Add the *finishing masala*.

Transfer to a white serving dish. Sprinkle the *garnish masala* and serve.

This is best eaten with boiled rice.

NOTE: Chillies may be increased or decreased to taste. If more gravy is required increase water and add a little extra salt.

The spices for the singe-fry masala can be hand pound in the traditional fashion or ground into a paste with a grindstone.

You can cook mixed vegetables, potatoes or cottage cheese in the same manner, but in these the cooking time will reduce considerably.

Largely diced fish, chicken or pork can also be substituted for the main ingredient.

Exceptionally tasty when jack fruits, yams or aubergines, are substituted for the main ingredient.

Minced Meat Curry (*Keema Curry*)

This is a simple dish. In it the best cuts of meat are seldom used, since it is the curry mixture that really matters. The mince meat used as the main ingredient should be coarsely ground or hand pounded.

Serves 3
Cooking Time: 40—45 minutes

British	Metric	Ingredients	American
18 oz	500 g	meat, beef, mutton, goat or lamb, coarsely ground, minced	18 oz
$\frac{1}{2}$ pt (2 cups)	300 ml	water	$1\frac{1}{4}$ cups
$\frac{1}{2}$ tbsp	7.5 g	salt, to taste	$\frac{1}{2}$ tbsp
5 oz (1 cup)	150 g	ghee	$\frac{5}{8}$ cup

161

5 oz (2 cups)	150 g	onions, finely sliced	1¼ cups
		singe-fry masala	
1 tsp	2.75 g	cumin powder	1 tsp
1 tsp	2 g	chilli powder	1 tsp
		follow-up masala	
1 tbsp	15 g	garlic paste	1 tbsp
1 tsp	5 g	ginger paste	1 tsp
		finishing masala	
1 tsp	2.75 g	garam masala	1 tsp
1 tsp	3.25 g	black pepper powder	1 tsp
		garnish masala	
1 tbsp	2 g	fresh green coriander, scissor-cut	1 tbsp
1 tsp	2 g	green chillies, scissor-cut	1 tsp

Method

After washing the mince meat, dry it with a kitchen towel and keep aside.

Heat the ghee till it smokes, add onions and brown them. Remove onions from ghee and keep aside. Reheating the same ghee, add the *singe-fry masala*. After it splutters for a few seconds, add the *follow-up masala* and stir fry for a few minutes. Now add the browned onions and salt, and mix well. Add the mince and stir fry till well browned for 8–10 minutes. Add 2 cups of water, cover, and cook on medium heat for 20–25 minutes. After the mince is done cook uncovered on high heat, stirring all the time.

The mince should be semi-liquid but well mixed like an emulsion. Add the *finishing masala* and mix. Do not cook any further.

Transfer to a white serving dish and put the *garnish masala* on top.

Serve with boiled rice or any Indian bread.

162

NOTE: Any vegetable may be added to make mince meat and vegetable curry. If 3 potatoes are added—boil, peal and quarter—sauté fry in ghee till brownish—and add after the follow-up stage and mix.

Cauliflower (5 oz/150 g) may also be added. Sauté fry cauliflower in ghee (2 oz/50 g). Add (when brownish) and mix after the follow-up stage.

Broccoli, lotus root and marrow are all adaptable. Sauté fry and follow the above procedure.

Mushrooms of any kind with capsicum also make a fine dish.

Royal Brain Curry with Persian Sauce

This is an exceptionally delicate dish. I remember eating it for the first time during my school days. It was made especially for very eminent friends of the then royal family of Afghanistan.

Serves 4–6
Preparation Time: 15–20 minutes
Cooking Time: 45–50 minutes

British	Metric	Ingredients	American
6 of sheep or 4 of veal		brain of sheep or veal or calf	6 of sheep or 4 of veal
1 tbsp	15 ml	lemon juice	1 tbsp
5 oz (1 cup)	150 g	ghee	$\frac{5}{8}$ cup
4 oz	100 g	butter	$\frac{1}{2}$ cup
1 tsp	5 g	salt (I), to taste	1 tsp
5 fl oz (1 cup)	150 ml	water	$\frac{5}{8}$ cup
		for the Persian sauce	
		singe-fry masala	
1 tsp	4g	turmeric powder	1 tsp

163

1 tsp	2 g	chilli powder	1 tsp

follow-up masala 1

1 tbsp	15 g	ginger paste	1 tbsp
1 tbsp	10 g	poppy seed paste	1 tbsp
1 tbsp	15 g	garlic, paste	1 tbsp
1 tsp	3 g	fenugreek powder	1 tsp
1 tsp	5 g	salt (II), to taste	1 tsp

follow-up masala 2

10	10	cardamoms	10
2 tbsps	40 g	almonds (I) / hazelnut paste	2 tbsps

follow-up masala 3

5 fl oz	150 ml	water	$\frac{5}{8}$ cup
6 oz (1$\frac{1}{3}$ cups)	200 g	yoghurt	$\frac{3}{4}$ cup
1 tsp	2.25 g	cornflour	1 tsp

finishing masala

2 tbsps	2.25 g	cream	2 tbsps
$\frac{1}{2}$ tsp	0.25 g	saffron, soaked in milk	$\frac{1}{2}$ tsp
2 tbsps	30 ml	milk	2 tbsps

garnish masala

20	20	almonds (II), roasted, chopped lengthwise into slivers	20

Method

To prepare the brains, soak them in salted water for 1–2 hours.

While the brains soak, prepare the Persian sauce. The sauce lends itself perfectly to the system and stages of the various masalas.

Grind the ginger, poppy seed, garlic, and fenugreek into a fine paste.

164

Unroasted hazelnuts can be substituted for almonds (which proved to be a most exciting innovation—as almonds are the traditional nuts). Soak almonds (I) in hot water for 10 minutes, skin them, grind to a paste and keep aside. After roasting almonds (II), chop them lengthwise, and keep aside. Adding 1 teaspoon of cornflour, cream the yoghurt and keep aside. This prevents the yoghurt from curdling and is akin to the traditional method when a little flour, sago or rice flour was added.

Soak saffron in warm milk and keep aside.

Take a wide and heavy saucepan and bringing ghee to high heat, add the *singe-fry masala*. Let singe for 10–15 seconds. Then add the *follow-up masala 1*, and stir fry for 2–3 minutes. Reduce heat and add the *follow-up masala 2* and cook on medium heat for 10–15 minutes and stir gently till ghee is released. Now add the *follow-up masala 3*, and simmer (not boil) on medium heat for 4–5 minutes. Keep the sauce aside in a warm oven at the lowest temperature.

Wash the brains, which had earlier been soaked, several times in cold water and de-membrane. No streaks of blood should remain. The next stage is the blanching. In this recipe we use lemon juice in water. Place the brains gently in water at room temperature with 1 tablespoon of lemon juice and bring to boil. Remove into a colander and wash again. If any membrane still remains, remove it. Place once again in water enough to cover them, at room temperature. Bring to boil and simmer for 1–2 minutes till they appear to curdle and are resistant to touch like bread dough. Again drain in a colander. Cut the brains into halves and keep aside.

Heat butter to near boiling and stir fry brains for a few minutes adding 1 teaspoon of salt till well coated in the butter.

Take a baking dish and pour one-third of the Persian curry sauce into it. Then place the cut brains, pour rest of the Persian curry sauce on top and bake on medium heat for 8–10 minutes.

Before serving sprinkle the *finishing masala* and the *garnish masala* on op.

This dish is best eaten by itself or with boiled fluffy rice, kulcha or white bread.

NOTE: Even if hazelnuts are used, the roasted and chopped almonds must go on top.

This dish needs careful handling to keep the brains soft and crunchy and good-looking.

Adapt this method for fish fillet and follow recipe.

Shell, de-vein and skin prawns and follow this recipe. The Persian sauce renders as a good example of the stages and systems of the masalas. The brains should be prepared ahead of time. While the brains are being soaked the sauce can be prepared. One has to be a bit ambidextrous for best results or two persons should assist in cooking this dish.

Garlic Meat Curry

This is a simple curry to make where one spice or herb predominates. It seems the Northern nomads who were accustomed to naan with meat suddenly discovered rice. The question arose as to how the rice could be eaten with meat. All they did was to expand the dry meats with water and increase salt and add herb or spice of their choice.

Serves 4–6
Cooking Time: 55–60 minutes

British	Metric	Ingredients	American
2¼ lb	1 kg	any meat, diced, medium	2¼ lb
9 fl oz (1⅔ cups)	250 ml	water	1⅛ cups
5 oz (1 cup)	150 g	ghee or any cooking oil	⅝ cup
		singe-fry masala	
1 tbsp	6 g	chilli powder	1 tbsp
1 tbsp	8 g	cumin powder	1 tbsp
1 tbsp	10 g	turmeric powder	1 tbsp

follow-up masala			
1 oz	30 g	garlic paste	2 tbsps
2 tsps	10 g	salt, to taste	2 tsps
finishing masala			
1 fl oz	30 ml	lemon juice	2 tbsps
garnish masala			
2 tbsps	4 g	green coriander, scissor-cut	2 tbsps

Method

Take a deep saucepan, pour ghee and bring to high heat. Add the *singe-fry masala*, with the turmeric coming last. Immediately after, add the *follow-up masala* and stir fry for 3–4 minutes. Now add the meat and stir fry till the ghee is released. This takes 30–35 minutes. Add water and simmer on slow fire till meat is done. Add the *finishing masala* and transfer to a serving dish. Finally, add the *garnish masala* and serve with boiled rice.

NOTE: Increase or decrease chillies, garlic and lemon juice to taste.

The recipe can be adapted to any meat, fish, poultry or vegetables keeping in mind the varying cooking time required for a particular meat or vegetable.

No aromatic spices or onions are used as their taste will be lost with so much garlic.

Kidney Tomato Curry

Kidneys need very careful preparation or else they tend to become dry. This dish can be made with any kidney—of calf, veal, lamb, goat or pork.

Serves 4–6
Preparation Time: 25–30 minutes

167

Cooking Time: 45 minutes

British	Metric	Ingredients	American
1 lb 6 oz	600 g	kidneys, about 10 of lamb, 5 of calf or veal & 6 of pig	1 lb 6 oz
9 fl oz (1⅔ cups)	250 ml	cooking oil, preferably peanut	1⅛ cups
1 tbsp	14 g	soda-bicarb	1 tbsp
1 tbsp	15 ml	vinegar	1 tbsp
½ tbsp	7.5 g	salt (I), to taste	½ tbsp
for tomato curry sauce			
singe-fry masala			
1 tsp	3 g	cumin seed, whole	1 tsp
⅓ oz (½ cup)	10 g	curry leaves, green	⅓ cup
follow-up masala 1			
2	2	onions, large, finely sliced	2
1 tsp	5 g	ginger paste	1 tsp
1 tbsp	15 g	garlic paste	1 tbsp
1 tsp	2 g	chilli powder	1 tsp
2 tsps	5.5 g	cumin powder	2 tsps
1 tsp	5 g	salt (II), to taste	1 tsp
follow-up masala 2			
3 lb 6 oz	1½ kg	tomatoes, large, red skinned & strained	3 lb 6 oz
follow-up masala 3			
⅓ oz (½ cup)	10 g	green coriander, leaves only	⅓ cup
2	2	green chillies, sliced	2

garnish masala

$\frac{1}{3}$ oz	10 g	green coriander, scissor-cut, leaves only	$\frac{1}{3}$ cup
3	3	green chillies, sliced	3

Method

First prepare the kidneys for cooking. Wash and blot with kitchen paper. Take a sharp knife and cut off the outer thin membrane. Then slice the kidneys horizontally in half. You will notice streaks of fat—trim them away keeping the kidneys flat on a cutting board and score the surface, both lengthwise and breadthwise. Keep the squares long or small according to the size of the kidney. For lamb kidney a small plus (+) score is enough. Never cut too deep or else they will split open during cooking.

Toss the kidney in the soda-bicarb and let them sit for 15–20 minutes. (In the meantime prepare the tomato curry sauce as in the recipe that follows.) After the kidneys are soaked wash them well in cold running water. Now toss the kidneys in salt and vinegar in a bowl for 10 minutes.

To prepare the tomato curry sauce, heat oil to near smoking and add the *singe-fry masala.* Cook for about 2 minutes till brown. Add the *follow-up masala 1,* first brown the onions and follow immediately with the rest. Stir fry for about 3 minutes, then add the *follow-up masala 2* and cook on moderate heat for 15–20 minutes till oil is released. Now add the *follow-up masala 3*. By now the consistency will be like thick tomato soup. Transfer to a large baking dish and keep aside.

Take a large saucepan, filled with water and bring to boil. After blotting the kidneys dry with a kitchen towel, put them in the boiling water. Turn off the heat and blanch for 3–4 minutes. Put them back in the colander and let them dry out.

When drained put the kidneys in the tomato curry sauce in the baking dish and spoon the sauce over the kidneys. Bake in an oven on moderate heat for 10 minutes. Sprinkle the *garnish masala* and serve.

This curry goes well with rice or with normal white bread. It may also be eaten by itself.

NOTE: This tomato curry sauce is very versatile and it can be used for practically eggs or any meat. Recipes using the sauce for eggs and prawns are already included.

Finely chopped spring onions about 2 tbsp (15 g) may also be included in the garnishing of this curry.

Sliced Lamb—Quick Curry

There are several quick curries and the technique used to cook the **meat** is identical to the Chinese method. Who made it first is not known. These curries are very popular and take very little time and labour.

Instead of lamb, beef or veal may also be used to prepare this curry.

Serves 3
Cooking Time: 12–15 minutes

British	Metric	Ingredients	American
18 oz	½ kg	lamb fillet, slices	18 oz
6 oz	150 g	butter or butter oil	¾ cup
singe-fry masala			
1 tsp	2 g	coriander powder	1 tsp
1 tsp	3.5 g	turmeric powder	1 tsp
follow-up masala 1			
1 tsp	3.25 g	black pepper, coarsely powdered	1 tsp
1 tsp	2 g	chilli powdered	1 tsp
follow-up masala 2			
1 tsp	2 g	ginger powder	1 tsp
1 tsp	5 g	garlic paste	1 tsp

170

1 tsp	5 g	salt, to taste	1 tsp
		finishing masala	
1 tsp	2.75 g	garam masala	1 tsp
		garnish masala	
1 tbsp	7.5 g	spring onions, finely chopped	1 tbsp
1 tbsp	6 g	green chillies, finely chopped, de-seeded	1 tbsp

Method

Slice the lamb across the grain about 1 cm apart. Keep aside.

Take a non-stick saucepan and bring half the butter to bubbling and sauté fry the meat slices on high heat in 2 or 3 lots as convenient. If butter is not enough use a little more. Sauté fry quickly, turning the meat over till it changes colour to white. Remove meat from the pan and place on kitchen paper.

Return the pan to fire and adding the remaining butter, bring to bubbling. Now add the *singe-fry masala* and as soon as it stops spluttering, after 5–10 seconds, add the *follow-up masala 1*. Stir fry for 5–10 seconds, add the *follow-up masala 2* and stir fry a few more seconds.

By now everybody should be at the table ready to eat. Only then should you proceed further—if there is any delay remove the saucepan from fire and wait till everybody is ready to eat. Now bring the pan with the cooked masalas to high heat—immediately add the meat and stir fry quickly on very high heat for a minute or so adding the *finishing masala*. If the cooking is delayed the juices from the meat are released and the meat toughens.

The time required for cooking should not be more than 12–15 minutes.

Transfer to a serving dish and sprinkle the *garnish masala* and serve.

Serve with rice or dumplings (gnocci) or boiled potatoes.

NOTE: This recipe may be adapted for chicken. It should also be sliced about 1 cm. The time taken to saute fry this will be less for chicken. Pork undercuts will also do.

Casserole Curries: Madras

This is a strong flavoured curry with a typical South Indian taste. The casserole helps to seal in the flavours. The dish may be made with fish, chicken or veal with cooking times adjusted. This is an innovative dish prepared by my daughter.

Serves 3
Cooking Time: 60–65 minutes

British	Metric	Ingredients	American
18 oz	$\frac{1}{2}$ kg	lamb meat, large, curry or goulash cut	18 oz
2 fl oz (4 tbsps)	60 ml	cooking oil, preferably groundnut	$\frac{1}{4}$ cup
$\frac{1}{2}$ tbsp	7.5 g	salt, to taste	$\frac{1}{2}$ tbsp
1 tbsp	10 g	white flour	1 tbsp
3 fl oz ($\frac{1}{2}$ cup)	75 ml	water	$\frac{3}{8}$ cup
		singe-fry masala	
10	10	curry leaves	10
		follow-up masala 1	
3	3	onions, finely chopped	3
		follow-up masala 2	
1 tbsp	10 g	turmeric powder	1 tbsp
1 tbsp	6 g	coriander powder	1 tbsp
1 tsp	2 g	chilli powder	1 tsp

½ tsp	1.25 g	cumin powder	½ tsp
during-cooking masala			
5 fl oz	150 ml	coconut milk	⅝ cup
2	2	soup cubes	2
5 fl oz (1 cup)	150 ml	water	⅝ cup
3	3	green chillies, slit lengthwise & de-seeded	3
2	2	lemons, juice of	2
other ingredients			
2	2	potatoes, quartered	2
6	6	cauliflower flowerettes	6
garnish masala			
2 tbsps	4 g	coriander, scissor-cut	2 tbsps

Method

Bring oil to smoking in a saucepan, add curry leaves and crisp fry for about 20 seconds. Add onions and glaze. Then add the *follow-up masala 2* and stir fry for 20–30 seconds. To this add the meat and brown and stir fry for another 5 minutes. Add salt and flour and mix well.

Transfer to a casserole dish, add the *during-cooking masala*, cover and bake for 40 minutes. Remove from the oven and add *other ingredients*. Cover and bake again for another 20 minutes or till meat is done.

Add the *garnish masala* and serve with rice.

Casserole Curries: Rampuri Lamb Meat Balls

Amongst the various kitchens of India, Rampur has a unique place. Its recipes are aromatic and not overpowered by chilli. Often they use milk products like khoya or cream in the recipes. This is obviously a recipe converted to casserole style by the educated younger generation of the House of Rampur. The previous Nawab was a contemporary at school.

Serves 3–4
Cooking Time: 70–80 minutes

British	Metric	Ingredients	American
18 oz	$\frac{1}{2}$ kg	mince lamb, coarsely ground	18 oz
1 tsp	2.75 g	garam masala	1 tsp
2 fl oz	50 ml	cooking oil (I)	$\frac{1}{4}$ cup
$3\frac{1}{2}$ fl oz	100 ml	cooking oil (II)	$\frac{1}{2}$ cup
$4\frac{1}{2}$ oz (1 cup)	120 g	semolina, enough to coat meat balls	$\frac{2}{3}$ cup
1	1	egg, white of	1
		singe-fry masala	
$\frac{1}{2}$ tsp	1 g	coriander powder	$\frac{1}{2}$ tsp
$\frac{1}{2}$ tsp	1.5 g	cumin, whole	$\frac{1}{2}$ tsp
		follow-up masala	
1 tsp	2 g	chilli powder	1 tsp
3	3	onions, finely chopped	3
$\frac{1}{2}$ tsp	2.5 g	garlic paste	$\frac{1}{2}$ tsp
$\frac{1}{2}$ tsp	2.5 g	ginger paste	$\frac{1}{2}$ tsp
1	1	egg-plant, medium, diced with skin	1
$\frac{1}{2}$ tbsp	7.5 g	salt, to taste	$\frac{1}{2}$ tbsp
		Rampur sauce	
a pinch		saffron, soaked in milk	a pinch

5 oz (1 cup)	150 g	tomato, puréed	$\frac{5}{8}$ cup
9 oz (1½ cups)	250 g	yoghurt, whisked	1 cup

Method

Mix lamb with garam masala and make medium-sized balls. Keep in refrigerator.

Bring oil to smoking in a deep saucepan, add the *singe-fry masala*, stir for a few seconds and add the *follow-up masala*. Stir fry for a few minutes and take off the fire.

Beat the egg white, do not make it frothy. Dip the meat balls in egg white and coat it with the semolina flour.

Take a clean sauce pan and bring oil (II) to smoking and stir fry meat balls till golden brown.

Blend Rampur sauce in a blender for 10–20 seconds.

Transfer all the contents kept aside, to a casserole—first the meat balls and then the masala and finally the Rampur sauce. Mix gently, cover and cook in an oven for 45–50 minutes.

Serve with rice or chapatis.

Aubergine Curry Meat Bolognese Casserole

Although this dish is oriental and has been eaten in India for many centuries, it perhaps originated in Turkey, Greece or what was Armenia and Sicily.

Serves 4–6
Cooking Time: 75–80 minutes

British	Metric	Ingredients	American
1¾ lb	800 g	auberguine, medium (about 4)	1¾ lb

2 fl oz (3 tbsps)	50 ml	cooking oil	$\frac{1}{4}$ cup
1 tsp	5 g	salt, to taste	1 tsp

curry meat sauce
bolognese a *l'Indienne*

18 oz	500 g	minced beef or lamb, coarsely hand chopped	$2\frac{1}{2}$ cups
$3\frac{1}{2}$ fl oz ($\frac{2}{3}$ cup)	100 ml	butter, ghee, sunflower oil or olive oil	$\frac{1}{2}$ cup
1 tsp	5 g	salt, to taste	1 tsp

singe-fry masala

$1\frac{1}{2}$ tbsps	10 g	coriander powder	$1\frac{1}{2}$ tbsps
1 tbsp	7 g	cayenne pepper	1 tbsp
1 tsp	2 g	ginger powder	1 tsp
$\frac{1}{2}$ tbsp	5 g	turmeric powder	$\frac{1}{2}$ tbsp

follow-up masala (coarsely chopped)

1	1	capsicum, green, large	1
1	1	capsicum, red	1
1	1	garlic, bulb, cloved & smashed	1
5 oz	150 g	onions	5 oz
$3\frac{1}{2}$ oz	100 g	tomatoes	$3\frac{1}{2}$ oz

during-cooking masala

3	3	bay leaves (*tejpat*)	3
1 tbsp	7 g	Hungarian sweet red paprika	1 tbsp
8 fl oz ($1\frac{1}{2}$ cups)	225 ml	water	1 cup
1 tsp	2.25 g	cornflour	1 tsp

garnish masala

$\frac{1}{2}$ tsp	0.75 g	nutmeg, fresh from mill	$\frac{1}{2}$ tsp

$\frac{1}{2}$ tsp	1.5 g	black pepper, freshly ground from mill	$\frac{1}{2}$ tsp
1 tsp	2g	green chilli, finely chopped	1 tsp
2 tbsps	4 g	green coriander, scissor-cut	2 tbsps

Method

Cut the aubergines in rings of thickness of about 1 cm and soak in water. Discard the crown and stem ends. Before cooking, take them out of the water and blot dry with a kitchen towel. Sprinkle salt evenly on all the pieces.

Bring oil to smoking and sauté fry the aubergine rings to light brown and set aside on kitchen paper.

Now to prepare the meat curry sauce coarsely chop garlic, onions, tomatoes, green and red capsicum, and keep them aside.

Heat the cooking oil to near boiling, add the *singe-fry masala*. As soon as it splutters and settles, add the coarsely chopped *follow-up masala*. Stir fry for 5–6 minutes. Now add meat, salt and *tejpat* and let it cook covered on a low heat for about 20 minutes, stirring every few minutes so that the meat does not stick to the bottom. Add the Hungarian paprika.

Meanwhile mix the cornflour in water and add to the meat. Cook on low heat for about 30 minutes or till the meat is done. Test the meat as you would test any other mince. When it is cooked the fat is released on top. Check the sauce, if too thick add a little more water but it should not be too liquidy and should be like the classical bolognese.

Take a baking dish or a large casserole. Pour some of the curry meat sauce, layer the aubergine rings on top, and repeat for the second layer. Cover and bake for 20–30 minutes on moderate heat. Transfer to a serving dish, sprinkle milled nutmeg on top along with the milled black pepper, and top it with the chopped green chillies and green coriander.

Serve with rice or on pizza bread. Excellent for lasagne.

NOTE: Hungarian paprika is substituted for *ratan jyot*, an Indian colouring **bark** which is fat soluble. Besides colouring, the paprika also improves flavour.

Mahmoos Banquet Meat Curry

An all-time favourite for special occasions, this dish is a little time-consuming and elaborate. It comes from friends closely connected with the Osmania kitchen of Hyderabad, where the Nizam's table was a legend.

Serves 4–6
Cooking Time: 60–70 minutes

British	Metric	Ingredients	American
2¼ lb	1 kg	meat, big chunks of good fatty lamb	2¼ lb
5 oz	150 g	ghee	⅝ cup
9 oz	250 g	potatoes (4 or 5)	9 oz
6	6	eggs, hard boiled & halved	6
9 oz	250 g	onions, finely sliced	2 cups
		water, as required in recipe	
2 tsps	10 g	salt, to taste	2 tsps
		singe-fry masala	
1 tsp	3.5 g	turmeric powder	1 tsp
1 tbsp	6 g	chilli powder	1 tbsp
		follow-up masala	
1 tbsp	15 g	ginger paste	1 tbsp
1 tbsp	15 g	garlic paste	1 tbsp
		during-cooking masala 1	
9 oz (1½ cups)	250 g	yoghurt, whisked	1 cup

during-cooking masala 2

5 oz (1 cup)	150 g	tomato puree	$\frac{5}{8}$ cup
2 tbsps	40 g	almond paste	2 tbsps
$1\frac{1}{2}$ tbsps	30 g	*chironji*, roasted OR pinenut paste	$1\frac{1}{2}$ tbsps
$1\frac{1}{2}$ tbsps	18 g	poppyseed, roasted & ground	$1\frac{1}{2}$ tbsps
$1\frac{1}{2}$ tbsps	13.5 g	coconut meat, finely ground	$1\frac{1}{2}$ tbsps
2 tsps	5.5 g	aromatic garam masala	2 tsps

finishing masala

2 tsps	5.5 g	garam masala	2 tsps
$\frac{1}{2}$ tsp	0.25 g	saffron, soaked in milk	$\frac{1}{2}$ tsp
$1\frac{1}{2}$ tbsps	20 ml	milk	$1\frac{1}{2}$ tbsps
2 tbsps	30 ml	lemon juice	2 tbsps

garnish masala

4	4	green chillies, scissor-cut	4
$\frac{2}{3}$ oz	20 g	green coriander, leaves only	$\frac{2}{3}$ cup

Method

Halve the potatoes, stir fry to light brown in ghee and keep aside on kitchen paper.

Brown the onions in the ghee and keep aside on kitchen paper.

Whisk the yoghurt for 3–4 seconds in a blender and keep aside.

Liquidize the during-cooking masala 2 and keep aside.

Soak saffron in milk and keep aside.

Take a large heavy-bottomed cooking pan and pour the remaining ghee. If the ghee is used up for frying potatoes and onions—take another $\frac{1}{2}$ cup/75ml/$\frac{1}{3}$ cup of ghee and bring to high heat. Add the *singe-fry*

179

masala, fry for about half a minute and then add the *follow-up masala*. Stir fry till light brown.

Now add the meat and cook for 10 minutes, stirring the meat all the time. Add salt. Add enough water to drown the meat—lower heat and cook till the meat is tender, evaporating the extra water.

Add the *during-cooking masala 1* that was set aside and let simmer (not boil) for 10–12 minutes. Keeping the meat at moderate heat, add the *during-cooking masala 2*. Mix vigorously and then boil for 10 minutes.

Transfer all the contents to a large, attractive, oven-proof serving dish. Spread the potatoes and boiled eggs on top and over it place the browned onions. Then sprinkle the *finishing masala* including the saffron in milk.

Cover the serving dish with foil and bake in an oven on moderate heat at 140 deg C for 15–20 minutes.

Remove foil, add *garnish masala* and serve with naan, roti or plain boiled rice.

Dry Lamb Curry

This dish is known as *sukha gosht* in India, meaning literally dry meat curry. The preparation stands halfway between barbeque and stir fry. The masalas make the meat a very tasty dish. This curry has acquired universal appeal.

Serves 3–5
Preparation Time: 3 hours
Cooking Time: 55–60 minutes

British	Metric	Ingredients	American
2¼ lb	1 kg	lamb, goulash cut	2¼ lb
7 oz (1⅓ cups)	200 g	ghee	⅞ cup
½ pt	300 ml	water	1¼ cups

180

marinade masala

1 lb	500 g	yoghurt	2 cups
1 tsp	3 g	meat tenderizer	1 tsp

singe-fry masala

1 tbsp	6 g	coriander powder	1 tbsp
1 tsp	3.25 g	black pepper powder	1 tsp
1 tbsp	10 g	turmeric powder	1 tbsp

follow-up masala

2 tbsps	30 g	ginger paste	2 tbsps
2 tbsps	30 g	garlic paste	2 tbsps
1 tbsp	6 g	chilli powder	1 tbsp
3–4	3–4	bay leaves (*tejpat*)	3–4

during-cooking masala

$\frac{1}{2}$ tbsp	3.75 g	*amchoor*	$\frac{1}{2}$ tbsp
1 tsp	1.75 g	allspice powder	1 tsp
$\frac{1}{2}$ tsp	2.5 g	sugar	$\frac{1}{2}$ tsp
2 tsps	10 g	salt, to taste	2 tsps

finishing masala

1 tsp	2.75 g	garam masala	1 tsp
3	3	*keora* essence, drops in 1 tbsp water (optional)	3

Method

Wash the lamb and dry with a kitchen towel.

Cream marinade masala for 5–10 seconds in a blender and keep aside.

Soak the lamb in the marinade and set aside for 3 hours. Remove and again dab the meat dry—do not wash. Keep aside.

Bring ghee to high heat in a large saucepan, add the *singe-fry masala* and singe for half a minute. Add the *follow-up masala* and stir fry for a minute. Do not brown it. Now put in the meat, mix well with the masala and stir fry till it turns brown. Add 1 cup (150 ml) water, cover and cook for 20 minutes on very slow fire, stirring from time to time. Check if meat is tender but firm, i.e. *al dente*. If still not tender add a little more water (this should be done within 30 minutes). Uncover the saucepan and keep browning the meat till all the water is evaporated. Add the *during-cooking masala* and stir fry on medium heat. By now the ghee will be released—test meat and salt.

Transfer to a preheated serving dish and sprinkle the *finishing masala*. If you can get *keora* essence, put three drops in 1 tablespoon (15 ml) of water and add on top.

NOTE: Can be eaten as a snack or with boiled rice but is best with romali roti, tortillas or plain soft white bread with the crust cut off.

Lamb can be substituted with beef, veal or pork. Cooking time will alter a little—less for veal, more for pork and the same for beef.

Give the leftover marinade to your pet cat.

Balloon Meat-Ball Curry (*Khol Kofta*)

This is a unique meat ball curry where the centre is hollow. It is believed to be have been innovated by the famous Wajid Ali Shah, Nawab of Oudh.

Serves 4
Preparation Time: 15–20 minutes
Cooking Time: 60–70 minutes

British	Metric	Ingredients	American
		for meat balls	
18 oz	$\frac{1}{2}$ kg	lamb, finely minced	18 oz

1½ tbsps	15 g	poppy seed	1½ tbsps
⅔ oz	20 g	roasted chick pea (Bengal gram), if available or roasted hazelnuts	4 tbsps
3 tbsps	18 g	arrow root powder	3 tbsps
4	4	cloves	4
1	1	cardamom, brown large, shelled	1
2	2	cardamoms, green small, shelled	2
10	10	black pepper corns	10
1"	2.5 cm	cinnamon (1 g)	1"
½ tsp	2.5 g	salt (I), to taste	½ tsp
		ice, crushed, as required	

for the sauce

2 oz (3 tbsps)	50 g	ghee (I)	¼ cup
3½ oz	100 g	ghee (II)	½ cup
3	3	onions, large, finely-sliced	3
1 tsp	5 g	salt (II), to taste	1 tsp

singe-fry masala 1

6	6	chillies, whole broken in several pieces or scissor-cut	6

singe-fry masala 2

1 tsp	2 g	coriander powder	1 tsp
1 tsp	3.5 g	turmeric powder	1 tsp
1 tsp	2.75 g	cumin powder	1 tsp

follow-up masala

1 tbsp	15 g	ginger paste	1 tbsp
1 bulb		garlic paste	1 bulb

		during-cooking masala	
4	4	bay leaves (*tejpat*)	4
6	6	large cardamoms	6
		finishing masala	
1 tsp	2.75 g	garam masala	1 tsp
		garnish masala	
$\frac{1}{3}$ oz ($\frac{1}{2}$ cup)	10 g	coriander green, scissor-cut	$\frac{1}{3}$ cup

Method

To prepare the meat balls grind poppy seed, roasted chick pea or hazelnuts as finely as possible and sprinkle it on the mince. Grind cloves, cardamom seeds, black pepper corns and cumin (these spices should be ground finely from the whole spices) and mix with the mince. As a relief measure powdered spices may be used. Sprinkle the arrowroot powder evenly on top and mix the mince well, kneading like dough, and put the whole mixture through the meat mixer. Use the attachments which will paste the mince rather than cut it. The finer this paste is the better—add half teaspoon of salt evenly when mincing.

Take ice, crush it and make ice balls of about the size of a large hailstone—keep the ice balls in the freezer.

Take the mince meat dough in the palm of the hand, take enough mince to make a medium-sized meat ball. Put the mince in the centre of your palm and press it flat. Place one ice ball in it and wrap the mince around it. You now have a meat ball with the ice ball in the centre—return to the freezer immediately so that the ice does not melt—repeat the process till all the mince dough has been made into balls. Refrigerate them.

The meat balls do not have any stages of masala as it is a mixture of mince meat, herbs and spices.

The curry sauce however has the normal distinct stages.

To make the curry sauce, take a heavy-bottomed cooking pan and bring ghee (I) to high heat in it. Put in the sliced onions and brown them.

Remove with a slotted spoon and set aside. Bring the remaining ghee to high heat, add the *singe-fry masala 1* and stir. When light brown add the *singe fry masala 2*. After singeing and spluttering for 60–90 seconds, add the browned onions and the *follow-up masala* and stir fry for 2–3 minutes, and keep aside.

Take a heavy-based saucepan and add ghee (II) to stir fry the meat balls.

Bring out the meat balls from the refrigerator, be careful not to damage them. Increase heat and fry till the meat balls are dark brown. Add the fried masala, 1 cup (5 fl oz/150 ml/$\frac{5}{8}$ cup) of water and salt. Then add the *during-cooking masala* and let simmer on medium heat for about 20 minutes. Finally add the *finishing masala*.

During this period the ice balls inside the meat balls will have melted, and the water released into the curry will have evaporated during simmering. When you break the meat ball it will now be hollow inside.

Transfer to a white serving bowl, sprinkle the *garnish masala* and serve it with boiled or steamed rice or Indian breads.

Emperor Lamb Curry (*Shahi Korma*)

This dish is definitely of Persian origin and the most exotic spices are used in it.

Shahi comes from Shah meaning the ultimate aristocrat. The royalty could not manage large pieces of meat or chillies—hence the name *Shahi Korma*.

Serves 4–6
Cooking Time: 40–45 minutes

British	Metric	Ingredients	American
2¼ lb	1 kg	lamb, smaller than goulash cut about 1½" cubes, may be irregular	2¼ lb

5 oz (1 cup)	150 g	ghee	$\frac{5}{8}$ cup
		singe-fry masala	
1 tsp	3.5 g	turmeric powder	1 tsp
1 tsp	2 g	coriander powder	1 tsp
		follow-up masala	
1 tsp	5 g	garlic paste	1 tsp
2	2	onions, finely chopped	2
1 tsp	5 g	green ginger root paste	1 tsp
1 tsp	3.25 g	black pepper powder	1 tsp
10	10	cardamoms, regular, seeds pounded	10
$\frac{1}{2}$ tsp	1.25 g	cloves, pounded	$\frac{1}{2}$ tsp
2 tsps	10 g	salt, to taste	2 tsps
1 tsp	3.5 g	turmeric powder	1 tsp
		during-cooking masala	
7 oz	200 g	almonds, soaked, peeled & well pounded with $1\frac{1}{3}$ cups water & strained through muslin	7 oz
8 fl oz	225 ml	water	1 cup
5 fl oz	150 ml	cream	$\frac{5}{8}$ cup
1 tsp	5 g	sugar	1 tsp
		finishing masala	
7 oz	200 g	yoghurt, creamed with cornflour in blender	$\frac{3}{4}$ cup
1 tsp	2.25 g	cornflour	1 tsp
3	3	lemon, juice of	3
		garnish masala	
$\frac{1}{2}$ tsp	0.25 g	saffron, soaked in milk	$\frac{1}{2}$ tsp
2 tsp	10 ml	milk	2 tsp

Method

Bring ghee to high heat in a heavy saucepan and remove from heat. Immediately put the *singe-fry masala* and as soon as it stops spluttering return to fire and put the *follow-up masala*. Stir fry for 3–5 minutes till the mixture is smooth.

Add the meat and continue stir frying for 10–15 minutes till the meat changes its colour, but is not completely brown.

Take the saucepan off the fire and add the *during-cooking masala*. Mix well with a wooden spoon, and if cold enough, with your hands.

Return the saucepan to fire and let it simmer on very low heat for 25–30 minutes or till meat is done and all the exotic aromas are flooding the kitchen.

Transfer to a shallow, white, attractive, oven-proof, serving dish. Add the *finishing masala*, leave in the oven on low heat till ready to serve.

Before serving sprinkle *garnish masala*. Serve with rice.

NOTE: This dish does not have any chillies and is soft and creamy to the palate. In regal homes the dish was also garnished variously with slivered pistachio nuts, whole pinenuts and covered on top with silver foil.

Pork Curry 'Double Fry'

Some friends describe this dish as 'smashing'.

It is almost certain that meat-eating Tamils created this dish with innovations from Portuguese mariners. A dish such as this could be called colonial. This recipe is however a gift from my late father's Chittagong cook who could cook practically from any kitchen in the world—some as originals, others innovated by him.

Serves 4–6
Cooking Time: 80–90 minutes

British	Metric	Ingredients	American
$2\frac{1}{4}$ lb	1 kg	pork, preferably undercuts 2"x1" (5 cmx2 cm) & natural thickness of $\frac{1}{2}$"	$2\frac{1}{4}$ lb
$3\frac{1}{2}$ fl oz ($\frac{2}{3}$ cup)	100 ml	cooking oil, preferably groundnut or sunflower seed oil	$\frac{1}{2}$ cup
2 tsps	10 g	salt, to taste	2 tsps
$\frac{1}{2}$ pt (2 cups)	300 ml	water	$1\frac{1}{4}$ cups
singe-fry masala			
12	12	curry leaves	12
1 tsp	3 g	fenugreek powder	1 tsp
1 tsp	3 g	mustard powder	1 tsp
1 tsp	2.75 g	cumin powder	1 tsp
1 tsp	2 g	coriander powder	1 tsp
1 tbsp	6 g	chilli powder	1 tbsp
4	4	red chillies, whole, broken in two	4
1 tsp	3.5 g	turmeric powder	1 tsp
follow-up masala			
1 tbsp	7.5 g	garlic, finely chopped	1 tbsp
3	3	onion, finely sliced	3
1 tbsp	9 g	ginger, finely grated	1 tbsp
20	20	black pepper corns	20
during-cooking masala			
6	6	cloves	6
2	4 g	cinnamon, 2" (5 cm) pieces	2
5	5	cardamoms, small green	5
1 tbsp	7.5 g	*amchoor*	1 tbsp

		finishing masala	
5 fl oz (1 cup)	≈ 150 ml	coconut cream	$\frac{5}{8}$ cup
		garnish masala	
1 tsp	3.25 g	pepper, freshly ground from mill	1 tsp
$\frac{1}{2}$ tsp	0.75 g	nutmeg, freshly grated	$\frac{1}{2}$ tsp
1	1	lemon, juice of	1

Method

Bring oil to full heat and add the *singe-fry masala* till it is brown. Add the *follow-up masala*. Stir fry till golden brown. Now add the pork and fry on high heat stirring and turning briskly ensuring that the pork is properly coated with the mixture. Add the *during-cooking masala* and stir fry for 5–10 minutes. Pour 2 cups (300 ml) water and salt, and cook on low heat till pork is tender for about 45–60 minutes. Add the *finishing masala* and cook uncovered for another 10–12 minutes.

Now comes the stage of 'double frying' the pork. Remove the gravy mixture from the pork with a spoon or any other method and keep aside leaving the pork in the saucepan plus whatever mixture sticks to it. Shallow fry the pork till dry and dark brown, ensuring that it does not stick to the bottom of the dish. Should the oil be insufficient, add a tablespoon of butter and fry.

When pork is evenly brown, pour back the gravy mixture into the saucepan. Cook till the gravy is thick.

Transfer to a white serving dish and sprinkle the *garnish masala* on top and squeeze a lemon.

Serve with boiled rice and Tabasco.

NOTE: This dish adapts beautifully for venison or Scandinavian elk meat.

Poor Man's Moghul Curry

The rich and the gourmet ate curries, examples of which are given in this book. The poor man also ate meat curries and would naturally make his preparation as close as possible to that of their master's. Nevertheless, the simplicity of the soup curry does not take away from it the pristine flavour.

Serves 4–6
Cooking Time: 50–55 minutes

British	Metric	Ingredients	American
2¼ lb	1 kg	any meat, goulash cut	2¼ lb
5 fl oz	150 ml	ghee or any fat, or cooking oil	⅝ cup
9 fl oz	250 g	water	1⅛ cups
singe-fry masala			
1 tbsp	8 g	cumin powder	1 tbsp
1 tbsp	6 g	chilli powder	1 tbsp
1 tbsp	10 g	turmeric powder	1 tbsp
follow-up masala			
5 fl oz	150 g	onions, as paste or from blender	⅝ cup
2 tsps	10 g	salt, to taste	2 tsps
during-cooking masala			
4	4	cardamoms, large	4
finishing masala			
1 tsp	3.25 g	black pepper	1 tsp
1 tsp	2.5 g	*amchoor*	1 tsp
garnish masala			
1 tbsp	2 g	green coriander, scissor-cut	1 tbsp

Method

Take a deep saucepan, pour ghee and bring it to high heat. Add the *singe-fry masala*, and immediately after it splutters, add onions. Stir fry till onions are brown. Add meat and the *during-cooking masala*. Stir fry till meat is dark brown and the oil is released to the top. Add the *finishing masala* and water, and let simmer on medium heat for 30–40 minutes till meat is done.

Transfer to a serving dish and sprinkle the *garnish masala*.

Serve with rice or *phulka*.

NOTE: No expensive spice or herb is used in this recipe. Chillies and souring can be controlled to suit your taste. One teaspoon of garam masala may be added to the finishing masala to make the dish spicier.

Yoghurt Mince Meat Curry

A very special dish created by Kashmiri Brahmins who knew how to handle both sweatmeats and meat. In this dish the techniques of both are combined to make a rich tasty dish.

Serves 3–4
Cooking Time: 40–50 minutes

British	Metric	Ingredients	American
18 oz	½ kg	mince meat, preferably lamb, coarsely ground	18 oz
1 lb 2 oz (3 cups)	500 g	yoghurt	2 cups
5 fl oz	150 ml	ghee, not cooking oil	⅝ cup
		singe-fry masala	
1 tsp	2.75 g	cumin powder	1 tsp
1 tsp	2 g	coriander powder	1 tsp

1 tsp	2 g	chilli powder	1 tsp

follow-up masala

1 tsp	5 g	ginger paste	1 tsp
1 tsp	5 g	garlic paste	1 tsp
½ tbsp	7.5 g	salt, to taste	½ tbsp
½ tsp	2.5 g	sugar	½ tsp

during-cooking masala

1 tbsp	6 g	beet root, grated	1 tbsp
2	2	bay leaves (*tejpat*)	2
4	4	cardamoms, regular	4
1"	2.5 cm	cinnamon stick (1 g)	1"
4	4	cloves	4

finishing masala

½ tsp	0.75 g	nutmeg, grated	½ tsp

garnish masala

2	2	*keora* essence, drops in 1 tbsp (15 ml) of water	2

Method

Take a heavy-bottomed cooking pan, bring ghee to high heat add the *singe-fry masala* and stir fry for a few seconds. Add the *follow-up masala* and stir fry for 2–3 minutes. Add the mince, and stir fry till it is brown. Liquidize yoghurt in a blender and add to the mince alongwith the *during-cooking masala* and simmer on moderate heat for 20 minutes stirring all the time. The yoghurt should start curdling and granulating and taking on the same look as the mince meat. Keep stir frying till the mince is done and all the water has evaporated. Add the *finishing masala* and mix.

Transfer to a serving dish and sprinkle the *garnish masala* and serve.

Goes with anything, especially suited as a canape topping.

Yoghurt Meat Curry

A complete curry dish renowned for its roundness of flavour and mild pungency. It comes from the original curry culture of Oudh, a famous culinary centre of India. It may be prepared with lamb, beef, pork or veal.

Serves 5–7
Preparation Time: 6 hours or overnight
Cooking Time: 40–50 minutes

British	Metric	Ingredients	American
2¼ lb	1 kg	lean meat lamb or beef, goulash cut	2¼ lb
3½ oz (⅔ cup)	100 g	ghee	½ cup
marinade masala			
11 oz	300 g	onions, coarsely chopped	11 oz
1⅓ oz	40 g	fresh ginger root, chopped, one piece	1⅓ oz
12 oz (2 cups)	330 g	yoghurt	1¼ cups
1 tsp	2.5 g	cornflour	1 tsp
singe-fry masala			
1 tsp	2.75 g	cumin powder	1 tsp
1 tbsp	6 g	coriander powder	1 tbsp
1 tbsp	10 g	turmeric powder	1 tbsp
1 tsp	2 g	chilli powder	1 tsp
1 tsp	3 g	fenugreek seed powder	1 tsp
during-cooking masala			
4	4	bay leaves (*tejpat*)	4
4	4	green chillies, whole, split	4
4	4	cardamoms, large brown	4

193

2"	5 cm	cinnamom (2 g)	2"
2 tsps	10 g	salt, to taste	2 tsps
finishing masala			
1 tsp	2.75 g	garam masala	1 tsp
garnish masala			
1 tbsp	2 g	green coriander leaves, chopped	1 tbsp
2 tbsps	12 g	spring onions, stems chopped	2 tbsps
2 to 4	2 to 4	garlic cloves, through press	2 to 4

Method

Put the marinade masala in a blender and purée. Transfer to a bowl and add the meat. Mix well with hand or wooden spoon and let sit for 6 hours or prepare the day before prepration and leave overnight.

Bring ghee to high heat, quickly add the *singe-fry masala* and stir fry for 20–30 seconds.

Add the marinated meat alongwith marinade. Reduce heat and add $1\frac{1}{2}$ cups (225ml) of water. Next, add the *during-cooking masala* along with salt. Stir the meat and simmer on medium to low heat for 35–40 minutes or till meat is done. The ghee will be released on top and the dish will have a golden-white colour.

Transfer to a serving bowl and sprinkle the *finishing masala* followed by the *garnish masala*.

Serve with rice or any oriental bread.

NOTE: Cornflour is added to yoghurt to keep it creamy and prevent curdling.

If you wish to make this dish intriguingly piquant, add $\frac{1}{2}$ tsp/1.7 g of Coleman's mustard powder to the marinade.

Curried *Dum Ke Pasanda*

A complete preparation with all the stages of Indian cooking plus baking. The quality of meat is the essence of the quality of the dish. Make sure good lean meat fillets are made by the butcher. Often made for special occasions. This delicious preparation is proof of the fact that so many different spices herbs and nuts can blend so beautifully.

Serves 4
Preparation Time: 2 hours
Cooking Time: 55–60 minutes

British	Metric	Ingredients	American
2¼ lb	1 kg	meat, lamb, fillet	2¼ lb
9 oz	250 g	onions (lot 1+lot 2)	9 oz
9 oz	250 g	ghee	1⅛ cups
		marinade	
9 oz	250 g	yoghurt	1 cup
a pinch	a pinch	salt, to taste	a pinch
		follow-up masala	
1 tbsp	15 g	ginger paste	1 tbsp
1 tbsp	15 g	garlic paste	1 tbsp
1 tsp	2 g	chilli powder	1 tsp
1 tbsp	10 g	poppy seed, roasted & ground	1 tbsp
1 tbsp	9 g	*chironji* (or pinenuts), roasted & ground	1 tbsp
1 tbsp	5 g	coriander, whole, roasted & ground	1 tbsp
		during-cooking masala	
1 tbsp	15 g	salt, to taste	1 tbsp
4½ oz	125 g	onions, fried & crushed (lot I)	4½ oz

1 tbsp	15 g	green coriander paste	1 tbsp
1 tbsp	15 g	chick pea, roasted split lentil powder	1 tbsp
		finishing masala	
4	4	cloves	4
3	3	cardamoms, small	3
1"	2.5 cm	cinnamom stick (1 g)	1"
$\frac{1}{2}$ tsp	1 g	allspice (*kebab chini*) powder	$\frac{1}{2}$ tsp
2	2	lemons, juice of	2
		ghee, remaining from first sauce (see method)	
$4\frac{1}{2}$ oz	125 g	onions, fried & crushed (lot II)	$4\frac{1}{2}$ oz
		garnish	
4	4	onions, rings of	4
$\frac{1}{2}$ oz ($\frac{1}{2}$ cup)	10 g	green mint leaves, whole	$\frac{1}{3}$ cup
3	3	whole green chillies, slit	3
12	12	wedges of lemon, slices	12

Method

Roast and grind poppy seeds, *chironji*, coriander, whole and split chick peas on a griddle and set aside. Cream yoghurt and salt in a blender for 10–15 seconds. Marinate the meat in it for 2 hours. Heat ghee in a heavy-bottomed saucepan to high heat, add onions and crisp fry till deep brown. Remove with a slotted spoon and crush while hot and keep aside on paper in two lots.

In the same ghee from which the onions have been removed add the *follow-up masala*, stir fry till light brown, add meat and salt. Next add the *during-cooking masala* and roasted split chick pea *dal* powder at the end.

Transfer all the contents including the meat, but not the ghee, into a baking dish and sprinkle the *finishing masala* on top and add the

196

remaining ghee from the first saucepan.

Cover with a foil and bake in moderate oven, both 'upper' and 'lower' till the meat is tender. Check meat with skewer right down to the bottom and also check salt.

When ready to serve transfer to a preheated serving dish. Sprinkle the *garnish masala*.

Goes best with romali roti or phulka.

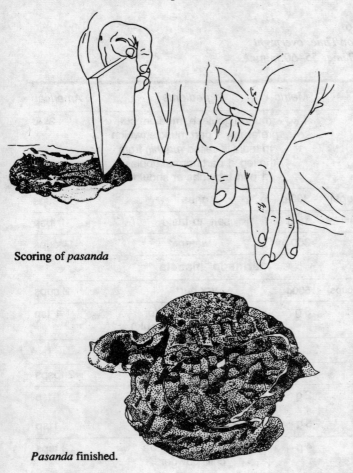

Scoring of *pasanda*

Pasanda finished.

Royal Mutton Curry: Oudh

With some variation by every cook, this remains the most sophisticated curry in the Indian kitchen. It must have been refined many times. The famous king of Oudh, Wajid Ali Shah, set down the recipe with more complex techniques.

This is my manageable version without sacrificing the original intent and flavour.

Serves 4–6
Preparation Time: overnight
Cooking Time: 55–60 minutes

British	Metric	Ingredients	American
2¼ lb	1 kg	mutton goulash, medium cut, preferably 1 part muscle (which in India is called *machli*) from the leg, 1 part normal goulash, 1 part fatty ribs or shoulder	2¼ lb
11 oz (2 cups)	300 g	ghee	1¼ cups
1 tbsp	15 g	salt, to taste	1 tbsp
½ pt	300 ml	water	1¼ cups
marinade masala			
1 lb 2 oz (3cups)	500g	yoghurt	2 cups
1 tsp	3 g	meat tenderizer (for temperate climates only)	1 tsp
singe-fry masala			
2 tbsps	15 g	coriander powder	2 tbsps
1 tsp	2 g	ginger powder OR	1 tsp
1 tsp	5 g	ginger root as paste	1tsp
2 tsps	4 g	cayenne pepper OR chilli powder	2 tsps
1 tbsp	8 g	cumin (white) powder	1 tbsp

1 tbsp	10 g	turmeric powder	1 tbsp
	follow-up masala		
9 oz	250 g	onion, purée	$1\frac{1}{8}$ cups
	during-cooking masala 1		
$1\frac{1}{2}$ bulbs		garlic (I), cloved	$1\frac{1}{2}$ bulbs
5–6		cardamoms, large brown	5–6
10	10	cardamoms, regular	10
6–8		cloves	6–8
4–6		bay leaves (*tejpat*)	4–6
1 tbsp	8 g	cumin powder	1 tbsp
	during-cooking masala 2		
7 oz	200 g	tomato, purée of	$\frac{7}{8}$ cup
	finishing masala		
$\frac{1}{2}$ tbsp	4 g	garam masala	$\frac{1}{2}$ tbsp
	garnish masala		
$\frac{1}{2}$ bulb		garlic (II), cloved	$\frac{1}{2}$ bulb

Method

Cream yoghurt, add 1 teaspoon meat tenderizer to cut down time for tenderizing in temperate climate. Marinate the meat overnight, do not refrigerate.

Purée onions and keep aside.

Purée tomatoes and sieve to remove seeds and skin and keep aside.

Smash cloved garlic (I), with the blunt side of a knife and keep aside

Bring ghee to high heat in a heavy pot preferably with a copper base. When very hot, add the *singe-fry masala*, till it bubble. Stir for 5–10 seconds. Add onion purée stirring all the time slowly, till brown. Now add the meat, and the *during-cooking masala 1*. Stir fry the mutton till it is brown and more than half cooked. The ghee will be partially released on top.

After the meat is brown, add salt and the *during-cooking masala 2* and cook on a slow fire for 40–50 minutes depending on the quality of the lamb or mutton.

At this stage when all the aromas are released and the tomato properly cooked, the ghee will appear on top. Check meat with a toothpick and cook for a few minutes if not done. DO NOT OVER-COOK.

Taste for salt.

Take out your best serving bowl, preferably white. Spoon the lamb curry in the bowl and sprinkle the *finishing masala* and press the garlic; (II), through a garlic press on top, as garnish Masala.

Traditionally this dish has a silver foil put on top—do so if you can get it.

It is served with boiled rice or whole wheat roti, chappati or any oriental bread and even with pizza bread.

VEGETABLE CURRIES

Single Step Whole Chick Pea Curry

A wayside favourite made throughout the length and breadth of North India. As one lot finishes, another is prepared.

Serves 4
Preparation Time: 3–4 hours
Cooking Time: 55–60 minutes

British	Metric	Ingredients	American
8 oz	225 g	chick pea (*kabli chana*), dry weight	$1\frac{1}{8}$ cups
$1\frac{1}{3}$ pt	750 ml	water	$3\frac{1}{4}$ cups
2 fl oz	50 ml	cooking oil	$3\frac{1}{4}$ cups
		masala	
1 tsp	3.25 g	black pepper powder	1 tsp
$1\frac{1}{2}$ tbsps	11 g	*amchoor*	$1\frac{1}{2}$ tbsps
$\frac{1}{2}$ tbsp	7.5 g	salt, to taste	$\frac{1}{2}$ tbsp
$1\frac{1}{2}$ tbsps	12.5 g	garam masala	$1\frac{1}{2}$ tbsps
$\frac{1}{2}$ tbsp	3 g	chilli powder	$\frac{1}{2}$ tbsp
1 tsp	3 g	grated ginger	1 tsp
2	2	*amla* (emblica berries)	2
		OR	
1	1	tea bags	1
		garnish masala	
		raw onion rings—to taste	
		green coriander, scissor-cut—to taste	
		green chillies, scissor-cut—to taste	

Method

Soak chick peas for 3–4 hours. Drain and boil in 5 cups (750 ml) of water along with the tea bag till the chick peas are done. This takes about 40 minutes. Drain in a colander and set aside.

Bring oil to smoking in a deep saucepan. Add all the masalas, except the tea bag which has already been added. Stir fry for about 10–20 seconds. Add the chick peas and stir for 3–5 minutes. Add 2 tablespoons (30 ml) of water and mix well. The *amla* or tea bag gives the required dark colour to the chick peas. Remove the tea bag or the amla berries.

Sprinkle the *garnish masala* on top and serve.

Goes best with bhatura or rice, kulcha, puri, etc.

Curried Eggplant Cottage Cheese Casserole

A simple dish for eggplant lovers. The cottage cheese used is easy to make, has excellent food value and readily absorbs flavours that are used.

Serves 4
Preparation Time: 15 minutes
Cooking Time: 40–45 minutes

British	Metric	Ingredients	American
14 oz	400 g	eggplants (about 2)	14 oz
$4\frac{1}{2}$ fl oz	125 ml	cooking oil	$\frac{5}{8}$ cup
2	2	onions, medium	2
7 oz	200 g	cottage cheese (*panir*)	7 oz
$\frac{1}{2}$ tbsp	7.5 g	salt (I), to taste	$\frac{1}{2}$ tbsp
1 tsp	5 g	salt (II) (for eggplant rings)	1 tsp
5 fl oz (1 cup)	150 ml	tomato purée	$\frac{5}{8}$ cup
		curry spices mix	

1 tsp	**5 g**	ginger paste	1 tsp
1 tsp	5 g	garlic paste	1 tsp
1 tsp	3.5 g	turmeric powder	1 tsp
1 tsp	2 g	coriander powder	1 tsp
1 tsp	2 g	chilli powder	1 tsp
$\frac{1}{2}$ tsp	1.25 g	caraway powder	$\frac{1}{2}$ tsp
		garnish	
		onion rings—to taste	

Method

Cut onions into rings and fry them to golden brown in oil. Set aside.

Slice the eggplant in round rings of thickness 1 cm and sprinkle with salt (II) and keep aside for 30 minutes.

Bring oil to smoking and sauté fry the eggplant slices to light brown. Remove and place on kitchen paper.

Take cottage cheese (*panir*) and mash or grate it, if too hard. Mix the ingredients of the curry mix with the cottage cheese with hand and sauté fry in the remaining oil in the saucepan for 3–5 minutes.

Transfer into a baking casserole laying the eggplant slices alternately with the cottage cheese mix. The topmost layer should be eggplant. Pour the tomato purée and salt (I) on the top.

Cover and bake for 20 minutes in moderate heat. Remove cover and bake for another 5 minutes.

Before serving *garnish* with browned onion rings and serve.

Usually eaten plain or with fried Indian breads like puri, paratha, etc.

Spicy Curry Aubergines

A typical Hyderabadi dish now famous the world over. This is a strong and piquant recipe with elaborate handling. Often becomes a conversation piece!

Serves 3–4
Cooking Time: 30–35 minutes

British	Metric	Ingredients	American
8	8	aubergines (eggplant), medium sized	8
7 fl oz (1⅓ cups)	200 ml	cooking oil (I), preferably groundnut	⅞ cup
2 fl oz	50 ml	cooking oil (II)	¼ cup
½ tbsp	7.5 g	salt, to taste	½ tbsp
		singe-fry masala	
1 tsp	3 g	cumin seed	1 tsp
1 tsp	4.25 g	fenugreek seed	1 tsp
⅓ oz (⅓ cup)	10 g	green curry leaves (optional)	⅓ cup
1 tsp	3.5 g	turmeric powder	1 tsp
1 tsp	2 g	chilli powder	1 tsp
		follow-up masala 1	
½ tbsp	5 g	coriander seed, roasted	½ tbsp
½ tbsp	4.25 g	cumin seed, roasted	½ tbsp
½ tbsp	4.5 g	sesame seed, roasted	½ tbsp
1 tbsp	12 g	peanuts, roasted	1 tbsp
1	1	onion, large, roasted	1

follow-up masala 2

5 fl oz (1 cup)	150 ml	tamarind pulp	$\frac{5}{8}$ cup
4	4	green chillies, slit lengthwise & deseeded	4
$\frac{1}{3}$ oz ($\frac{1}{2}$ cup)	10 g	green coriander, leaves only	$\frac{1}{3}$ cup

Method

Slit the aubergines halfway lengthwise and let rest in salt water. Prepare the tamarind pulp and keep aside. Mix together the follow-up masala 1 and blend in a blender for about 2 minutes. Keep aside.

Bring oil (I) to high heat and add the *singe-fry masala* and fry, stirring quickly for about half a minute. Now add the aubergines after draining the salt water, taking care that the aubergines do not break. Stir fry for 6–8 minutes, turning them over after every 3 minutes. Set the pan aside.

Take a fresh saucepan, add oil (II) and bring to high heat. Add salt, *follow-up masala 1* and stir fry for 5–7 minutes. And then add the *follow-up masala 2* and simmer on moderate heat till the sauce is thick. Remove from fire.

Now take the cooked aubergines and lay them over the thick sauce in the pan. Cover the pan and let simmer on low heat for about 10 minutes till oil is released at the top. Remove the cover and let the extra water evaporate. Serve by transferring gently into a preheated silver or EPNS platter.

NOTE: May be served with pulao or romali roti. Tortillas also do splendidly as a roll.

In the traditional mode, this dish is prepared and eaten the next day, so that the cooked aubergines are fully marinated in the sauce. They taste even better like this. To reheat, if eaten the next day, transfer the contents to a baking dish, cover with a foil and bake on moderate heat for about 15 minutes and serve in the baking dish.

Scrambled Cottage Cheese Curry Delight

This is another dish credited to our ancestors. It is simple to make, delicious to eat and not overpowered by 'curry' *per se*. This curry is extremely nutritious and a good diet stabilizer.

Serves 3–4
Preparation Time: 75 minutes
Cooking Time: 10–15 minutes

British	Metric	Ingredients	American
18 oz	$\frac{1}{2}$ kg	soft cottage cheese	$2\frac{1}{4}$ cups
1 oz	30 g	ghee	2 tbsps
2 oz	50 g	green peas	$\frac{1}{3}$ cup
1	1	onions, finely chopped	1
1	1	capsicum, finely square cut, about $\frac{1}{2}$ cm x $\frac{1}{2}$ cm	1
2	2	green chillies, whole, slit lengthwise & deseeded	2
$\frac{1}{2}$ tbsp	7.5 g	salt, to taste	$\frac{1}{2}$ tbsp
singe-fry masala			
1 tsp	3 g	cumin whole	1 tsp
1 tsp	3.5 g	turmeric powder	1 tsp
garnish masala			
1 tbsp	2 g	green coriander, scissor-cut	1 tbsp

Method

The cottage cheese for this recipe should not be ready-made but should be prepared as according to the recipe on page 281.

Single boil all the vegetables, except the green chillies, with enough water to cover them. Take off the fire and keep aside.

Bring ghee to high heat in a pan, add the *singe-fry masala*, and as soon as the turmeric sizzles, take off the fire.

Strain the water from the vegetables through a colander. Take the pan with masala and bring to heat. Add the strained vegetables and stir fry for 3–4 minutes. Add salt. Now add the *panir* loosening it with the hand—the consistency should look like şoft scrambled eggs. Add the green chillies, stir fry for 3–5 minutes till the extra water evaporates, and the *panir* and vegetables are evenly mixed.

NOTE: This curry goes well with any kind of Indian breads or rice.

A can of mixed vegetables may be used instead of the vegetables as stated.

A little garlic may be used if preferred—about 2 cloves through garlic press. Other vegetables of personal choice may be used, but they should not be more than one-third of the complete dish.

Makes an excellent stuffing for parathas. It is also a good filling for hot grilled sandwiches.

Kidney Beans or Butter Beans with Aubergine Curry Sauce

Several kinds of long beans are available, but kidney beans or butter beans do best for this curry. A preparation popular with aubergine lovers, this curry is a combination of Greek, Spanish and North Indian cuisine. It was created on the spot for friends from abroad.

Serves 2–3
Preparation Time: 3–4 hours
Cooking Time: 30–35 minutes

British	Metric	Ingredients	American
3½ oz	100 g	beans	½ cup
2½ pt (10 cups)	1½ l	water	6 cups
3½ fl oz	100 ml	cooking oil, preferably olive	½ cup

209

2	2	aubergines, medium	2
1 tsp	5 g	salt, to taste	1 tsp
1 tsp	5 g	citric acid	1 tsp
		OR	
1 tbsp	15 ml	lemon juice	1 tbsp
		singe-fry masala	
½ tsp	1.5 g	cumin seed, whole	½ tsp
½ tsp	1 g	thyme seed or carum (*ajwain*) seed, whole	½ tsp
½ tsp	1 g	chilli powder	½ tsp
		follow-up masala	
1 tsp	5 g	garlic paste	1 tsp
1 tsp	5 g	ginger paste	1 tsp
2	2	onions, large, finely sliced	2
		finishing masala	
½ tsp	0.25 g	saffron, soaked in milk	½ tsp
2 tbsps	30 ml	milk	2 tbsps

Method

Wash and soak beans in water for 3–4 hours.

Soak saffron in warm milk and set aside.

Boil aubergines for about 10–15 minutes, skin and immediately purée in a blender with citric acid or lemon juice (this prevents oxidation). Set aside.

Drain soaked beans through a colander and boil in enough fresh water for 15–20 minutes till soft and well done. Drain and keep aside.

Bring olive oil to high heat, add the *singe-fry masala* and let it splutter for 20–30 seconds. As soon as it splutters add the *follow-up masala* and salt, and stir fry for 2–3 minutes. Now add the aubergine purée and cook on moderate heat for 8–10 minutes, stirring now and then. When the oil is released take off the fire.

Transfer the cooked beans to a baking dish or flat casserole and pour the aubergine sauce and the *finishing masala* evenly on top. Cover and bake on moderate heat for 5–10 minutes. Serve in the baking dish.

Goes well with boiled rice or on pizza bread.

Green Peas in Green Pea Curry Sauce

A unique 'conversation piece' curry which tastes good too. My grand aunt (*Chachi ma*) from West Uttar Pradesh is credited with the preparation of this recipe.

My father's kitchen garden sometimes had a surplus crop of peas and his favourite aunt created this recipe to consume all the peas. She also made pea koftas, pea pancakes, samosas filled with peas, potato cutlets filled with peas, sweatmeat of green peas (a mock pistachio *burfi*) with a smattering of chopped real pistachio on top. Also pea pulao, cottage cheese with pea, peas soup, etc. The most unimaginable dish would be prepared with peas.

Serves 3–4
Cooking Time: 30–35 minutes

British	Metric	Ingredients	American
18 oz	$\frac{1}{2}$ kg	green peas, shelled	$3\frac{1}{2}$ cups
$\frac{1}{2}$ tsp	1.75 g	baking powder	$\frac{1}{2}$ tsp
$3\frac{1}{2}$ oz ($\frac{2}{3}$ cup)	100 g	ghee	$\frac{1}{2}$ cup
5 fl oz (1 cup)	150 ml	water (I)	$\frac{5}{8}$ cup
5 fl oz (1 cup)	150 ml	water (II)	$\frac{5}{8}$ cup
	singe-fry	**masala (liquidized)**	
4	4	green chillies	4
1 oz ($1\frac{1}{2}$ cups)	30 g	green coriander, leaves only	1 cup
8–9	12–15 g	garlic cloves	8–9

211

British	Metric	Ingredients	American
1 tsp	3.5 g	turmeric powder	1 tsp
2 tsps	10 g	salt, to taste	2 tsps
		garnish masala	
1 tbsp	8.5 g	cumin, powdered, roasted	1 tbsp

Method

Take one third of the shelled green peas, boil with water (I) and baking powder; liquidize and keep aside. Baking powder maintains the green colour and adds to the softening of the raw peas.

In a deep cooking pan bring ghee to high heat, add the liquidized *singe-fry masala* and stir fry till oil appears on top. Now add the remaining shelled green peas and stir fry till well coated with the masala for 2–3 minutes. Add water (II) and simmer on medium heat for 15–20 minutes till the peas are done. Add the liquidized peas. Transfer to a baking dish. Heat for a few minutes in an oven and transfer to a serving dish.

Sprinkle the *garnish masala* and serve with steaming boiled rice.

Royal Cottage Cheese Morel Curry (*Chaman Gucchi*): Kashmir

This is the most exclusive of all the Kashmiri vegetarian dishes, and once eaten is seldom forgotten.

Serves 5–6
Preparation Time: 45 minutes
Cooking Time : 35–40 minutes

British	Metric	Ingredients	American
9 oz	250 g	soft cottage cheese, 26 pieces, 2" square & 1" thick	9 oz
2 oz	50 g	dry morel (*gucchi*)	2 oz

5	5	tomatoes, medium to large, ripe & red	5
7 oz	200 g	ghee	$\frac{7}{8}$ cup
		singe-fry masala	
6	6	red chillies, whole, dried Indian or Chinese, crushed by hand	6
1 tbsp	6 g	chilli powder	1 tbsp
$\frac{1}{2}$ tsp	1.25 g	fennel seed or aniseed	$\frac{1}{2}$ tsp
$\frac{1}{2}$ tbsp	4 g	cumin powder	$\frac{1}{2}$ tbsp
		follow-up masala	
1 tbsp	15 g	ginger paste	1 tbsp
1 tbsp	10 g	poppy seed paste with added water	1 tbsp
1 tbsp	20 g	almond paste	1 tbsp
2 tsps	10 g	salt, to taste	2 tsps
		during-cooking masala	
9 fl oz (1$\frac{2}{3}$ cups)	250 ml	water	1$\frac{1}{8}$ cups
1 tbsp	7 g	Hungarian red paprika	1 tbsp
$\frac{3}{4}$ tsp	4 g	sugar	$\frac{3}{4}$ tsp
$\frac{1}{2}$ tbsp	4 g	garam masala	$\frac{1}{2}$ tbsp
		finishing masala	
9 oz (1$\frac{1}{2}$ cups)	250 g	yoghurt, creamed	1 cup

Method

Soak the morel in water for 45 minutes till fully rehyderated and keep aside.

Single boil tomatoes, peel off skin, slice and wash. Chop finely with a cleaver or a knife and keep aside.

Put ghee in a wok or a heavy saucepan and bring to high heat. Put the cottage cheese pieces and sauté fry to light brown. This may be done in two lots. Take them out and place on a paper and keep aside.

Bring to high heat the ghee that is left in the saucepan, add the *singe-fry masala,* and as soon as it stops spluttering add the finely chopped tomatoes. Let simmer for 5–10 minutes till it becomes a smooth sauce, tomatoes still being palpable. After squeezing morel of all the water, add and stir fry for 2–3 minutes. Now add the *follow-up masala,* and let cook for another 5 minutes. Add the cottage cheese pieces and let simmer for about 10 minutes. Turn the cottage cheese and the morel gently. Finally add the *during-cooking masala*, mix gently and cook on slow fire till oil is released.

Transfer to a baking dish, add the *finishing masala* and keep on low heat in the oven for 10 minutes. The dish should not be allowed to boil.

Serve immediately with rice or by itself. Also goes well with any oriental bread.

NOTE: The cottage cheese (*panir*) in this dish should be soft and prepared as according to the recipe on page 282.

Traditionally *ratan jyot* was used as colouring. It can be used if available. A few pieces of the bark are used instead of the Hungarian paprika in the during-cooking masala and removed before serving.

Madras Vegetable Soup Curry

This dish is made with the cheapest vegetables that are in season. Potatoes, onions, beans, yam, raw bananas, cabbages, cauliflowers and all the gourds may be used here.

Serves 6–8
Cooking Time: 20–25 minutes

British	Metric	Ingredients	American
2¼ lb	1 kg	vegetables, roughly chopped	2¼ lb

214

3½ fl oz (⅔ cup)	100 ml	cooking oil	½ cup
5 fl oz (1 cup)	150 ml	water	⅝ cup
		singe-fry masala	
1 tsp	2 g	chilli powder	1 tsp
1 tsp	3.5 g	turmeric powder	1 tsp
		follow-up masala	
1 tsp	5 g	ginger paste	1 tsp
1 tsp	5 g	green chilli paste	1 tsp
1 tsp	5 g	green coriander paste	1 tsp
		during-cooking masala	
5 fl oz (1 cup)	150 ml	coconut milk	⅝ cup
1 fl oz	30 ml	tamarind pulp	2 tbsps
2 tsps	10 g	salt, to taste	2 tsps
		garnish masala	
1½ tbsps	5 g	grated coconut, leftover	1½ tbsps

Method

Wash vegetables and keep in a colander. Take a deep cooking pot and heat oil to smoking. Add the *singe-fry masala*, and after 3–5 seconds add the *follow-up masala*. Stir fry till oil is released. Add the vegetables and again stir fry. Mix them well with the masala. Stir fry on high heat for 5 minutes till the vegetables are well coated with the mixture. Now add the *during-cooking masala* and water and let simmer on medium heat for 15 minutes or till vegetables are done.

Transfer to a serving bowl, sprinkle *garnish masala* and serve with the cheapest boiled rice.

NOTE: Increase water if more soup is required along with a little more salt.

215

Sesame Seed Potato Curry: Nepal

This is a staple vegetable dry curry preparation in Nepal and many hill regions. Distinct and exhilirating.

Serves 4
Cooking Time: 25–30 minutes

British	Metric	Ingredients	American
2¼ lb	1 kg	potatoes	2¼ lb
5 fl oz (1 cup)	150 ml	cooking oil, preferably mustard	⅝ cup
singe-fry masala (as paste)			
4	4	green chillies	4
1 oz (1½ cups)	30 g	green coriander, chopped	1 cup
1 bulb	15–20 g	garlic, cloved	1 bulb
1½ tbsps	15 g	turmeric powder	1½ tbsps
2 tsps	10 g	salt, to taste	2 tsps
follow-up masala			
2 tbsps	18 g	sesame seed (I), roasted & ground with a little water	2 tbsps
during-cooking masala			
1 tbsp	7.5 g	*amchoor*	1 tbsp
½ tbsp	4.5 g	sesame seed (II), roasted	½ tbsp
garnish masala			
½ tbsp	4.5 g	sesame seed (III), roasted & powdered	½ tbsp

Method

Boil, peel and quarter the potatoes and keep aside.

Take 3 tablespoons of the sesame seeds and roast dry till light brown on

216

a griddle and keep aside. When cold, keep half a tablespoon for the during-cooking masala, grind the rest. Keep ½ tablespoon of the powder for the garnish masala. Make the remaining powder into a paste with a little water for use in the follow-up masala. Keep aside.

Liquidize the singe-fry masala in a blender with 1 teaspoon of water and keep aside.

Take a wok or a cooking pan, bring oil to smoking, add the liquidized *singe-fry masala* and stir fry till oil is released. Add the potatoes and stir fry. Now add the *follow-up masala*. Keep stir frying and add the *during-cooking masala*. Check for salt and sourness. Before serving, sprinkle the *garnish masala*. This curry is semi-liquid.

NOTE: It goes well with Indian fried bread like puri, paratha. May also be eaten with boiled rice.

This is a common wayside preparation for trekkers and commuters in the hilly areas. Boiled and quartered potatoes may be stored. Similarly the singe-fry masala is ground and kept as paste. The sesame seeds roasted-pasted and roasted-powered are kept in separate bottles. When a traveller turns up at one of the wayside tea shops, he is served almost instantly with this curry along with hot puries.

Dried Broken Beans Curry

In every Indian household large beans of all descriptions are used. In the conventional recipe, quite a few broken beans are left over. My personal cook used to collect these and make a curry dish for the attendants. On tasting the dish there was no doubt in my mind that it qualifies for wider custom.

In this curry the more the types of beans the better—broad beans, kidney beans, black eye, butter beans, etc. The beans should be smashed in odd-sized pieces.

Serves 3–4
Preparation Time: 4–6 hours
Cooking Time: 45–50 minutes

British	Metric	Ingredients	American
7 oz (2 cups)	200 g	dry large beans	1 cup
6	6	onions, finely chopped	6
3⅓ fl oz (⅔ cup)	100 ml	cooking oil	½ cup
1 tsp	5 g	salt, tó taste	1 tsp
1⅓ pt (5 cups)	750 ml	water	3¼ cups
		singe-fry masala	
1 tsp	3 g	cumin seed, whole	1 tsp
1 tbsp	6 g	chilli powder	1 tbsp
		follow-up masala	
1 tsp	2 g	ginger powder	1 tsp
1 tsp	5 g	garlic paste	1 tsp
8 oz (1½ cups)	225 g	tomato purée	1 cup
		finishing masala	
1 tsp	2.75 g	garam masala	1 tsp
		garnish masala	
3	3	green chillies, scissor-cut, de-seeded	3

Method

Soak the beans for 4–6 hours or overnight.

Wash and drain through colander.

Bring water to boil in a heavy-bottomed pot and add the beans. The water should be at least 2–3 fingers above the beans. After about 40 minutes, when the beans are done, set them aside.

Take another heavy-bottomed pan and bring oil to smoking and brown the onions. Remove them and drain on kitchen paper.

Bring the remaining oil to smoking and add the *singe-fry masala* and stir fry for 5–10 seconds. Add the *follow-up masala* along with 1

218

teaspoon salt and continue stir frying till oil appears on top. Now add the browned onions, stir and mix well. Drain the beans and add to the mixture. Stir fry for 2–3 minutes. Add the *finishing masala* and mix and add water. Simmer on slow fire for 10–15 minutes or till oil is released.

Check salt and flavour, transfer to a white serving dish. Sprinkle the *garnish masala* and serve with rice, tortillas or any oriental bread. Goes best with kulcha.

NOTE: To make almond paste, soak almonds for 2 hours in water, peel and pound to paste in a mortar and pestle.

To make poppy seed paste, soak poppy seed in hot water for 2 hours and pound to paste along with almonds in mortar and pestle or in a grinder.

Semolina Ball Curry or Vegetarian 'Meat' Curry

I had semolina koftas for the first time as a vegetarian meal dish in a wayside *dhaba* somewhere in Rampur. But never could find it again. With luck an octogenarian from that city gives this recipe.

Serves 4–5
Preparation Time: 15–20 minutes
Cooking Time: 35–40 minutes

British	Metric	Ingredients	American
		for semolina kofta	
10 oz	250 g	semolina, dry weight	$1\frac{1}{3}$ cups
5 fl oz (1 cup)	150 ml	water (l)	$\frac{5}{8}$ cup
1	1	egg	1
1 tsp	3.5 g	baking powder	1 tsp
1 tsp	5 g	salt, to taste	1 tsp

219

½ tsp	2.5 g	curry leaves, as paste	½ tsp
1 tbsp	15 ml	onions, very finely grated or chopped & squeezed for the juice	1 tbsp
1 tsp	2 g	chilli powder	1 tsp
		additionally	
16 fl oz (3 cups)	450 ml	water (II)	2 cups
5 fl oz (1 cup)	150 ml	cooking oil	⅝ cup
		singe-fry masala	
1 tbsp	8.5 g	cumin seed, whole	1 tbsp
1 tbsp	10 g	turmeric powder	1 tbsp
		follow-up masala	
2 tbsps	30 g	onions paste	2 tbsps
1 tsp	5 g	garlic paste	1 tsp
1 oz (½ cup)	25 g	croûtons from leftover bread, well browned	⅓ cup
2½ oz (½ cup)	75 g	tomato purée	⅜ cup
1 tsp	5 g	salt, to taste	1 tsp
		finishing masala	
1 tsp	2.75 g	garam masala	1 tsp
		garnish masala	
¼ tsp	0.13 g	saffron, soaked in milk	¼ tsp
1 fl oz	30 ml	milk	2 tbsps

Method

Make a medium dough of all the ingredients for the semolina kofta, and let sit for 15 minutes. Then shape them into balls. They will make about 15–20 balls depending on size.

Take a wok or a deep saucepan and bring oil to smoking. Then sauté fry the semolina balls. When light brown remove and drain on kitchen paper.

When oil is drained put them in hot water for 10–15 minutes.

Meanwhile mix the follow-up masala in a food processor, and keep aside.

Bring the remaining oil to smoking and add the *singe-fry masala*. After 5–10 seconds add the liquidized *follow-up masala*, and stir fry till oil is released. Now add the semolina balls and stir fry gently for 3–5 minutes. Add the *finishing masala* and mix gently. Add water (II). Simmer on low heat for 10–15 minutes till the semolina balls have absorbed the curry sauce and appear to be larger than their original size. Check salt.

Transfer to a serving dish and sprinkle the *garnish masala*.

The curry may be eaten with rice or any of the breads.

NOTE: Saffron has been used for better taste and effect. It was not included in the original recipe.

Lentil Curry (*Sambar*)

This is the only genuine lentil curry and it is from South India. It may very well have been the genesis of the curry kitchen.

Serves 5–6
Cooking Time: 50–55 minutes

British	Metric	Ingredients	American
2 oz	60 g	pigeon pea lentil (*tuar dal, arhar*), dry weight	$\frac{1}{4}$ cup
7 fl oz (1$\frac{1}{3}$ cups)	200 ml	water	$\frac{7}{8}$ cup
1 tbsp	15 g	ghee (I)	1 tbsp
2 oz (4 tbsps)	60 g	ghee (II)	$\frac{1}{4}$ cup

221

during-cooking masala

1 tsp	5 g	split beans lentil (bengal gram, *chana ki dal*), roasted & ground	1 tsp
1 tsp	5 g	split black gram (*urad dal*), roasted & ground	1 tsp
1½ tbsps	7.5 g	coriander, whole, roasted & ground	1½ tbsps
1 tsp	2 g	chilli powder	1 tsp
1 tsp	4.25 g	fenugreek, whole, roasted & ground	1 tsp
1 tbsp	10 g	turmeric powder	1 tbsp

vegetables

6	6	lady-fingers or okra (*bhindi*), small & medium, whole	6
8	8	shallots or small onions	8
1	1	brinjal (aubergine), with skin medium cut in rings ½" thick	1
10 pieces		drumstick, chopped in 2" pieces	10 pieces
1¼ tsps	6 g	salt, to taste	1¼ tsps

finishing masala

1 fl oz	30 ml	tamarind pulp	2 tbsps

garnish masala

Here, there is a departure from the cooking of meats & vegetables. The normal singe-fry masala is made & then poured on top of the cooked sambar dal & vegetables. This is known as tempering or baghar.

singe-fry masala

½ tsp	2 g	mustard seed	½ tsp
½ tsp	2 g	fenugreek seed	½ tsp

3	3	red chilli, whole, cut in half & de-seeded	3
$\frac{1}{4}$ tsp	1 g	asafoetida powder	$\frac{1}{4}$ tsp
20	20	curry leaves	20
1 tbsp	7.5 g	onions, finely chopped	1 tbsp

Method

Prepare tamarind pulp and set aside.

Roasting of split bengal gram, black gram, coriander seed and fenugreek seed should be done on a griddle and kept aside. This constitutes the basic sambar masala.

Wash *tuar* dal in running water through a sieve. Take a large heavy-bottomed cooking pot and add water and the lentils and boil. Once the water boils, turn down the heat and add the *during-cooking masala* and salt and simmer on moderate heat for about 30 minutes, till nearly done. Now add the *vegetables* and continue to simmer for another 20–25 minutes till the vegetables are done. Check salt and add the *finishing masala* and stir gently to mix all ingredients. Remove from fire.

Take a frying pan, add ghee (I) and bring to high heat. Now add the mustard seeds of the singe-fry masala and let them splutter. Add the remaining singe-fry masala except the onions and fry gently for about 15–20 seconds. Now add the onions. When they glaze, pour the *singe-fry masala* on top of the dal and stir gently.

The dal and vegetables should be very hot. If not, heat for a few minutes.

Just before serving add ghee (II) and serve with fluffy white rice—not the long-grained variety.

NOTE: Although the masala sequences are in the reverse to those of meat and vegetables curries, this method of cooking is the classical sequence for dals and lentils.

Mushroom Curry: Coriander Greens

When morels were cheap this dish was made of morels. It has of late been adapted for champignon (button) mushrooms and is equally tasty.

Serves 3–4
Cooking Time: 15–20 minutes

British	Metric	Ingredients	American
18 oz	500 g	fresh mushrooms	18 oz
3½ oz (⅔ cup)	100 g	ghee or butter	½ cup
singe-fry masala			
1 tsp	2.75 g	garam masala	1 tsp
follow-up masala			
1 tbsp	15 g	ginger paste	1 tbsp
1 tbsp	15 g	garlic paste	1 tbsp
2½ oz (½ cup)	75 g	onions paste	⅜ cup
during-cooking masala			
1 tsp	2 g	chilli powder	1 tsp
⅔ oz (1 cup)	20 g	green coriander, scissor-cut	⅔ cup
3	3	green chillies, slit lengthwise	3
½ tbsp	7.5 g	salt, to taste	½ tbsp
finishing masala			
9 oz (1¼ cups)	250 g	yoghurt	1 cup
½ tsp	1 g	cornflour	½ tsp
		OR	
½ tsp	1.25 g	chick pea flour	½ tsp
2 tbsps	20 g	poppy seed paste	2 tbsps
garnish masala			
1 tbsp	5 g	coriander seed, whole, roasted	1 tbsp

Method

Wash and dry mushrooms and slice according to the shape preferred and keep aside in a colander. Liquidize the finishing masala in a blender and keep aside.

In a saucepan bring ghee to high heat. Take away from the heat and add the *singe-fry masala* and stir. Return to heat and add the *follow-up* masaia and stir fry till ghee is released. Now add the *during-cooking masala* and stir fry for 2–3 minutes. Add the mushrooms and stir fry for 3–4 minutes. Add the *finishing masala* which has been liquidized. Simmer on slow fire for 5–8 minutes—the mixture should attempt to boil but not actually boil.

Transfer to a serving dish and sprinkle the *garnish masala*.

NOTE: May be eaten with rice or on pizza bread.

An unusual departure in this recipe is the singe-fry of the garam masala—a reversal of the traditional sequence.

Also, many cooks boil the onions before making a paste to give it a creamy texture. No water is used as mushrooms release enough liquid, which is full of flavour, during cooking.

Bengali Vegetable Curry

There are so many vegetable curries in India that it is almost impossible to select a representative one. The one that has found universal favour in our homes is the Bengali version.

Any vegetables may be used here, except peas and potatoes. The ones recommended are turnips, carrots, cabbage, white radish, knol khol and pumpkin or·any marrow, in equal proportions.

Serves 4–5
Cooking Time: 25–30 minutes

British	Metric	Ingredients	American
$2\frac{1}{4}$ lb	1 kg	vegetables	$2\frac{1}{4}$ lb
5 fl oz (1 cup)	150 ml	cooking oil	$\frac{5}{8}$ cup
$\frac{1}{2}$ pt (2 cups)	300 ml	water	$1\frac{1}{4}$ cups
		singe-fry masala	
1 tsp	3 g	cumin, whole	1 tsp
$\frac{1}{2}$ tsp	1.25 g	cumin powder	$\frac{1}{2}$ tsp
$\frac{1}{2}$ tsp	1 g	coriander powder	$\frac{1}{2}$ tsp
1 tsp	3 g	mustard powder	1 tsp
$\frac{1}{2}$ tsp	2 g	fenugreek seed, whole	$\frac{1}{2}$ tsp
1 tsp	2 g	chilli powder	1 tsp
1 tbsp	10 g	turmeric powder	1 tbsp
		follow-up masala	
1 tsp	5 g	ginger paste	1 tsp
4	4	green chillies, slit lengthwise	4
2 tsps	10 g	salt, to taste	2 tsps
		during-cooking masala	
1"	2.5 cm	cinnamon (1 g)	1"
4	4	cardamoms, large brown	4
2 tbsps	20 g	poppy seed, roasted & ground	2 tbsps
		finishing masala	
2 oz	50 g	coconut, freshly grated	$\frac{5}{8}$ cup
4	4	*bori* (*vari*)	4
		garnish masala	
1 tsp	2.75 g	garam masala	1 tsp

2 tbsps	4 g	green coriander, scissor-cut	2 tbsps
1 tbsp	15 ml	mustard or rapeseed oil, cold	1 tbsp

Method

Dice the vegetables to about the same size, cutting them into various shapes.

Take a saucepan and bring oil to smoking and add the *singe-fry masala*. When the spluttering stops, add the *follow-up masala* and stir fry for a few minutes. Now add the vegetables and stir fry for 5 minutes till all the vegetables have been properly coated with oil and partially cooked.

Add the *during-cooking masala* and stir fry for another minute or so. Add water and simmer for 15 minutes or till vegetables are done. The dish should be a semi-liquid by now.

When ready transfer to a serving dish. Sprinkle the *finishing masala*, with grated coconut first and then coarsely pounded *bori*.

Finally sprinkle the *garnish masala* with the mustard oil coming last.

Serve with fluffy boiled rice or puri or any Indian fried bread.

NOTE: *Bori* or *vari* is made from various fermented lentils, pasted and sun dried. They come in the shape of irregular balls. Preference for flavour is the *vari* made from *urad* lentil. The best flavour is when you sauté fry them first and then coarsely pound them for sprinkling on top of the dish. If not available, deep fry $2\frac{1}{2}$ oz/75 g/$\frac{1}{3}$ cup split chick pea (*chane ki dal*) till it is crisp and sprinkle on top.

Gourd and Marrow Vegetable Curry

Because of their annoying simplicity the humble gourds and marrows have always been looked down upon. Many members of my family as well as friends have turned up their noses at the mere mention of their name. Yet they can be converted into some of the most elusive but delectable meals, a derivative from the Southern and Gujarati kitchens. Here is one of them, a favourite with vegetarians.

Gourds and marrows of any kind, including squash, may be used here. Zucchini (*tori*) and courgettes, may also be included.

Serves 4–5
Cooking Time: 30–35 minutes

British	Metric	Ingredients	American
2¼ lb	1 kg	gourds and marrows, any kind	2¼ lb
7 oz (1⅓ cups)	200 g	ghee	⅞ cup
½ pt (2 cups)	300 ml	water	1¼ cups
singe-fry masala 1			
1 tsp	3.75 g	mustard seed (small)	1 tsp
singe-fry masala 2			
1 tsp	2.75 g	nigella (*kalonji*)	1 tsp
1 tsp	4.25 g	fenugreek seed	1 tsp
1 tbsp	6 g	coriander powder	1 tbsp
1 tbsp	6 g	chilli powder	1 tbsp
25	25	curry leaves	25
½ tbsp	5 g	turmeric powder	½ tbsp
follow-up masala			
6	6	green chillies, slit lengthwise	6
2 tsps	10 g	salt, to taste	2 tsps
during-cooking masala (creamed in blender)			
6	6	yolk of eggs	6
11 oz	300 g	yoghurt	1¼ cups
1 tsp	5 g	sugar	1 tsp
½ tbsp	3.5 g	cornflour	½ tbsp

228

finishing masala			
½ tsp	1 g	mace powder (*javitri*)	½ tsp
½ tsp	2 g	asafoetida powder	½ tsp
garnish masala			
⅔ oz (1 cup)	20 g	green coriander, scissor-cut	⅔ cup

Method

The gourds and marrows should be peeled and cut into squares, rectangles, oblongs and thick juliennes. Keep aside.

Cream the yoghurt and yolk of eggs, sugar and cornflour in a blender for 10–20 seconds and keep aside.

Bring ghee to high heat. Add the *singe-fry masala 1*. When it splutters add *singe-fry masala 2* and after a few seconds of stirring add the cut gourds and stir fry for 5–8 minutes. Add the *follow-up masala* and stir fry for a minute or two, take off the heat. Add water, bring to boil and cook for 10–15 minutes till the extra water has evaporated. Take off from heat and add the *during-cooking masala* slowly and stir. When properly mixed, simmer on moderate heat for 10–15 minutes stirring now and then till the ghee appears on the top and the vegetables are done. The consistency should be creamy. Check salt. Add the *finishing masala* and turn off the heat.

Transfer to a white serving bowl and add the *garnish masala*.

Serve with fluffy boiled rice.

NOTE: If asafoetida is not available or is not agreeable, substitute by 1 teaspoon (5 ml) of garlic through press.

Curried Okra: South Indian

My children have Keralite spouses. This dish has been asked to be repeated several times since it was first prepared by my daughter. Okra is now a popular vegetable the world over.

Serves 3
Cooking Time: 20–25 minutes

British	Metric	Ingredients	American
18 oz	$\frac{1}{2}$ kg	okra (*bhindi*), tender	18 oz
		groundnut oil (I), to deep fry okra	
1 tbsp	15 g	split chick pea lentils	1 tbsp
20	20	curry leaves	20
2–3 fl oz	50–75 ml	groundnut oil (II)	$\frac{1}{4}$–$\frac{3}{8}$ cup
singe-fry masala			
1 tsp	3.75 g	mustard seed	1 tsp
1 tsp	2 g	coriander powder	1 tsp
1 tsp	3.5 g	turmeric powder	1 tsp
1 tbsp	6 g	chilli powder	1 tbsp
$\frac{1}{2}$ tsp	1.5 g	cumin seed, whole	$\frac{1}{2}$ tsp
follow-up masala			
2	2	onions, finely chopped	2
1 tsp	2.5 g	ginger, finely chopped	1 tsp
during-cooking masala			
$\frac{1}{2}$ tsp	1.25 g	*amchoor*	$\frac{1}{2}$ tsp
1 tsp	5 g	salt, to taste	1 tsp
3	3	green chillies, cut in half and de-seeded	3
finishing masala			
3 oz ($\frac{1}{2}$ cup)	85 g	yoghurt, whisked	$\frac{3}{8}$ cup
garnish masala			
2 tbsps	9 g	grated coconut	2 tbsps

1 tbsp	2 g	green coriander, scissor-cut	1 tbsp

Method

Wash and dry okra. Cut into 2–3 pieces each. Take enough oil to be able to deep fry the okra, and deep fry till brownish. Drain on kitchen paper.

In the same oil deep fry curry leaves till crisp for about one minute. Remove with a slotted spoon and drain on kitchen paper. In the same oil deep fry the split chick pea dal for about 30 seconds. Remove with a slotted spoon and keep aside.

Take another saucepan and bring 50 g of oil to smoking. Add the *singe-fry masala* with turmeric coming last. When it stops sizzling, immediately add the *follow-up masala* and stir fry till the onions soften. Add deep fried okra, curry leaves and split chick pea. Stir fry for a few minutes and add the *during-cooking masala* and continue stir frying for 2 minutes. Add the *finishing masala* and reduce heat. Simmer for 4–5 minutes stirring gently. The curry should be semi-viscous. Transfer to a serving dish. Mix ingredients of the *garnish masala* and sprinkle on top.

This curry is eaten with rice or puri.

Cucumber Curry in Orange Juice

In India there are times and places when cucumbers alone are in season and cheaply available. It is almost certain that this derives its origin from the Chinese kitchen. A curry of distinct flavour.

Serves 3
Cooking Time: 20–25 minutes

231

British	Metric	Ingredients	American
18 oz	$\frac{1}{2}$ kg	cucumber (*kheera*), julienne cut	18 oz
5 fl oz (1 cup)	150 ml	orange juice	$\frac{5}{8}$ cup
2 fl oz (3 tbsps)	50 ml	cooking oil	$\frac{1}{4}$ cup
singe-fry masala			
1 tbsp	10 g	turmeric powder	1 tbsp
1 tsp	2.75 g	cumin powder	1 tsp
during-cooking masala 1			
1 tsp	5 g	ginger paste	1 tsp
1 tsp	5 g	garlic paste	1 tsp
during-cooking masala 2			
3	3	onions, boiled & liquidized	3
1	1	lemon, juice of	1
1 tsp	5 g	salt, to taste	1 tsp
finishing masala			
4	4	red chillies, dried, crushed by hand & de-seeded	4
garnish masala			
2 tbsps	4 g	green coriander, scissor-cut	2 tbsps

Method

Bring oil to smoking in a saucepan and add the *singe-fry masala* adding turmeric last of all. Immediately after adding turmeric, add the cucumbers and stir fry for 3–4 minutes. Add the *during-cooking masala 1* and stir fry for about 5 minutes till the oil is released. Now add the *during cooking masala 2* and simmer on moderate heat for 10 minutes. When oil starts appearing on top again, add the orange juice. Stir for a minute or two, take off the fire, and add the *finishing masala*.

Check for 'sour and sweet' flavours. Transfer to a serving dish and sprinkle the *garnish masala*.

It is best eaten with rice.

NOTE: Make sure that the orange juice does not cook for more than 2 minutes or so, as it will lose flavour and is likely to turn bitter. Very palatable when eaten cold as salad. The solid part may also be used for canapes.

Cucumbers should be peeled and the bitter stem end of about $1\frac{1}{2}$" cut off. Taste cucumbers for bitterness before cooking. Use only those cucumbers that are sweet. Boiled and liquidized onions give a creamy consistency and a milder onion flavour.

Accompaniments

On Rice

The method of rice preparation can be as varied as the number of persons preparing it. Each family has its own way of cooking rice, so much so that each one insists that there is no better way of cooking it.

There are 100–200 varieties of rice in each rice-growing country—China, India, Thailand, Burma, Indonesia, the Philippines—and in each country there are several sub-varieties for each region.

Gourmet and hobby cooks have divided these various types of rice into three basic varieties. The first type is the long-grained one, famously known by its Indian name basmati, which means 'imitating the bamboo'. The second variety is the common rice which is used all over the world. It is of medium length and tends to have more free starch. The third type is the round rice which is very appropriate for many dishes and is grown in many parts of the world, including Hungary.

The basic preparation of rice involves boiling or steaming. Pulaos, rice salads and Chinese fried rice have two stages of cooking. As to the boiling of rice, the water and rice proportions, the timing and the heat at which to be cooked, are varied and debatable points.

I am in full agreement with most eminent cooks on how to cook rice. This involves washing a fixed quantity of rice in running water till the water runs clean and all the free starch has been washed away. Then one measure of rice and two measures of water are taken preferably at room temperature or lukewarm, and put into a boiling pot. Initially on high heat and then on medium heat. Almost without exception, the rice will bloom in 10–15 minutes and will have typical rice holes, like geysers, emitting steam. The rice is then felt between the fingers—it should be almost cooked but not totally cooked. Loosen the rice with a wooden spoon or fork, cover again and turn off the heat. In the next 10–12 minutes, the rice will cook in its own heat and steam. Thereafter, follow the recipe which says what to do with the boiled rice.

For cooking rice all measures are volumetric. Use the same container to measure rice and water. The family advise on cooking rice includes soaking the rice in water for half to one hour and adding butter or ghee to the water when boiling the rice to prevent sticking. The adding of butter or ghee, however, is optional. It is not usually popular in the Chinese or the South Indian methods of rice preparation. This is mainly done in Gujarat and West UP.

In case you are using any packaged rice like Uncle Ben or any other brand it is best to follow the printed instructions.

For special pulaos, oil or fat forms an essential constituent along with the water.

On Indian Breads

Many cookery books describe Indian breads and their preparation in great variety and detail. Since this book is mainly about curries, it would be appropriate to discuss the most common Indian breads, which are referred to as accompanying the various curry dishes. The ones included in this book are phulka, chappati, romali roti, bhatura, naan, puri and parathas. Any of these recipes for oriental breads may be confidently used.

Puffed Whole-Wheat Bread *(Phulka)*

The phulka is the commonest of all Indian breads, and is eaten daily with meat and vegetables curries and *dals*. Very often it is called a chappati, but the chappati is generally flat and not puffed. The origin of the word *chappati* seems to be from the word *chapat* which means to slap and the word *chapta* which means flat. In both cases the dough, when prepared, is made into balls and flattened between the two hands, as if you were slapping the dough.

Phulka means one that is puffed, and derived from the Hindi *phulna* meaning to swell.

British	Metric	Ingredients	American
8 oz (2¼ cups)	225 g	white plain flour or whole wheat flour	2 cups

238

$\frac{1}{4}$ tsp	1 g	salt (optional)	$\frac{1}{4}$ tsp
5 fl oz (1 cup)	150 ml	water	$\frac{5}{8}$ cup
		some dry flour for dusting	

Method

The preparation of the phulka itself is very quick, but maturing the dough takes 30–40 minutes. First the dough is kneaded for 5–10 minutes, depending on the quality of flour, till it is smooth and pliable and definitely not sticky. The classical way to knead is with the knuckles. Most people go by this process and it is widely used the world over to make any kind of bread. The dough is placed on a lightly floured board, covered with a wet cloth and kept aside for 20–30 minutes.

Then the dough is divided, for the quantities given, into six pieces. These pieces are rolled into a ball using some dry flour so that the dough does not stick to the palm. The balls of dough are flattened between the palms and rolled out with a rolling pin into a diameter of 5"–6". The thickness should be about a quarter centimeter or less. The process is repeated for all the pieces.

The cooking accessory required to bake these flattened circles of dough is called the *tawa*. It is also called the griddle. The *tawa* is heated and the rolled out dough is slapped onto it. It is cooked for a minute or so, till it browns lightly. It is then turned over and cooked on the reverse side. When both sides are lightly brown, the *tawa* is removed quickly from the fire, the heat is raised and the browned phulka is placed directly on the flame (gas-burner assumed). It is turned around quickly with a pair of metallic tongs (in India this is done by hand). The phulka will immediately begin to bloat on the fire. Turn it over to the other side, when a few brown scars appear. Bring it down from the fire. (This undoubtedly takes some practice for persons not used to preparing Indian bread.) But preparing this becomes easier with constant practice. The phulka is now ready to be served.

When made fresh and served hot it is one of the most delectable whole-wheat oriental breads.

239

NOTE: In many homes it is customary to lightly apply, on the thin side of the phulka, a little butter or ghee.

To make a chappati, the same process is used except that the rolled out dough is not placed directly on the fire to bloat. This is done on the *tawa* itself.

The phulka and chappati are a staple diet throughout Central and Northern India.

Roti is any unleavened bread like phulka, chappati or romali roti.

Paratha

Depending upon the stuffing for the filling inside, many kinds of parathas are possible. But here, only the plain paratha has been discussed as this is the one that is usually eaten with the various curries.

Parat means layer, and therefore paratha is a layered fried bread. The layering for this is done by folding the dough while rolling it out.

British	Metric	Ingredients	American
40 oz	120 g	whole wheat flour, sifted	1 cup
$\frac{1}{2}$ tsp	2.5 g	salt (optional)	$\frac{1}{2}$ cup
9 fl oz	250 ml	water	$1\frac{1}{2}$ cups
$3\frac{1}{2}$ fl oz	100 ml	vegetable oil	$\frac{1}{2}$ cup
		some dry flour for dusting	

Method

Sift the flour not in a very fine sieve but in number 2 or 3 mesh so that the whole wheat fibre is not wasted. Add oil and gradually rub it into the flour. Then add water and salt and knead the dough for 10 minutes till it is soft. Gather the dough into a ball, put it in a bowl, cover with a damp cloth and let it sit for about half an hour.

Before beginning to make the paratha, knead the dough again, divide it into six parts, make round individual patties of the six parts. Take one, covering the others completely with a damp cloth. Roll it out with a rolling pin to reach around 6" diameter. Keep dusting with flour while rolling to avoid sticking. Smear the rolled out dough with 1 tablespoon of oil, fold it in half, again smear it with 1 teaspoon of oil and then fold it in a quarter. Dust it with flour and roll it out again to any shape preferred. This may be triangular, round or square. The classical shape is the triangular one. The triangle should be approximately equal on each side, the size being about 6".

Now take the *tawa*, concave side up. Heat and spread a tablespoon of oil on it. Slap the paratha on the *tawa* and cook one side for 2 minutes. Lift it, put a teaspoon of oil and slap it on the uncooked side. Put a little more oil around the paratha, turn down the heat and let it fry. To make it crisp it should be golden brown on both the sides. The amount of oil used to dry fry the paratha in this manner is gradually adjusted by practice. When the reddish brown spots appear, the paratha is ready. This process is repeated for making more parathas. They are delicious when served hot and crisp. But this cannot be done too quickly when there are too many guests and family members. Therefore many parathas are prepared before the meal and served semi-warm, though at this stage they are not all that crisp.

NOTE: To make stuffed parathas the stuffing is added before folding and layering the flour. The stuffing used may be boiled peas, potatoes, cauliflower or radish. For non-vegetarians a popular stuffing used is minced meat or left over canteen keema.

The same dough as that used for the phulka may be used to prepare parathas.

Leavened Bread *(Naan)*

Many of the curry preparations that appear in the book have this bread as an accompaniment. This most certainly is of Persian and Afghan origin and is extremely popular. It is a combination of a regular European bread and the Indian chappati and has therefore acquired a universal appeal. In this bread we use processes which are familiar in making the normal European white bread.

British	Metric	Ingredients	American
8 oz	225 g	plain white flour	2 cups
$\frac{1}{2}$ tsp	2 g	dry yeast	$\frac{1}{2}$ tsp
2 fl oz	50 ml	water or milk, warmed	$\frac{1}{4}$ cup
1 tsp	5 g	sugar	1 tsp
2 oz	50 g	yoghurt	$\frac{1}{4}$ cup
1 tsp	3.5 g	baking powder	1 tsp
1	1	egg, beaten	1
2 tbsps	30 ml	ghee melted	2 tbsps
$\frac{1}{2}$ tsp	2.5 g	salt	$\frac{1}{2}$ tsp
2 tsps	5.5 g	nigella (kalonji)	2 tsps
2 tsps	6 g	poppy seed	2 tsps

Method

The flour is raised by the administration of yeast. The yeast used may be dry—as in the case of this preparation—or fresh, where the amount of yeast used would be 1 teaspoon.

As in the case of bread preparation, sprinkle the yeast in warm water or milk (this should not be hot), stir in sugar and leave it to ferment for 10 minutes. If the yeast is good it will rise. If it does not, ferment again with another brand of yeast. When the yeast is frothy, mix the yoghurt, baking powder, beaten egg, salt and melted ghee or any cooking oil (butter will also do). Make sure the mixture is smooth and creamy. A hand beater may be used to mix.

Now put the flour in a large bowl, make a well in the centre and pour the mixture with the yeast. Rub well and knead with the knuckles and stretch out with the palms—this is the classical movement for hand made breads.

242

In this particular bread a food processor with a dough kneading attachment may be used initially for kneading, but the dough will still have to be stretched with the hands for elasticity.

After this is done roll the dough into a large bowl, brush it with a little cooking oil or ghee and leave it covered in a bowl with damp cloth and put it away in a warm cupboard without any draught, to rise.

This should be left for 3–4 hours till the size doubles.

Bring it out after the size has doubled, knead it once again with the hands and cut it into eight portions. The portions should be shaped into balls and left in a greased dish covered with a damp cloth for another 10–15 minutes.

During the time you are waiting for the dough to rise for the second time, preheat the oven to 500 deg F/260 deg C. Lightly oil 2 or 3 flat baking sheets—not trays with raised sides. If baking sheets are not available use aluminium foil over the grill tray.

Heat a tawa or a large flat heavy griddle on low heat. Flatten a ball of dough with hand. Stretch the dough from one end to make a tear drop shape. Again stretch and pull to make it 6″ long 4″ wide at one end. Moisten one side with a little water and stick wet side down on the hot griddle. Brush the top with a little ghee and sprinkle with nigella and poppy seeds. When under surface is half cooked the nan will come off the griddle easily with the wrong side of a table spoon. Remove and repeat one or two.

Once this is done place 2 or 3 nans on the baking sheet depending on the size of the oven and bake at moderate heat for 5-7 minutes. If the dough is right they will puff and have a crisp golden brownish appearance.

Bhatura

This is a popular Punjabi deep fried bread and is commonly eaten with curried chick pea or *chole*.

This bread is semi-leavened and it is fermented with yoghurt and baking powder.

243

British	Metric	Ingredients	American
14 oz (4 cups)	400 g	white flour plain	$3\frac{1}{2}$ cups
$3\frac{1}{2}$ oz	100 g	semolina	$1\frac{1}{8}$ cups
$\frac{1}{4}$ tsp	1 g	soda-bicarb	$\frac{1}{4}$ tsp
$\frac{1}{2}$ tsp	1.75 g	baking powder	$\frac{1}{2}$ tsp
1 tsp	5 g	salt	1 tsp
1 oz	30 g	yoghurt	2 tbsps
2 tsps	10 g	sugar	2 tsps
1 fl oz	25 ml	ghee	2 tbsps

groundnut oil to apply on the surface and for deep frying

Method

First sieve the flour along with semolina, soda-bicarb, baking powder and salt. Cream and whisk the yoghurt with sugar, pour the sieved flour along with the other ingredients into a bowl, make a well, pour in the water and yoghurt mixture. First mix with hand and then collect the dough and knead for 10 minutes or so. Then, knead in the ghee and make sure the dough is soft. Cover again to rise for 40 minutes to 1 hour.

When you are ready to start the meal divide the dough into 12–15 equal portions making balls and greasing your hands with either cooking oil or ghee. Put the frying oil in a deep wok or *karahi* and while it is heating to smoking point start flattening each ball of dough between your two greased palms to reach 4"–5" diameter then put them in the heated oil. They will immediately start puffing up; turn them over for very short time.

It may be better to flatten all the balls of dough to a diameter of 4"–5" before beginning to fry. Heat the oil accordingly.

If you find it difficult to make the round shape with the hands use a rolling pin. The shape of the dough may be varied from round to elongated or from thinner to thicker, as you please.

244

Before serving put into a basket or container lined with kitchen paper.

NOTE: If you are having a party the advantage of bhatura is that you can single fry or half fry them and keep them in a colander lined with kitchen paper. When the dinner is to be served they can be fried again very quickly and because they are semi-leavened they will puff up.

Deep Fried Bread *(Puri)*

The puri is considered to be the queen of all fried breads. It takes a few minutes to deep fry and many can be made in little time. It is the staple oriental bread at parties, marriages and receptions and is served mostly with vegetarian food.

The word *puri* means complete. The dough for the puri takes a little over an hour to prepare, but the making of the puri itself takes half a minute to a minute in one batch of 6–8 deep fried at a time.

British	Metric	Ingredients	American
9 oz (2¼ cups)	250 g	white flour plain or whole wheat flour, sifted	2¼ cups
1 tbsp	15 ml	cooking oil	1 tbsp
5 fl oz(1 cup)	150 ml	water	$\frac{5}{8}$ cup
		oil—for deep frying	

Method

The flour and salt are sifted in a bowl. The oil is rubbed in properly, and water is added and mixed to make a firm dough. The first kneading is to be short and for around 4–5 minutes, and no elasticity is to develop. After kneading, it should be set aside and covered with a wet cloth for 1 hour.

For the quantity given, this dough is divided into 8 portions and made into balls with a drop of oil to grease the palms. The dough balls are then flattened to little discs and rolled out with a rolling pin to around

4" diameter. The thickness of these will be around a quarter cm or less. The oil is heated to around smoking, and should the wok or *karahi* be large enough, all the 8 are deep fried at a time, if not, in 2 lots.

As soon as they are placed in the hot oil, they will begin to rise. When they are fully puffed, turn them over for a very short while. Then take them out with a large slotted spoon into a basket or a container lined with kitchen paper. In a few minutes any extra oil will be absorbed or drained out. Serve immediately while still puffed up.

NOTE: Bhatura and puri are both fried breads. The former is semi-leavened while the latter is unleavened. Both can be eaten with the main dish.

Romali Roti

Literally 'handkerchief bread', this kind of fine chappati originated sometime during the Moghul days. It gets its name from its texture and size, though not shape—for it is circular and not rectangular. The dough for this is prepared in almost the same way as that for the phulka. But unlike the phulka it does not puff when cooked and remains flat.

British	Metric	Ingredients	American
$4\frac{1}{2}$ oz	125 g	plain white flour, sifted	1 cup
$3\frac{1}{2}$ oz	100 g	whole wheat flour, sifted	$\frac{2}{3}$ cup
$\frac{1}{4}$ tsp	1 g	salt	$\frac{1}{4}$ tsp
5 fl oz	150 ml	water	$\frac{5}{8}$ cup

Method

The plain white and whole wheat flour along with the salt are sifted together. Water is mixed in this so as to make normal dough. It is kneaded for 5–10 minutes till the dough gets soft. It is then set aside for 45 minutes to 1 hour.

The dough is split into 3 portions, making small balls as in the case of phulka and then rolled out in a circle as large and thin as possible, making sure that the circumference of the rolled out dough is not more than that of the *tawa*.

The convex side of the *tawa* is used for 'baking' the romali roti. The *tawa* is a round parabolic form and both sides are used as required for making Indian breads. Many attempts have been made to make the romali roti on a large flat pan, but only the thick black iron *tawa* with a convex top seems to work.

The *tawa* is heated and the rolled out roti is picked up with the help of the rolling pin. The edges of the roti are stretched as it is slapped onto the *tawa*. It is turned over as soon as the colour of the dough changes to very light brown. Some experience is needed to know when all the moisture has been mopped up by the roti and that the bread is not raw.

Since the roti is very thin, it cooks very quickly. The process is repeated for each roti. This form of bread, if not eaten immediately, is folded twice—once in half and then quarter—and piled one on top of the other and kept in a container in which a moistened cheese-cloth or muslin has been placed. The folded rotis are covered with the muslin and another cover is placed on the container.

Before serving, the rotis should be steamed or the container placed in an oven on medium heat for 5–10 minutes. It is important that this bread be eaten moist, for otherwise it tends to become papery and rather unpalatable.

On Raitas

With the recently discovered importance of yoghurt as a dietetic necessity, it has become a great favourite in all parts of the world. Yoghurt, also called curd, contains a bacteria called lactobacellus, which is an important component of the intestinal flora.

Raitas are essentially salads with yoghurt dressing, and in practically all the recipes the main ingredient of the raita is blended yoghurt, which has a sauce-like consistency. Any of the raitas explained here may be accompanied with any of the curries.

In many European countries a dill and yoghurt dressing with cucumbers is often served.

For the recipes given, it is best to use cultured yoghurt instead of the factory-manufactured one. This may be prepared at home according to the recipe on pg 280. If this is not possible the factory-manufactured yoghurt may be used.

Cucumber with Ginger

One of the great family favourites.

Serves 4

British	Metric	Ingredients	American
3½ oz (2 cups)	100 g	cucumber, julienne cut	1¼ cups
18 oz (3 cups)	500 g	yoghurt	2 cups
1 tbsp	9 g	ginger, finely cut or grated	1 tbsp
1 tsp	5 g	salt, to taste	1 tsp
1 tbsp	5 g	sugar	1 tbsp
1 fl oz	30 ml	lemon juice	2 tbsps
½ tsp	1.75 g	turmeric powder	½ tsp

Method

Cream the yoghurt in a blender alongwith ginger, salt, sugar and lemon juice and turmeric powder for 20–30 seconds. Transfer to an attractive glass or any other dish, add the cucumbers and keep in the refrigerator for about half an hour before serving.

Adjust the salt, lemon juice, ginger and sugar to your taste. This raita is extremely healthy and piquant.

Radish with Powdered Mustard Seed

This raita is very popular with East Europeans. When mature its taste resembles that of strong horse radish.

Serves 4

British	Metric	Ingredients	American
3½ oz (2 cups)	100 g	radish, finely grated	1¼ cups
18 oz (3 cups)	500 g	yoghurt	2 cups
1 tsp	5 g	salt, to taste	1 tsp
½ tsp	2.5 g	sugar	½ tsp
2 tbsps	20 g	mustard seed, freshly powdered in spice/ coffee grinder	2 tbsps

Method

The radish should be finely grated, or matchstick cut or julienne cut and kept aside.

Cream yoghurt, salt, sugar and the freshly powdered mustard seed for 20–30 seconds. Pour into a serving bowl and add the radish. Set aside for 30–40 minutes at room temperature. This raises the mustard to impart the characteristic mustard flavour. Chill before serving.

NOTE: The mustard seed should be of the small red variety. These are seeds of the Chinese mustard greens, and are known as *rye* in India.

Cachumber Raita

This contains onions, tomatoes, cucumbers and fresh green and red chillies.

Serves 4–5

British	Metric	Ingredients	American
1½ oz (½ cup)	40 g	onions, diced	⅓ cup
11 oz (½ cup)	25 g	tomatoes, diced	¼ cup
1 oz (½ cup)	25 g	cucumber, diced	¼ cup
2 tbsps	12 g	fresh green & red chillies, scissor-cut	2 tbsps
21 oz (3½ cups)	575 g	yoghurt	2⅜ cups
1 tsp	5 g	salt	1 tsp
1 tsp	5 g	sugar	1 tsp
1 tbsp	15 ml	lemon juice	1 tbsp

Method

Cream yoghurt in a blender alongwith salt, sugar and lemon juice for 20–30 seconds. Transfer to a serving dish and add all the ingredients. Chill before serving.

Mint Raita

The mint attains a unique flavour to this raita.

Serves 2–3

British	Metric	Ingredients	American
1½ oz (2 cups)	45 g	mint leaves	1½ cups
12 oz (2 cups)	330 g	yoghurt	1¼ cups
1 tsp	5 g	salt	1 tsp
½ tsp	2.5 g	sugar	½ tsp
1	1	green chillies, finely scissor-cut	1

Method

Liquidize the mint in a wet grinder and mix well with salt and sugar. Mix with yoghurt. Put them through a blender and cream for 20–30 seconds. Transfer to a serving bowl and sprinkle the finely-cut, green chilli on top. Serve chilled.

NOTE: Another very interesting version is to use one jigger of *creme de minth* eliminate sugar from the recipe and add 1 teaspoon (5 ml) lemon juice.

Tulsi Basil (*Ocimum Sanctum*) also makes a fine raita and is a good alternative to the mint in the raita.

Garlic   Capsicum   Raita

This newly created raita is very popular with garlic fans. It goes well with all curries.

Serves 3–4

British	Metric	Ingredients	American
3½ oz (2 cups)	100 g	capsicum, finely sliced	1¼ cups
18 oz (3 cups)	500 g	yoghurt	2 cups
1 tbsp	15 g	garlic paste	1 tbsp
1 tsp	5 g	salt, to taste	1 tsp
1 tsp	2 g	chilli powder	1 tsp

British	Metric	Ingredients	American
$\frac{1}{2}$ tsp	2.5 g	sugar	$\frac{1}{2}$ tsp
1 tbsp	15 ml	lemon juice	1 tbsp

Method

Cream yoghurt in a blender alongwith garlic paste, salt, chilli powder, sugar and lemon juice. Pour the mixture into a serving bowl, add capsicum and place in the refrigerator for half-an-hour before serving. Increase or decrease chillies, as required.

For an attractive look, use 50 g (1 cup) green capsicum and 50 g (1 cup) red capsicum. Serve chilled.

Potato Raita

A very common everyday raita made all over India. Very popular with vegetarians.

Serves 4

British	Metric	Ingredients	American
8 oz (2 cups)	220 g	potatoes, boiled	$1\frac{3}{4}$ cups
21 oz ($3\frac{1}{2}$ cups)	575 g	yoghurt	$2\frac{5}{8}$ cups
1 tsp	5 g	salt	1 tsp
$\frac{1}{2}$ tsp	1.75 g	black pepper powder	$\frac{1}{2}$ tsp
1 tbsp	8.5 g	cumin, freshly roasted and powdered	1 tbsp

Method

Dice the boiled potatoes to cubes of about 1 cm and keep aside.

Cream yoghurt, salt, black pepper (not the cumin powder) in a blender for 20–30 seconds. Transfer into a serving dish and sprinkle the powdered cumin on top. Chill before serving.

Dill Green Raita

This raita is being made for over 150 years in India. It is also popular in central and eastern Europe. More often this is used as a salad dressing for cucumbers and chilled boiled potatoes.

Serves 3

British	Metric	Ingredients	American
2 oz (1 cups)	50 g	dill greens, finely chopped	$\frac{1}{2}$ cup
18 oz (3 cups)	500 g	yoghurt	2 cups
1 tsp	5 g	salt, to taste	1 tsp
$\frac{1}{2}$ tsp	2.5 g	sugar	$\frac{1}{2}$ tsp
$\frac{1}{2}$ tsp	2.5 ml	lemon juice	$\frac{1}{2}$ tsp
$3\frac{1}{2}$ oz (1 cup)	100 g	cucumber, diced	$1\frac{1}{4}$ cups
		OR	
$3\frac{1}{2}$ oz	100 g	potatoes, boiled	1 cup

Method

Put the dill greens through a wet grinder for a few seconds to break open the aromatic pores. They need not be finely ground.

Cream yoghurt with all the ingredients alongwith the dill. Transfer to a serving bowl and chill. When ready to serve have diced cucumbers or diced boiled potatoes ready. Pour the dill yoghurt on the cucumbers or potatoes. Serve chilled.

Eggplant Raita

This is a bit different from the normal raita. It has a singe-fry process and uses mustard or rapeseed oil. Olive oil also goes well if the mustard or rapeseed are not available.

Serves 4

British	Metric	Ingredients	American
2	2	eggplant, medium to large (round ones preferred)	2
18 oz (3 cups)	500 g	yoghurt	2 cups
1 tablet	500mg	ascorbic acid/vitamin C	1 tablet
		OR	
2 tbsps	30 ml	lemon juice	2 tbsps
		OR	
1 tsp	4.5 g	citric acid	1 tsp
2 tbsps	30 ml	mustard, rapeseed or olive oil	2 tbsps
singe-fry masala			
1 tsp	3.75 g	mustard seed	1 tsp
3	3	dry red chillies, whole, break in 2 pieces, de-seeded	3
$\frac{1}{2}$ tsp	1.75 g	turmeric powder	$\frac{1}{2}$ tsp
1 tsp	5 g	salt, to taste	1 tsp
garnish masala			
2 tbsps	4 g	green coriander, scissor-cut	2 tbsps
1 tsp	2 g	green & red chillies, scissor-cut	1 tsp

Method

Oil the eggplants and roast in medium heat for 10 minutes. Skin, mash and mix with 1 tablet ascorbic (vit C) or 1 teaspoon of citric acid in 1 tablespoon water, or 1 tablespoon of lemon juice and keep aside.

Take a frying pan, pour oil and bring it to smoking. Add the *singe-fry masala*—first putting the mustard seeds, and when they stop spluttering remove pan from the fire and add the red chillies and turmeric. Add the mashed eggplant and mix well with a fork. Keep aside.

Cream yoghurt with salt. Transfer to a serving bowl and add the

254

eggplant with the masala—stir gently to mix well. Chill and sprinkle the *garnish masala* before serving.

NOTE: Any kind of brinjals may be used here, keeping a proportion of 2 of the main ingredients to 3 of the yoghurt by cup measure.

Citric acid, ascorbic acid or lemon juice is used to prevent oxidation.

Chutneys and Relishes

Traditionally chutneys were ground manually in grindstones, which made the task quite tedious. The electronic era has brought in food processors which have made the preparation of this unique relish extremely simple. But even now the traditional method of preparation with the grindstone is often preferred. An interesting scientific fact about these grindstones is that the two parts of the grindstones are made from a single piece of granite or rock. The fact that both the mortar and pestle are made from the same piece of rock imparts equal hardness to the lower stationary part and the upper grinding stone. This prevents any harder part to chip off a softer part into the chutney. The grindstone in North India consists of a flat board type of mortar and a semi-round stone for the pestle. Grinding is done in a rocking motion. In South India the mortar is bowl-shaped and the pestle is oblong-shaped. The grinding in this is done in rotatory motion.

Green Coriander Chutney

Perhaps the most widely consumed chutney in India.

British	Metric	Ingredients	American
3 ½ oz	100 g	coriander greens	3½ oz
1	1	green chilli, hot	1

255

2 tbsps	30 ml	juice of lime or lemon	2 tbsps
½ tsp	2.5 g	salt to taste	½ tsp

Method

The ingredients are put through the wet grinder and when they form a semi-liquid paste the chutney is ready. A pinch of sugar often improves the flavour.

This is eaten with all vegetable dishes and with batter fry fish. It also goes well with dry meats.

Mint Yoghurt Chutney

This is the most common and palatable chutney in North India. A special souring is required for this. Dried sour pomegranate seeds, called *anardana,* which were first used in north-west India and Kandhar in Afghanistan, make excellent souring agents besides imparting a unique taste and texture to the chutney.

British	Metric	Ingredients	American
3½ oz	100 g	green mint leaves	3½ cups
2 tbsps	30 g	yoghurt	2 tbsps
1½ tbsps	15 g	sour pomegranate seeds (*anardana*)	1½ tbsps
½ tsp	2.5 g	salt	½ tsp
a pinch		sugar	a pinch
½ tsp	2.5 ml	lemon juice	½ tsp

Method

Pound the pomegranate seed. Put these alongwith all the ingredients in a wet grinder and make a sauce-like consistency of the whole mix. Do not over-grind since the yoghurt might turn lumpy like butter.

This chutney is eaten with raw onions, all dry meats and batter fried dishes. It goes well with practically any dish.

Green Mint Chutney

The method of preparation is exactly same as for the green coriander chutney, except that the green mint is substituted for green coriander.

British	Metric	Ingredients	American
3½ oz	100 g	green mint, leaves	3½ cups
1	1	green chilli, hot	1
2 tbsps	30 ml	juice of lime or lemon	2 tbsps
½ tsp	2.5 g	salt	½ tsp

Method

Put the ingredients through a wet grinder. When they are properly converted to a semi-liquid paste the chutney is ready.

Best eaten with dry meats and batter fry fish and vegetables. Also with roasts.

Mango Chutney

This is the king of oriental chutneys. Since in most parts of the world raw mangoes are not available, it is best to use the standard brands marketed the world over. Your supplier will give you the best ones. Sherwood Major Grey, Bolst Venkat are some well-known names.

In India every household has its own singular method of preparation. Mango chutney is eaten with all rice dishes and roasts.

Quince Chutney

The quince is often overlooked except in Greece and a few other countries. According to my experience, it is the best chutney for Indian as well as some European roasts. It can easily claim to be an alternative to the mango chutney.

British	Metric	Ingredients	American
18 oz	½ kg	quince, peeled and julienne-cut on a 'universal slicer'	18 oz
50 oz	150 g	brown sugar	1 cup
3 tablets 1000 mg		ascorbic acid redoxin vitamin C, powdered	3 tablets 1000 mg
1 tsp	5 g	salt	1 tsp
10–12	10–12	cardamoms, small	10–12
10–12	10–12	garlic cloves	10–12
3–4	3–4	dry red chilli, whole	3–4
½ tsp	1 g	ginger powder	½ tsp
3 fl oz (½ cup)	75 ml	water, warm	⅜ cup
3 fl oz (½ cup)	75 ml	water, normal	⅜ cup

Method

The quince fruits used for this should not be too ripe or too raw.

Soak the cardamoms in half a cup of warm water for 1 hour and keep aside.

Mix well the brown sugar and the julienne cut quince and put in a heavy-bottom cooking pan. Add the cup of normal water and let the mixture simmer on very low heat. Stir so that the sugar does not stick. The best vessel to use would be a Teflon casserole. When the sugar has melted and the quince is semi-soft—after 30–40 minutes—add the cardamoms alongwith the water, salt, garlic cloves, red chillies, vitamin

258

C and ginger powder, and again let it simmer for 15–20 minutes. Check for sweet, sour and salt. Have an appropriate size pickling jar ready. Transfer to the jar and seal immediately. Let it rest for a few days in the open: if hot climate in the shade, if cool, in the sun. Then it's ready to be stored.

NOTE: Eaten in the place of mango chutney but is excellent with roast pork and other roasts.

Vitamin C is used as an anti-oxidising agent and to balance the acid content.

As a matter of abundant caution and for a longer shelf life, add 1 salt spoon of potassium meta-bisulphite or 2 salt spoons of sodium benzoate, after the chutney is prepared.

You can also cut 'cheeks' from the quince and again cut them into half laterally to give the 'mango' effect.

Tomato   Chutney

A chutney which must have been the origin of the Hungarian Lecso. In any case it has been in use since tomatoes first arrived in India.

British	Metric	Ingredients	American
9 oz	250 g	tomatoes, ripe, chopped de-seeded	9 oz
3	3	capsicum, de-seeded, ring cut	3
3	3	green chillies, coarsely chopped	3
2 oz	50 g	onions, sliced medium	2 oz
1 tbsp	15 g	garlic paste	1 tbsp
3 tbsps	45 ml	vinegar	3 tbsps
1 tsp	5 g	salt	1 tsp

2 tbsps	30 ml	oil, preferably olive oil	2 tbsps
1 tbsp	15 g	sugar	1 tbsp

Method

Bring oil to high heat and put in all the ingredients. Stir gently on low heat for 15 minutes. Raise heat and keep stirring till a thick amalgam is produced—if too liquidy evaporate water at the highest heat, stirring all the time. As soon as the oil shows on top remove and let cool. Transfer to a pickling jar and eat after 2 days. Goes extremely well as a pizza topping and with plain rice and with all meat curries.

The tomatoes should be red, fresh and ripe.

Raw Tomato Capsicum Chutney

This chutney was made as a matter of necessity in London when nothing except some horrible-looking, unripe tomatoes and a few capsicums were available in my friend's kitchen.

British	Metric	Ingredients	American
5 oz	150 g	raw green tomatoes, chopped	¾ cup
1	1	capsicum, finely diced	1
1	1	onions, finely diced	1
3 cloves	3 cloves	garlic, through press	3 cloves
1 tbsp	15 ml	vinegar (wine vinegar preferred)	1 tbsp
½ tsp	2.5 g	salt	½ tsp

Method

Put the chopped green tomatoes alongwith garlic, vinegar and salt in a food mill and wet grind to medium consistency. Before serving add the capsicum and onions. Check the sweet, sour and salt. These may be increased or decreased to taste and eaten with anything.

NOTE: This chutney is eaten fresh and is not a preserve like the quince chutney.

Add 1 teaspoon of olive oil and some thyme on top to give it a Mediterranean flavour.

Chilli Garlic Chutney

This is very much like the Moroccan harissa, and is commonly used all over India. It is hot, strong and full of garlic.

British	Metric	Ingredients	American
2 oz	50 g	hot red pepper	2 oz
2 tbsps	30 g	garlic paste	2 tbsps
1 tbsp	15 ml	groundnut oil	1 tbsp
½ tsp	2.5 g	salt	½ tsp
1 tbsp	15 ml	juice of lime or lemon	1 tbsp
1 drop	1 drop	red food colour (optional)	1 drop

Method

The red chillies are soaked in hot water for half-an-hour. They are then placed in a wet grinder along with all the ingredients and made into a semi-smooth paste. The chutney is set aside for 3 hours before use.

Only a little is used at a time.

One tablespoon of this chutney whisked in a cup of yoghurt makes an excellent relish.

Coconut Chutney 1

There are innumerable ways of preparing coconut chutneys. They are commonly used and go well with all dishes—with rice or fried breads as an accompaniment.

This is the first of the three methods discussed here.

British	Metric	Ingredients	American
3½ oz	100 g	coconut, grated	1 cup
2 tbsps	30 ml	lime or lemon, juice of	2 tbsps
½ tsp	2.5 g	salt	½ tsp
1 tsp	2 g	chilli powder, coarsely ground	1 tsp

Method

The coconut may be grated on a hand grater or in a food processor.

Mix them together and serve immediately.

Coconut Chutney 2

Coconut chutney along with powdered peanut and yoghurt makes a very tasty relish.

British	Metric	Ingredients	American
3½ oz	100 g	coconut, finely grated	1 cup
2 tbsps	12 g	peanut roasted, coarsely powdered	2 tbsps
2 oz	50 g	yoghurt	3 tbsps
1 tsp	5 ml	juice of lime or lemon	1 tsp
½ tsp	2.5 g	salt	½ tsp

262

Method

Mix together or put all the ungrated ingredients in a wet grinder and grind to a coarse paste.

Keep the chutney for half-an-hour in the fridge before serving.

Coconut Chutney 3

Take all the ingredients of the green coriander chutney and add finely grated coconut, sugar, extra lemon juice and salt. Another alternative to this is as given below.

British	Metric	Ingredients	American
3½ oz	100 g	finely grated coconut	1 cup
3½ oz	100 g	coriander greens	3½ oz
1½–2	1½–2	green chilli, hot	1½–2
3 tbsps	45 ml	juice of lime or lemon	3 tbsps
1 tsp	5 g	salt	1 tsp
2 tsps	10 g	sugar	2 tbsps

Method

All the ingredients are put through a wet grinder. When they are properly converted into a semi-liquid paste the chutney is ready.

This is a sweetish chutney and may be used as a spread to prepare excellent 'English type' sandwiches.

May also be eaten with vegetarian dishes.

Peanut and Cucumber Relish

This is staple relish of the western region of India and can be eaten by itself. It goes best when oriental breads accompany the main dish.

British	Metric	Ingredients	American
2 oz	50 g	peanuts, roasted, skinned	2 oz
$3\frac{1}{2}$ oz	100 g	cucumber, peeled and diced small	$1\frac{1}{4}$ cups
1 tbsp	2 g	green coriander, scissor cut	1 tbsp
2 tbsps	30 ml	juice of lime or lemon	2 tbsps
1 tsp	5 g	sugar	1 tsp
$\frac{1}{2}$ tsp	2.5 g	salt	$\frac{1}{2}$ tsp

Method

Coarsely pound the peanuts and mix all the other ingredients and keep them in the fridge for half to one hour before serving. For those who like it a little hot, crush a few whole red peppers and mix before serving.

White Radish Relish

This is a unique relish. It has a flavour and pungency akin to that of the horse radish. So much so that I am often asked by European friends as to whether horse radish is available in India.

British	Metric	Ingredients	American
$5\frac{1}{2}$ oz	150 g	white radish, finely grated	$1\frac{3}{4}$ cups
2 tsps	5 g	mustard seed, small variety, freshly ground OR	2 tsps
1 tbsp	7 g	Coleman's mustard	1 tbsp
3 tbsps	45 ml	juice of lime or lemon	3 tbsps
1	1	green chillies, finely round cut	1

$\frac{1}{2}$ tsp	2.5 g	salt, to taste	$\frac{1}{2}$ tsp
2 tbsps	30 ml	water	2 tbsps

Method

Salt the grated radish with about 1 tablespoon of salt and set aside for 1 hour. This releases water and concentrates the essential flavour of the radish.

Mix the mustard in 2 tablespoon of water for 15 minutes.

Squeeze the radish of any extra water and place in a glass bowl. Add the mustard and half teaspoon salt and lemon/lime juice and mix well. Keep the chutney away for half-an-hour outside, and for another half-an-hour in the fridge.

Before serving, add the finely cut round green chillies.

Makes delightful 'English' or 'open' sandwiches using a generous amount of butter and relish on the bread.

On Sweets

Indian sweets fall into two categories—those which form a part of the main course in an Indian meal and those especially prepared for special occasions, i.e. sweetmeats. Only the former type have been listed in this section.

Most of the sweets have milk as one of the main ingredients. This is perhaps because milk is mostly prescribed in the diet during fasts and festivals in the Indian tradition. It is fascinating to see the versatility of milk and the variety of ways milk is used to create these exotic dishes. Indians were certainly the first people to convert milk into *khoya*—its condensed form. Milk is also converted to cottage cheese, butter and refined butter (*ghee*). And of course it is converted to the all-important yoghurt which forms an integral part of the Indian kitchen. The entire range of biochemical constituents of milk have been exploited in the preparation of Indian sweets.

Kheer is made with rice and milk boiled together with sugar and flavours like saffron, cardamoms, rose-water and dry fruits like almonds, etc. *Shrikhand* is made from hung and dried yoghurt. *Phirnee* is a rice pudding which is an Indian gift to world cuisine. It is made with ground rice and milk, and is similar to *blancmange. Rasgoolas* are cottage cheese balls and are quite a favourite the world over. *Kulfi*, the forerunner of modern ice-cream, is made with condensed milk and is flavoured with nuts and other aromatics.

Apart from the milk-based dishes there are those made from lentils and vegetables such as carrots, gourds, etc.

The Indian meal is like a mini-buffet where all the dishes of the menu are served together, including the sweets. The following are the sweet preparations that are served with meals.

Kheer I—with Rice

The word *kheer* comes from the sanskrit *akshir* meaning thickened milk, and is used for any dish made of thickened milk. It is normally used for what might be called a 'rice pudding' in the West. The *kheer* with rice is very popular for any occasion. It can be simply rice, sugar and milk or more exotic with nuts, saffron, rose water, *keora* and raisins.

In South India *kheer* is called *payasam*. The word comes from the Sanskrit *payas* meaning milk preparation; and the preparation itself is *payasam*. In the South parboiled rice or *sela chawal* is used and is often preferred by many.

Serves 6

British	Metric	Ingredients	American
$1\frac{3}{4}$ pt	1 l	milk, full cream	$4\frac{1}{4}$ cups
$2\frac{1}{3}$ oz	65 g	rice	$\frac{1}{3}$ cup
$4\frac{1}{2}$ oz	125 g	sugar	$\frac{5}{8}$ cup
2 pinches	2 pinches	saffron	2 pinches

Method

Soak the rice in lukewarm water for 1 hour. Strain and keep aside.

Bring milk to boil and reduce heat. Add rice, sugar and saffron and simmer till the quantity of milk is reduced by one-third, or if lighter *kheer* is preferred, by one-fourth. Stir gently throughout.

Serve hot or cold. For more embellishment add slivers of pistachio nuts and/or almond nuts and raisins (pre-soaked for half-an-hour).

Kheer II—from Cottage Cheese

A very delectable variation.

Serves 6

British	Metric	Ingredients	American
1¾ pt	1 l	milk	4½ cups
9 oz	250 g	cottage cheese (*panir*)	9 oz
4½ oz	125 g	sugar	⅝ cup
1 tbsp	15 ml	rose water	1 tbsp
1 pinch		salt	1 pinch

Method

Dice the cottage cheese 1 cm x 1 cm x ½ cm and keep aside.

Bring milk to boil on medium heat. Add sugar and cottage cheese and simmer till milk is reduced to half or one-third approximately.

Add rose water. Serve hot or let it cool. Refrigerate and cover with silver foil (if available). Stir gently throughout cooking. Nuts do not go with this preparation.

Kheer III—with Gourd

One would not imagine that a vegetable like gourd can make such a delicious sweet dish—but it does.

Serves 6

British	Metric	Ingredients	American
1¾ pt	1 l	milk full cream	4½ cups
5 oz	150 g	finely grated gourd	1¾ cups

British	Metric	Ingredients	American
$4\frac{1}{2}$ oz	125 g	sugar	$\frac{5}{8}$ cup
1 tbsp	15 ml	butter	1 tbsp
$\frac{1}{2}$ tsp	2.5 ml	*keora* essence	$\frac{1}{2}$ tsp

Method

Take a frying pan, add butter and bring to bubbling. Sauté fry the grated gourd till glazed but not dried and keep aside.

Bring milk to boil on medium heat, add the gourd and sugar, and simmer—stirring all the time till milk is reduced by one-third or by half. This takes about 45 minutes. Add the *keora* and stir just before serving.

Serve hot or cold. When cold put silver foil on top. No other aromatics other than *keora* or rose water go with this.

Phirni

Derived from the word *pherna* meaning to turn around, which implies processes like grinding, stirring and mixing. This is a very common household preparation and is perhaps the forerunner of the French *blancmange*. Rice belongs to older civilizations and rice-flour is used for the preparation of this dish. Wheat flour came later and was used in the *blancmange*.

Serves 6–8

British	Metric	Ingredients	American
$1\frac{3}{4}$ pt (7 cups)	1 l	milk, normal	$4\frac{1}{2}$ cups
$1\frac{1}{3}$ oz (3 tbsps)	40 g	rice	3 tbsp
$4\frac{1}{2}$ oz	125 g	sugar, to taste	$\frac{5}{8}$ cup
1 tsp	2.5 g	cardamom seeds, freshly powdered	1 tsp

Method

Soak the rice for 2 hours in water. Strain and put through a wet grinder for a few seconds, it should remain marginally granular. Keep aside. Bring milk to boil on medium heat, add the ground rice a little at a time and keep stirring on moderate heat till the mixture comes to thicken after 30–40 minutes. Immediately add the sugar and bring to boil while stirring. Reduce heat and again increase heat for a second boiling. Keep on stirring to avoid sticking and burning. Take off the heat and pour with the help of a ladle into 6–8 separate ice-cream bowls or any other containers having a broad mouth. Cool outside for 30 minutes and refrigerate. While serving add a pinch of the cardamom powder on each portion. Cover with silver foil, if available.

Shrikhand

One of the oldest ancient Indian desserts or sweet dishes. *Shri* is from *akshir* now simplified to *shri* meaning as in *khir,* a thickened milk preparation. *Khanda* means sugar candy. *Akshir-khanda* is colloquially shrikhand. Perhaps the American word candy is derived from *khanda.* We therefore have 'thickened milk sugar candy' and that's exactly what *shrikhand* is. This might also have been the origin of the cheesecake.

Serves 3–4

British	Metric	Ingredients	American
18 oz	$\frac{1}{2}$ kg	hung dried yoghurt	18 oz
$3\frac{1}{2}$ oz	100 g	sugar, preferably confectionary sugar	$\frac{1}{2}$ cup
15	15	saffron strands, best quality	15
$\frac{1}{2}$ tsp	0.75 g	nutmeg freshly grated	$\frac{1}{2}$ tsp
1 pinch	1 pinch	salt	1 pinch

Method

Make sure that the curd used is absolutely devoid of water—for this the curd should be hung at least overnight.

Soak the saffron in 1 tablespoon of hot milk. Cover and set aside.

Personally I am a great believer in the 'kitchen maid', i.e., the food processor. Add all the ingredients into the wet grinding bowl and grind at low speed for 5–10 seconds and then at full speed for another 5–10 seconds. Taste for sugar and check for any granular pieces. Sugar should be homogenous with the yoghurt and there should be no granulations—put through the grinder again if necessary.

The *shrikhand* is ready. A version which is recently very popular is to freeze it as ice-cream. Both the unfrozen and frozen are equally delicious.

Do try this 'sweet' if you want to be pleasantly surprised.

Kulfi

The origin of this word is not traceable, but the Persian word *kalaf* is the closest and it means to starch or apply a stiffening agent. *Kulfi* is basically a concentrated milk ice-cream with a high fat content which may be termed as the stiffening agent.

Serves 6–8

British	Metric	Ingredients	American
$1\frac{3}{4}$ pt (7 cups)	1 kg	milk, full cream	$4\frac{1}{2}$ cups
$4\frac{1}{2}$ oz	125 g	sugar	$\frac{5}{8}$ cup
2 tbsps	10 g	pistachio slivers	2 tbsps
1 tbsp	4.5 g	almond slivers	1 tbsp
as required		*keora* essence	as required

Method

Reduce milk by boiling to half the quantity. Add nuts and sugar, and stir till dissolved.

Normally there are special containers for *kulfi* and these are conical in shape with a threaded cap to seal in the contents. If not available use normal small size ice-cream paper-cups. Pour the concentrated milk liquid into the available containers and put them in the freezing

271

compartment of your refrigerator and let freeze 'to stone' for 4–5 hours.

Before serving empty the contents onto a serving plate or ice-cream bowls. Add a drop of *keora* essence in each and serve.

Traditionally *kulfi* was served with *phalooda* or vermicelli. The bland and partially salty flavour of the vermicelli naturally enhances the flavour of the *kulfi*. Try it, cook vermicelli as you would do normally and let cool.

Sweet Rice (*Zaffrani Pulao*)

Simple and extravagant in appearance and appeal. *Zaffarani pulao* means saffron rice—only this one is sweet.

In this preparation the quality of rice and saffron are most important. The rice must be best quality—basmati or long-grain *pulao* rice. The saffron must be of a rich vermillion colour and highly aromatic. The brand Spanish No. 1 is the best.

Serves 3–5

British	Metric	Ingredients	American
9 oz	250 g	rice, basmati	$1\frac{1}{4}$ cups
$3\frac{1}{2}$ oz	100 ml	ghee (no other oil or fat will do)	$\frac{1}{2}$ cup
2 oz	50 g	sugar	$\frac{1}{4}$ cup
$\frac{1}{2}$ tsp	0.25 g	saffron	$\frac{1}{2}$ tsp
3 tbsps	15 g	almond slivers	3 tbsps
2 oz	50 g	sultanas	$\frac{1}{3}$ cup

Method

Soak the sultanas in 1 cup (5 fl oz/150 ml/ $\frac{1}{8}$ cup) warm water and keep aside. Soak the saffron in half a cup (3 fl oz/75 ml/ $\frac{1}{8}$ cup) of warm water. Cover and keep aside.

Clean and wash rice and soak in water for 2 hours or more—strain through a colander and keep aside.

Take a large heavy deep fry pan and bring ghee to high heat. Add rice and stir well to coat it with ghee and stir fry for a few minutes. Immediately add luke warm water to cover the rice. Normally one volume of rice should have $1\frac{1}{2}$ volumes of water—this may be adjusted as required. Add sugar and again stir fry to mix well together. Cover the pan on moderate heat, let cook like any pulao for 20–30 minutes. Uncover and, if still wet, cook uncovered for another 5–10 minutes.

Rice should be *al dente*. Mix almonds, sultanas (after straining) and saffron well into the rice. Serve immediately while hot.

Rasgoola

Ras means juice which is tasteful and *goola* means round. *Rasgoola* is therefore a 'juicy ball' perfected by the Bengalis of India. Each home has its own secret formula to make the *rasgoola* as juicy and as soft as possible. These *rasgoolas* have now been canned and have become popular worldwide.

British	Metric	Ingredients	American
$2\frac{1}{4}$ lb	1 kg	cottage cheese (*panir*) (or *chhana* as known in Bengal)	$2\frac{1}{4}$ lb
1 tbsp	15 g	flour	1 tbsp
2 tsps	10 g	sugar (I)	2 tsps
1 tsp	5 ml	rose essence or rose water	1 tsp
$\frac{1}{2}$ oz	15 g	crystal sugar (*mishri*) (large crystals about $\frac{1}{2}$ cm)	20–25 crystals
syrup			
1 lb 10 oz	750 g	sugar (II)	$3\frac{3}{4}$ cups
$1\frac{3}{4}$ pt (7 cups)	1 l	water (I)	$4\frac{1}{2}$ cups
7 fl oz ($1\frac{1}{3}$ cups)	200 ml	hot water (II), as required to make the syrup	$\frac{7}{8}$ cup

273

Method

Take the cottage cheese (*chhana*), add flour, baking powder, rose essence and sugar (I). Knead into a dough several times to make it smooth and pliable.

Roll the dough into 1 or 2 cylinders depending on the quantity. The cylinder diameter should be about 1". Cut the dough cylinder at $\frac{1}{2}$" length into several pieces. In this case they will make 20–25 pieces. Press and flatten each in the palm of your hand and place one piece of crystal sugar in the centre and fold it into a round ball. Repeat for all the pieces.

Cover the balls with a wet cloth and set aside.

Meanwhile make the syrup by boiling sugar (II) in water (I) till the sugar is fully dissolved. Continue boiling. While the syrup is boiling, quickly add the *chhana* balls one at a time. Continue to boil and cook for 20 minutes per lot and keep adding hot water (II) a little at a time. Make sure the balls do not stick to each other, with the help of a wooden spoon. Remove the syrup (with balls in it) from the fire and cool. When cold, transfer to an attractive glass or silverware bowl and keep in the refrigerator before serving. Serve with the syrup.

I have often served *rasgoolas* with a tablespoon of Quantreau Liquer to 2–3 balls alongwith the syrup. It is the most 'physical' experience!

Halwa

Halwa is an amalgam of sugar, grains, ghee, lentils (or vegetables) and water. The word comes from the Persian *hal* meaning to solve, resolve and dissolve.

This is a sweet dish which is common to the Indian cuisine from all regions. Since ghee is most important and sugar its chief accompaniment, both of which come from India, the dish gained worldwide eminence as a result of the applied consummate skill of Indian cooks.

274

Semolina Halwa (*Suji Halwa*)

Servers 6–8

British	Metric	Ingredients	American
18 oz	500 g	semolina	3 cups
9 oz	250 g	ghee	$1\frac{1}{8}$ cups
1 lb 6 oz	625 g	sugar	$3\frac{1}{8}$ cups
$2\frac{1}{2}$ pt (10 cups)	1.5 l	water	6 cups

Method

Roast the semolina in a griddle or a wok till it is light brown. Keep aside.

Dissolve sugar in water on high heat—when fully resolved keep aside.

Take a heavy-bottomed frying pan or a wok and add ghee. When it melts add the roasted semolina and stir fry till darker brown but not too deep brown. When ghee appears to be released add the sugar syrup and keep stir frying till all the water has evaporated and it forms a homogenous 'amalgam' and releases the proverbial aroma of cooked wheat. Keep stirring if too thin. Serve hot.

NOTE: This may be garnished with chipped copra and sultanas.

Carrot Halwa (*Gajar ka Halwa*)

This is a special North Indian version and has found acceptance by all palates.

Serves 6–8

British	Metric	Ingredients	American
$4\frac{1}{2}$ lb	2 kg	carrots	$4\frac{1}{2}$ lb
$1\frac{3}{4}$ pt (7 cups)	1 l	milk, full cream	$4\frac{1}{2}$ cups

275

9 oz	250 g	sugar	$1\frac{1}{4}$ cups
7 fl oz	200 ml	ghee	$\frac{7}{8}$ cup
2 oz	50 g	walnuts (preferred) or almonds, shelled and chopped	$\frac{1}{3}$ cup

Method

Finely grate the carrots and set aside.

If using walnuts quarter or half them and keep aside. If almonds are used half them lengthwise and keep aside.

Bring milk to boil on medium heat and add the grated carrots. Simmer for 30–40 minutes till carrots are completely tender. Remove to another dish. Add ghee and bring to high heat. Add the tenderized carrot to the ghee and stir fry till all the water has evaporated and continue stir frying till ghee is released and the carrots are dark brownish red in colour. Now add the sugar and mix well on the fire for a few minutes. Finally add the nuts. No further cooking is required. It is important that after adding the sugar ghee is released and no water is present.

Serve hot.

NOTE: It is delectable when served with clotted cream.

Roasted hazelnuts instead of walnuts and almonds is a tasty substitution.

The same recipe can be adapted for pumpkin *halwa*. The yellow common pumpkin is used. Peel and grate as for carrots in the same quantity and then follow the recipe.

Silver foil may be applied on top for special occasions.

On Drinks

It is more than certain that alcoholic beverages were drunk in ancient and medieval India with food. The two-tier system in alcohols, one such as distilled hard alcohol and the other such as beer, was prevalent.

From my personal experience and those of my friends the following drinks go well with Indian curries.

Aperitif
Bloody Mary, well spiced
Pina Collada

With Meals
Full bodied Burgundy
Rose chilled
Pilsner or draft beer

After Dinner
Creme de Menthe Frappé
Sambocca Frappé
Coffee

Light buttermilk, Indian teas or Chinese jasmine also do very well and may be had during the meal.

Apart from alcoholic beverages and buttermilk, tea, etc., the drinking of fresh fruit juices is quite common in India. Having a climate, both temperate and tropical, fruit juices may consist of:

Apple
Pineapple
Mango
Oranges
Tangerine
Red Pomegranate
Water Melon
Tomato
Grape
Papaya

These can be served before the meal and may be had during the meal as desired.

Last but not least, water is the real companion to the Indian curry dishes. However, today, mineral water is drunk with the meal, either with gas or without gas. This is a universal accompaniment with meals of all kinds.

CULINARY ADVISER
On Basic Preparations

In the recipes given in this book there are 6 very important preparations that are best done at home. In fact it might be necessary to do so because in many parts of the world these preparations are not readily available, and often if they are available they are not of the required quality.

The preparations detailed in order of importance are given here.

> Garam masala
> Ghee, clarified butter
> Yoghurt, curd
> *Panir*, Indian cream cheese or Indian ricotta
> Tamarind pulp
> Coconut cream and milk

Garam Masala

Special Garam Masala

The garam masala given here is the one used throughout in the recipes.

Peppercorn	4 tbsps + 1 tsp	$= 35$ g/$1\frac{1}{6}$ oz
Caraway	4 tbsps	$= 30$ g/1 oz
Cumin	5 tbsps + 1 tsp	$= 45$ g/$1\frac{2}{3}$ oz
Cardamom seed	8 tbsps	$= 60$ g/2 oz
Cardamom brown seed	$1\frac{1}{2}$ tbsps	$= 10$ g/$\frac{1}{3}$ oz
Cloves	3 tbsps less 1 tsp	$= 20$ g/$\frac{2}{3}$ oz
Cinnamon broken pieces	3 tbsps less 1 tsp	$= 20$ g/$\frac{2}{3}$ oz
Nutmeg grated	2 tbsps + 1 tsp	$= 10$ g/$\frac{1}{3}$ oz
Mace crushed	1 tbsp + 2 tsp	$= 10$ g/$\frac{1}{3}$ oz

All the ingredients are ground together (could be done in a spice grinder) and the powder is passed through a fine sieve. The coarse powder is ground again. The masala is then put in an air-tight brown or blue glass bottle and kept in a cool place, because light, heat and air destroy much of the quality of a good garam masala.

Equal proportions of regular cardamom, cinnamon and cloves are finely ground together for aromatic garam masala.

NOTE: Buy the best quality whole spices to get good results. When using a grinder for spices pound these first and then grind.

Ghee

Ghee is the purest form of butter fat with practically no milk solids. It has been prepared in India from times immemorial and has been described in ancient texts, which are dated by scholars to around 8000 BC! Ghee is the colloquial form of the Sanskrit word *ghrith*.

At the time when there were no mechanization or refrigeration, cow's milk or buffalo's milk and in some regions even yak milk and goat milk was converted to butter either by a curd intermediary or by a cream intermediary. This was done manually, with ceramic or wooden implements.

Once converted to butter, it was melted on very slow heat till most of the water evaporated and the solid precipitated. What remained in the vessel was ghee.

Ghee resembles olive oil. Without the impurities this clarified butter or ghee is stable and can be stored indefinitely.

Besides, it is an excellent cooking medium because it does not change colour under heat and can be reheated and re-used many times without change in its characteristics.

For the developing countries ghee has become very expensive and vegetable oils are being used as an alternative. However, with the surplus of butter in many developed nations, butter oil has come to be prepared and extensively used. Butter oil, because of its high-tech processing, tends to lose the original flavour of ghee but is technically the same product.

Where butter is cheap and available in plenty, ghee can be made at home by simply keeping it on slow fire for a few hours till the water evaporates. The melted butter, which is now converted to ghee, is then decanted.

Most of the cooks in India use no other cooking medium except ghee, specially for red meats, vegetables and pulaos.

If you cannot buy **ghee** or make it, use any cooking oil as recommended in the recipes.

Yoghurt, Curd *(Dahi)*

Yoghurt has a fascinating history of its own. It certainly originated in India and was taken to the West by the nomadic tribes and gypsies of Eastern and Central Europe via Asia Minor. It is probable that milk which was a staple food for all nomads might have been kept to ferment. Thereafter the milk curdled and came to be known as curd. In the Sanskrit language the word curd is almost identical for curdling.

Yoghurt is one of the most nutritious foods and is a complete diet in itself. Besides, it restores the intestinal flora after an imbalance created by antibiotic therapy.

Yoghurt lends itself to conversion for cheese or butter and is extensively used in the Indian kitchen as a meat tenderizer and a sour creaming agent. In its whisked or liquidized form it constitutes a medium for all the raitas, a kind of Indian salad. Recipes for the raitas are included in this book.

Yoghurt is eaten with sugar, with jams, flavoured with salt, with condiments. It is also made into buttermilk. Today it is being added to practically anything—crackers, potato wafers, cheese soups, flams, salad dressing, toppings, savoury dishes, goulash, strogonoff and what not!

In case it is not possible to prepare yoghurt at home, buy the cultured yoghurt. If that too is not available use factory yoghurt.

Method of Preparation

Yoghurt is a result of the activity of the lactobacillus bacteria in milk. The technique of making yoghurt is to have a yoghurt culture from the yoghurt prepared every day. Cultured yoghurt can also be bought in the market these days. Bring 7 cups ($1\frac{1}{4}$ pt/1l) of milk to room temperature and mix properly 2 tbsps (30 ml) of the yoghurt culture into it.

In Indian homes the culture is mixed by rubbing the yoghurt between the palms of the hand and pouring over the milk so that the yoghurt acquires body temperature and creates the ideal incubation environment for the lacto-bacillus.

After mixing the yoghurt culture in the milk let it stand covered in a warm corner of the room. Normally it takes 3 hours, sometimes longer depending on the climate and the quality of the milk and the culture, for the curd to set.

Hung Drained Yoghurt (*Bandhi Dahi*)

Means literally yoghurt which has been 'tied up'. This is required for some of the curry recipes in this book.

Method of Preparation

The preparation is very simple. Take 6 cups ($2\frac{1}{4}$ lb/1 kg/4 cups) of yoghurt, tie it in a muslin cloth and hang it up for the night. Put a receptacle underneath to catch the dripping water. The water will drain out overnight and what is left is very close to the European cream cheese. This is what is called hung yoghurt.

Panir

Panir is cottage cheese, and might have originated in India or in southern Italy where it is called ricotta. The English refer to it as the Indian cream cheese, though this is not really appropriate because it is closer to ricotta and also perhaps to the Chinese bean curd or dofu.

Panir is very refreshing, neutral, spongy and has a healthy count of protein and fat. Though available in the market, it is best prepared at home and takes very little time to prepare.

The *panir* may be loose, soft or hard depending on the method of preparation. The three forms are discussed here.

Method of Preparation

To make 18 oz/$\frac{1}{2}$ kg of loose *panir* take $2\frac{1}{8}$ pt/$1\frac{1}{2}$ l/$6\frac{1}{2}$ cups of full cream milk and bring slowly to boil. Remove from the fire. Add juice of 1 lemon or 2 small lemons. Stir, and when the milk curdles and the water is separated from the caesine, take a muslin cloth or a cheese-cloth, put it over the colander and allow it to strain by itself for about 1 hour. *Panir* is left behind in the cloth. Do not use a mould or a weight to drain the water. This makes the loose *panir*.

To make the soft *panir* use a mould to drain the water, but do not use any weight.

To make the *panir* hard, use the mould and then use a weight to strain away the water. A medium weight is used for the soft texture, a heavier one for harder cheese, like in the case of bean curd. Let the weight stay on the cheese for a couple of hours, unwrap, and cut to any form you like—diced, diamond cut, julienne cut or squared.

Panir makes a delectable salad by itself with any dressing you like—French, Italian, etc.

If used in the curry recipes, the *panir* is prepared as given here and then the recipe is followed.

Tamarind Pulp

India perhaps has the maximum number of souring agents in the world. Each with its own subtle flavour and tartness. Tamarind is the one most extensively used. Because of its sugar content it gives a rounded off tartness. It also imparts a characteristic aroma and colour to the dish.

Tamarind has been dealt with in the glossary which gives the history and use of its genre and homeland. The tamarind bean with its characteristic pods is now available throughout the world. By and large it is available either de-seeded or with seeds in its light to dark brown colour as mature pods packed in different measures.

If the pods have an outer shell it should be removed. The soft pulp is then seen. Soak the peeled tamarind directly in hot water. For general household cooking usually a cup of tamarind soaked in three cups of hot water is required.

Let the mixture sit for about half an hour and if the tamarind is not de-seeded rub off the pulp after it has been softened in water by hand and remove the seeds. If de-seeded just strain the mixture through a strong cloth and this is the tamarind juice or more technically tamarind liquid pulp.

The tamarind juice is then used as prescribed in the recipe.

Coconut Cream or Milk

The coconut is supposed to be a divine fruit. According to Indian texts it is considered to be an auspicious holy symbol. It has all the five elements and it has water inside. Each and every part of this nut can be utilized.

When in its green form the coconut water is the best thirst-quencher having additionally properties and minerals which act as electrolytes.

During the war in Southeast Asia coconut water was given intravenously to the troops as a life saving parental liquid.

In its intermediary form, i.e. when the green outer shell converts to brown known as *naryal* it is then used for what is required for the recipes, namely making of coconut cream and milk. The ripened coconut develops a very hard brown shell covered with matted brown strands. After removing the strands the bare coconut with the hard shell is obtained. This has coconut water inside.

Method of Preparation

There are several ways of cracking the coconut to reach the meat or the pulp. Some use saws, some pierce the eye with a nail and some bake it in the oven to expand the liquid inside and thus crack the shell.

In Indian homes however two coconuts are hit hard against each other over a receptacle, one of them cracks and the water is collected in the receptacle. Once broken the white meat is exposed which has to be scraped or scooped out. The water from this coconut is extremely nutritious and pleasant to drink and should not be wasted.

Crush the meat to pulp in a blender and to this (for an average coconut) add 2 cups ($\frac{1}{2}$ pt/300 ml/ $1\frac{1}{4}$ cups) of boiling water for the cream and 2 cups ($\frac{1}{2}$ pt/300 ml) for the second pressing with the leftover liquidized pulp. If you should have a strong blade blender it is easiest to put this scooped out meat in the blender pouring boiling water while you blend it. Once it is fully liquidized pour the whole mixture into a strong muslin cloth and squeeze it into a container. This is known as the first pressing and is the one that is used for making the heavy coconut milk, known as coconut cream. An average coconut should give you 2 cups ($\frac{1}{2}$ pt/300 ml) of coconut cream.

The creaming process is better achieved by leaving this first pressing extract in the refrigerator for 6–8 hours till it looks like cream both in texture and colour.

With the residue left after the first pressing, you once again liquidize it with another lot of water and repeat the process of pressing through the muslin. This becomes the second pressing and is known generally as coconut milk.

The best flavouring from the coconut is obtained when it is in the coconut cream form.

Today in many parts of the world canned coconut cream and coconut milk can be obtained. The nations who do it best are Thailand, Malaya and Taiwan. Any recognized brand could be used from specialist shops or super market. The Thai coconut cream or milk is of a very fine quality. This is not surprising because many dishes in the Thai kitchen consist of two basic parts, one is the paste compounded with many exotic spices and herbs and the other is coconut cream or milk.

When the coconut is completely dry with no water inside it is known as *copra*. This food has the highest calorie count per 100 mg as compared to any other food in the world. Diced pieces of the *copra* are carried by pilgrims who go to remote shrines and mountains as a basic ration.

On Cooking Oils

Ghee

In India the cow is regarded as a sacred animal. It is obvious that this was inducted as a religious concept only because of its importance as the best re-cycling agent for converting grass and fodder into milk which in turn is converted into butter, cream, ghee, yoghurt, *panir*, cheese and condensed milk called *khoya*. These derivatives from milk provide all the essential energy principles required such as fats, protein, sugar and enzymes as well as many beneficial baccili.

Ghee is clarified butter and is largely prepared from the milk of cows and buffaloes and to some extent from sheeps and goats as in the

Himalayas and Tibet. The greater proportion is from buffalo milk because of the yield and the higher fat content which makes it cheaper and more readily available.

In many recipes ghee is the main cooking oil and there is no real substitute for this very important cooking medium. Once the butter is clarified and the water evaporated it can be preserved for many years.

Over the years, however, many other oils have gained popularity both for economic reasons and ready availability.

Other Oils

India is one of the few countries which uses so many oils for cooking, each being representative of a certain area and their existence is almost pre-historical.

In tropical countries there is a natural environment for the cultivation of oilseeds unlike in temperate climates.

Amongst the oils which are predominantly in use are groundnut, sesame, mustard, rapeseed, kardi seed oil, sunflower seed oil and coconut oil. Corn oil and rice-barn oil are very recent developments.

As their names suggest they are extracted from the various oilseeds—groundnut oil from groundnuts, sesame oil from sesame seeds, etc.

Today groundnut oil and sunflower seed oil are extremely popular all over the world for various reasons, including their ability to be re-heated without affecting flavour. Mustard oil and sesame seed oil have strong taste and aroma with distinct flavour and can only be recommended for special dishes belonging to certain regions of India.

Wherever oil is mentioned it is best to use either groundnut or sunflower seed oil if ghee is not preferred.

Olive oil which is considered the ultimate in oils in Europe and is from the Mediterranean region seems not to blend with the flavours of the Indian cuisine. It can however be used for any or all vegetables except where mustard oil is specifically prescribed.

In the Chinese contemporary kitchen the oil used is generally groundnut with a flavouring of highly aromatic roasted sesame seed oil.

On observation it appears that optimum flavours are developed by different oils for different kitchens and different recipes.

Today with the gourmet culture supported by medical research practically all oils are available in all super markets.

On Frying

There are several types of frying which although practiced may not have been appropriately defined. This is more applicable to some of the Indian frying techniques such as singe fry and dry fry.

It is to be remembered that in all frying processes the oil has to be brought to near smoking or to high heat.

Frying is done with oil and an ingredient which is fried in it.

The various frying techniques in existence attributed to Italy and the mother kitchen of Europe (France) include shallow fry, sauté and deep fry.

> *Shallow fry:* generally means that the oil should not cover the ingredient which is either shaken in the frying pan or turned over quickly.

> *Sauté:* is a French word which is almost similar to shallow frying but the oil may be even less than for shallow frying and again you may or may not turn the ingredient with a spatula. In this process as in shallow frying the ingredient is cooked rapidly in a small amount of fat or cooking oil.

> *Deep fry:* as the term suggests there should be plenty of oil in a wok, *kardai* or a deep frier and the ingredient is able to either drown in it or pop up and down. The oil used has to be on very high heat. Potato wafers, pomfret fish, and many ingredients which are covered with batter, and bread crumbs are generally deep fried.

Apart from these common frying techniques the Chinese introduced a very important frying process called stir fry.

> *Stir fry:* is a process where you cook any ingredient with very little oil on high heat and keep stirring the ingredient quickly swirling it around the wok. Never let it stand still and never let the ingredient release its own liquid content.

Stir fry is also a process extensively used in India particularly in Gujarat and Bengal for cooking vegetables. In the local language the ingredient cooked in this fashion is known as *kacha pacca* that means literally half cooked. It is an excellent form of frying to retain the colour and the original flavour of the ingredient.

In the Indian system apart from using all the given frying techniques, 2 techniques need special mention.

As you will observe, in the special section on cooking stages, especially when you use spices and herbs, by and large the first process is to singe fry spices or herbs.

Singe fry: is to bring the required amount of oil to high heat and put the spices which are required to be singe fried in a particular recipe. These spices will splutter and bubble producing a characteristic singeing sound.

Usually after the singe fry is over you either immediately add the follow-up spices or the main ingredients. Never leave the singe fry ingredients on the fire by themselves.

This is a term which has been very recently codified by the collective genius of friends and relatives.

The other frying technique used in India is the dry fry. This is usually where oil or cooking fat is used with such items where the ingredient remains dry and oil is continuously added in small quantities.

Dry fry: this process is very necessary for cooking parathas, dosa and some fried vegetable cutlets or meat patties.

As you will observe in the section for breads the paratha after being folded and put on the griddle or *tawa* is continuously fed spoonfuls of oil at fairly high heat which immediately disappears after it interacts with the moisture in the paratha dough.

The principal function in this process is to burn out the water by putting oil but not the ingredient. In all this you will never find any surplus oil or water in the ingredient and therefore it has now been defined as dry fry.

We now have the following systems of frying:

Shallow Fry	Stir Fry
Sauté Fry	Singe Fry
Deep Fry	Dry Fry

On Meat Cuts

The meat cuts that are commonly used in India are fine mince, coarse mince, hand-chopped coarse mince, the curry cut similar to the goulash cut and bone meat cuts.

The other cuts such as shoulder, leg, fillet and rib chops are the same as in international cuisine.

The recipes give the type of meat cuts that are required.

The various cuts used in the Indian kitchen are more or less the same as used in international kitchen.

The meat cuts are illustrated with the recipes.

On Salt

It is amazing that salt is not dealt with adequately in most cookery books. The Bible says:

> If the salt loses its savour
> wherewith shall it be salted.

There can be no better statement for the importance of salt.

If for one moment we were to remove salt from all the cooking you can imagine what will happen. Despite all the exotic spices, herbs and condiments used nobody will ever enjoy a dish without salt.

There are three basic aspects of salt which should be considered.

Firstly the type of salt that one should use for cooking; secondly the timing for putting salt into a particular dish and finally the amount of salt as an individual and universal index.

Basically salt is sodium chloride, which, although a mineral, is regarded more as a condiment, and along with potassium and oxygen constitutes the main kinetic force of the heart.

Sodium as the element to the mineral salt is present in practically all the foods that are eaten.

288

There are today several types of salt and because of their marketing and research back-up, the salts that were originally used are being forgotten.

Amongst the salts that can be identified as different types are sea salt, rock salt, table salt and iodized salt. As far as cooking in India is concerned the gurus of the culinary arts recommend the use of rock salt, freshly ground, particularly for meats. The natural impurities in rock salt retard the formation of hydrochloric acid and thereby prevent the meat from becoming shredded or mushy. From experience I find this to be largely true and if for nothing else certainly for good mutton or lamb.

Sea salt is the salt that is mostly used these days and I have nothing against it.

However, sea salt when converted to table salt to ensure free flow has magnesium chloride in small quantities. Although it may not be noticeable free flow salt tends to be less salty when used in the same quantities as pure rock salt or pure sea salt. It also reacts adversely for delicate foods such as mushrooms, asparagus, morel and milk products.

It is true that natural salts are not easily available. On the other hand if you are particular you can always find them. Recently there has been a revival in the use of rock salt.

There are many names to these categories of salt which are often referred to as common salt, kitchen salt, crystal salt, etc. They all fall in the basic categories above, with the exception that these salts do not have additives for flow, for oxidization and whiteness.

In the case of quantity of salt to be used there has been some statistical analysis of the salt index related to various ethnic groups. Without complicating the issue it is generally true that a flat teaspoon of common salt to half a kilo of product or 2 flat teaspoons for a kilo of product is a safe measure. Every family controls its measure of salt according to what the members demand.

When using souring ingredients such as tomatoes, yoghurt or tamarind a little extra salt may be required.

To add salt when cooking at a specified time is no longer a conscious act. Nevertheless there is a time for adding salt which varies with the dish. By and large in cooking Indian meat curries it is advisable to add salt when the main ingredient is put into the pot. This helps permeation as well as assists in tenderizing. Adding of salt after a dish has been prepared or nearly prepared does not give an even saltiness to the dish and if there are large chunks as the main ingredient they tend to remain short of salt whereas the rest of the dish tends to have more salt. In other words the quantities of salt that have been described should be used at the time the recipe prescribes.

It is never advisable to add salt too early when cooking red meat. This tends to release the blood and reduces the succulence and flavour of meat. On the other hand fish is generally salted before cooking. This represents different interaction of salt with different meats.

The use of iodized salt for cooking is neither recommended nor practised since the objective of iodized salt is not achieved by its use in cooking. The thermal effect tends to free the iodine and besides some rice and vegetable dishes change their flavour and colour.

This short note on salt is not written to make anyone uneasy about the type of salt they use, the timing and the quantity— but largely for insight and perhaps some perfection!

On Cooking Utensils, Serving Dishes and Appliances

Utensils used for the Indian kitchen have not changed since time immemorial—from as early as Mohenjodaro, 4000 BC or even earlier!

Contrary to common belief any kind of utensil will do for cooking Indian curry dishes. Personally I have found the *kardai* and the Chinese wok the most practical. But any heavy cooking pan or casserole dish may be used.

If you are just beginning to cook curries it is safer to use a Tafflon-lined utensil.

In the Indian kitchen the names of utensils commonly used are *degchi* and *kardai*. For unleavened bread a *tawa* is indispensible.

Kardai is the forerunner or similar to the traditional Chinese wok. It has a round bottom and is excellent for all kinds of frying as well as all types of cooking.

Degchi is a flat-bottomed utensil with a flat cover. The flat cover mates perfectly with the dish so that it can be sealed with dough for 'sealed pot' curries.

For slow fire cooking it is well-known that the utensil should be one with a heavy bottom preferably copper. This renders even conductivity of heat and prevents burning.

In case, for one reason or another, you have to use an aluminium dish—either a wok or casserole—make sure to use a stand over the gas or the electric hot plate.

As for turning over the meat or vegetables one can either use a flat wooden spatula or any large shallow serving spoon.

What is important in the curry kitchen is the control of time and heat for singe-frying and for slow cooking rather than the utensils used.

Serving dishes are important to the Indian kitchen. Each recipe suggests what to use for serving for the best effect. Indian dishes also require that saucers or several individual bowls be used alongside the main *thali*.

The curries and vegetables are eaten individually with rice or Indian breads and as such they must be kept separately. It is not commended nor palatable to have a curry run into a 'dal' or rice. The European kitchen generally has boiled vegetables around the main course and thus presents no conflict of taste, aroma and flavour, when served in a common plate.

Recently the pressure cooker has been modified in India to a pressure pan. In my opinion this is a very practical development since in a pan all the stages of cooking can be carried out till the main ingredient is put as prescribed in the recipe. Thereafter the pressure lid on the pan may be placed and used as a pressure cooker thus reducing the cooking time by half or less.

If you are used to a pressure cooker by all means use the pressure pan to save time. Your experience in pressure cooking will allow you to determine the various timings required for cooking the main ingredient after the earlier stages have been carried through.

Amongst other gadgets used for convenience and as time saving devices, is a good blender that may be made the maximum use of. This can whisk your yoghurt and with different attachments can do wet grindings for pastes and dry spices grinding.

Whenever you use the coffee grinder as a spice grinder, first pound the whole spices as far as possible and then ground them finely in the coffee or spice grinder.

The mincing attachment could be used for mincing various meats but the best effect is obtained in hand-chopped coarse mince for the various recipes.

Roasting of spices can be done in a heavy-bottomed frying pan or the tawa or any griddle. In case of pounded masala spices the spices have to be hand-pounded. For roasted or pounded spices use the coffee or spices grinder.

On Gas and Electric Oven Temperatures

All temperatures are stated in degrees Centigrade and as generally expressed levels of heat, such as high, medium and low.

Level of heat	Mark/Gas	Centigrade	Fahrenheit
Low	1	140	275
	2	150	300
Medium	3	170	325
	4	180	350
Fairly hot	5	190	375
Hot	6	200	400
	7	220	425
Very hot	8		
	9	240	475

Indian Culinary Words and Terms

PULAO
Pilav

Persian *Pileh* means stair or step, it also means doing things by degrees or gradually. This aptly describes the pulao which is supposed to have distinct layering. The ultimate pilav or pulao is the biryani.

BIRYANI   Persian

Biryani means to roast. This a pulao where the meat is supposed to be roasted with some oil and as is the boiled rice. *Biryani* therefore becomes a dish of meat and rice, oil roasted.

KOFTAH   Persian
Kofta

From *koftan, kobidan,* to beat or pound. Thus the meat balls are made from pounded meat. Now a days it is also applicable to mincing, which is a mechanized process.

NAAN   Persian

From *n'an aan* which means to temper like in steel. When dough is tempered, in other words baked, it becomes *naan.* The baker is called naanbai.

PASANDA   Persian

Derived from the word *pasandida* meaning 'likeable looking' personified as very likeable. Short culinary word is *pasanda* and applies to the most likeable cut of meat—in this case the undercut or fillet.

ROMALI   Persian

Ro is face in Persian and *malidan* is to rub—that which rubs the face meaning handkerchief. The quality of the handkerchief aptly describes the romali roti which is thin, large, chappati-like bread.

MASALA   Persian

Compound word with *ma + asal.*

| | **Arabic** | *Ma* in Arabic means 'which, what, whatever' *all that which* and in Arabic *asal* means the 'taste of the dish'. In Persian it means the 'real thing'. It follows that masala would mean 'all that which is real'. The masala is all that a curry is about. |

DEGCHI — Persian

Deg is a basic word meaning 'pot' in Persian, with the suffix *cha*, it is *degcha* big pot, with the suffix *chi* it is *degchi*, small pot.

MAHMOOS — Arabic

Derived from the word *muhamas* which means to put one thing together with another without any delay. The word *mahmoos* is a mutiliation of the original Arabic as used in India.

You will observe from the recipe that there are many ingredients including pastes, yoghurt, nuts, meat, eggs and vegetables and each has been put together with the other without delay.

KEEMA — Turkish

Basic word meaning to hash.

KORMA — Turkish

Probably originates from the word *gorma,* where *gor* means vegetables and *ma* for *mas* is meat. Korma the word now used is usually the combination of meat and vegetables.

TARKARI — Hindi

Whereas *kari* is of Tamil origin as already stated, the adjunct *tar* is originally Persian for wet. It follows then that a curry which uses water is *tarkari.*

PANIR — Hindi

For *pan-nir. Par* is to 'go yonder' and *nir* is water. When the water is separated or 'goes yonder' by the chemi-

		cal action of adding citric acid to milk, what remains is curd and casein called *panir*.
KARDAI	Hindi	The Indian wok alongwith its Chinese counterpart is perhaps one of the world's earliest cooking utensils. Derives from the word *kardana* meaning to concentrate liquid+substance by boiling. The utensil is therefore called *kardai*. The wok and the *kardai* are scientifically devised—they have a semi-circular receptacle which distributes heat evenly and can be used for any of the various frying techniques. Alongwith the *tawa* it is one of the most important cooking utensils which has not changed till the present day.
TAWA	Hindi	*Taav* in Hindi is to 'give it heat' and *tava* is that which gives heat to whatever is put on it. This particular device is indispensible for making Indian breads, phulka, roti, chappati and parathas. It is used both by the wheat-eating belt of the Indo-Gangetic plains and the rice-eating region of the South.

On Spices and Other Foods to be Stored

If there is an outlet, either a speciality store or a good super market, which sells spices and herbs, it would be better to plan what you wish to cook a day ahead and buy only as much as is required.

The list of spices given is based on their frequency of use and the recommended quantity.

Ingredient, Common English Names	Indian Names	Recommended Quantity
i) Primary whole spices		
Bay leaves	tejpata	
Cardamom large brown	bari illachi	
Cardamom green whole	illachi	2 oz/50 g
Wild onion seed, Nigella	kalonji	each
Coriander whole seeds	dhania	
Cloves	laung	
Cinnamon quills	dalchini	
Nutmeg	jayphal	
Mace	jaivitri	
Fenugreek seeds	methi	
Poppy seeds	khas-khas	
Peppercorns, black pepper	kali mirch	4 oz /100 g
Dried red chillies	lal mirch	each
Cumin seed white	zira	
Anise/fennel seed	saunf	
Mustard seed	rye	
Sesame seed	til	
ii) Primary ground spices		
Black pepper	kali mirch	
Chilli powder	lal mirch	
Coriander powder	dhania	
Cumin powder	zeera	4 oz /100 g
Turmeric powder	haldi	each
Dry raw mango powder	amchur	
Red Hungarian sweet paprika		
iii) Secondary whole spices		
Cumin seeds black	shah-jeera	
Dried ginger	sonth, adrak	4 oz /100 g
Lovage seed, carum	ajwain	each
Tamarind	imli	
Coconut, fresh	nariel	2
Coconut, dry	copra	1

Ingredient, Common English Names	Indian Names	Recommended Quantity
Bay leaves	tejpatta	If dried,
Fenugreek leaves dry	methi	2 oz/ 50 g each
Curry leaves	kari patta	
Green coriander	hara dhania	If green
		4oz /100 g each
Green fenugreek	hari methi	
Ginger	adrak	

(iv) Special spices

Asafoetida	hing	
Saffron stamens	kesar zafran	
Ratanjot	ratanjyot	1 oz /25 g
	ratanjot	each
Silver foil	chandi ka varq	10 foils

v) Other Foods

Basmati rice	basmati	4 lb/2 kg
Gram flour	besan	2 lb/1 kg
Cornflour	-	8 oz $\frac{1}{4}$ kg
Lentils	masur	
Red Gram split	tuar-dal	$\frac{1}{2}$ kg each
Split chick pea	chana-ki-dal	
Almonds	badam	
Pea nuts	mungphali	
Pine nuts	neoza	4 oz/100 g
		each
Hazel nuts	-	
Chironji	chironji	
Pistachio	pista	

All dried spices or herbs must be kept in air-tight containers and after use must be sealed properly again.

Weight and Volume Equivalents

Ingredients	Weights in grammes	
Whole Spices	tsp	tbsp
All spice	1.75	5.0
Cardamom brown seed	2.25	6.75
Cardamom seed	2.5	7.5
Carum seed	2.0	6.25
Chironji	3.0	9.0
Cinnamon broken pieces	2.5	7.5
Cloves	2.25	6.75
Coriander	1.75	5.0
Cumin seed	3.0	8.5
Fennel seed	2.5	7.5
Fenugreek seed	4.25	12.5
Mustard brown	3.75	11.0
Mace	2.0	6.0
Nigella seed	2.75	8.25
Pepper black corns	2.75	8.0
Poppy seed	3.5	10.0
Saffron	0.5	1.5
Sesame seed	3.0	9.0
Shah zeera, whole	2.5	7.5
'For control'		
Water	5.0	15.0
Salt	5.5	15
Powdered spices	tsp	tbsp
Allspice	1.75	5.0
Amchoor	2.5	7.5
Black caraway/cumin	2.5	8.0
Cardamom brown	2.5	7.5
Cardamom seed powder	2.75	8.25
Carum	2.75	8.0
Chilli powder	2.0	6.0
Cinnamon	2.75	8.5
Cloves	2.5	7.5
Coriander	2.0	6.0

Powdered Spices	tsp	tbsp
Cumin	2.75	8.0
Fennel	2.75	8.0
Fenugreek	3.0	8.25
Garam masala special	2.75	8.25
Ginger	2.0	6.0
Mace	2.0	6.0
Mustard	3.0	10.0
Nutmeg grated	1.5	4.5
Pepper black	3.25	10.0
Salt	5.0	15.0
Shah zeera	2.5	8.0
Turmeric	3.5	10.0

Glossary on Spices

ALLSPICE
Botanical Name: Pimenta officinalis
Family: Myrtaceae
Hindi: *Kabab chini*
Dried fruits of the evergreen Pimenta officinalis have an aroma similar to a mixture of cloves, cinnamon and nutmeg. Allspice has been known to Europe and Asia for only 500 years.

Whole berries are called pimento.

AMCHUR
Dry, raw mango
Botanical Name: Mangifera indica
Family: Anacardiaceae
Hindi: *Amchur*
From its indigenous home in India. Sanskrit mythology mentions it in many of the old tales and folklore of the Hindus. The unripe fruits are peeled and the flesh cut into thin slices which are then dried in the sun. Usually available in powder form. Used as an acid flavouring ingredient in Indian cookery.

ANARDHANA

Pomegranate seed-dry

Botanical Name: Punica granatum

Family: Lythraceae

Hindi: *Anardhana, Anardana*

Anardana comprises the dried seeds (dried with flesh) of pomegranate—a shrub or a small tree 5–8 metres high, considered to be a native of Iran. It grows in the Himalayas between 900 and 1800 m. These seeds with pulp when sun-dried or dehydrated, constitute the condiment *anardana*. Like *amchur*, *anardana* too is used as an acidulant in Indian curries.

ANISE

Botanical Name: Pimpinella anisum

Family: Umbelliferae

Hindi: *Saunf, saonf*

Are dried fruit of Pimpinella anisum. Anise is amongst the oldest of medicines and spices mentioned in many classical writings. It is used as a carminative and de-obstructant, also as water of Anise, Araq Badian. Aniseed possesses a sweet aromatic taste and emits when crushed, a characteristic agreeable odour. In India it is employed to a considerable extent as a flavouring agent in confectionery. The Kashmiri chefs use this in preparing dishes.

ASAFOETIDA

Botanical Name: Ferula foetida

Family: Scorodosma

Hindi: *Hing*

Is the resinous gum of a plant growing in Afghanistan and Iran. Asafoetida is a sedative, expectorant, digestive and laxative. Used in minute quantities in Indian cooking, its main purpose is to prevent flatulence and it adds a distinct flavour not dissimilar to garlic.

BAY

Bot: Laurus nobilis

Fam: Lauraceae

Universally used in European cooking. Rather similar to the *tejpatta*, used in Indian cooking.

BLACK CARAWAY
(Black cumin)
Botanical Name: Carum nigrum
Family: Umbelliferae
Hindi: *Shah-jeera, Zira siyah*
Useful in flatulent colic, atonic dyspepsia and spasmodic afflictions of the
bowels. Seed is used parched and powdered or raw and entire. In the former
case it is employed to flavour curries. Used as a condiment with curries and
in batter for frying fish, chicken and vegetables.

CAPSICUM
Botanical Name: Capsicum frutescens or Capsicum annum
Family: Solanaceae
Hindi: *Mirch*
Includes cayenne pepper (capsicum frutescens), paprika (capsicum annum), red pepper, chilli peppers and pimento. All chillies are capsicum,
but all capsicums are not chillies. Capsicums have now travelled around
the world, there are more varieties than one can even imagine. The larger
the capsicum, the milder; the smaller, the hotter. Hotter varieties are
referred to as chillies. Chilli was not known to Indians until about 400
years ago when this crop was first introduced into India by the Portuguese
towards the end of the 15th century.

CHILLIES
Botanical Name: Capsicum annum
Hindi: *Lal mirch*
Cultivated throughout the plains of India. Considered to be stomachic and
stimulant. Green chillies are used for pickling, and ripe ones are mixed
with other ingredients to make sauce. Dried and ground for use like
cayenne pepper. The consumption of chillies is enormous. Principal ingredient in all chutneys and curries. Important ingredient of curry powders.
It is a valuable adjunct to bitters, tonics, and all stimulants. Chilli powder
is made up of powdered chilli and red pepper—cayenne and paprika—
cumin, cloves, marjoram and garlic.

Asian chilli powder is made from ground chillies. It is much hotter than
the Mexican style chilli powder.

CAPSICUM PEPPER
Green, Red, Yellow, Paprika
Botanical Name: Capsicum grossum
Hindi: *Simla mirch*
A spice used for flavouring food—dried fruit of certain varieties of capsicum annum. Also known as 'capsicums' and 'sweet' or 'bell' peppers. This large variety is very mild and sweet in flavour. Used as a vegetable or salad ingredient. Szent Gyorgi, a Hungarian scientist, isolated vitamin C from paprika because early sailors on spice voyages were prone to the disease scurvy. Paprika is the ground red powder of the pepper plant; it is the Hungarian name for sweet pepper.

CARAWAY
Botanical Name: Carum carui
Family: Umbelliferae
Hindi: *Shah jeera, Zira siyah*
Has a pleasant, slightly sharp flavour with a sweet undertone. Seeds are similar to black cumin in appearance but differ in flavour, cannot be used in place of cumin seeds.

  Characteristic agreeable aromatic odour, warm semi-sharp taste in between dill and cumin.

CARDAMOM
Botanical Name: Elettaria cardamomm
Family: Scitamine
Hindi: *Illachi*
Helps after-dinner digestion. Next to saffron, the world's most expensive spice. Cardamoms grow mainly in India and Ceylon. Used in curry powder and used in whole, mixed pickling spice. For full flavour it is best to grind them just before use. Indian cooks prefer the green cardamom.

CARDAMOM BROWN
Greater Cardamom
Botanical Name: Amomum subulatum
Family: Scitamineae
Hindi: *Bari illachi, Bara elachi*
A native of Nepal and Bhutan. The greater cardamom has a fruit about the

size of a nutmeg. Invaluable in certain disorders of the digestive system, marked by scanty and viscid secretion from the intestines, promotes elimination of bile, and is useful in congestion of the liver. The seeds yield a medicinal oil. It is an agreeable, aromatic stimulant. The seeds are aromatic. The greater cardamom is used in the preparation of sweetmeats on account of its cheapness and in curries as a substitute for the small true cardamom.

CARUM
Bishop's Weed, Lovage
Botanical Name: Carum copticum
Family: Umbelliferae
Hindi: *Ajwain*
Same family as parsley and cumin, having the flavour of thyme. *Ajwain* water is used as a medicine in stomach ailments. It has stimulant, tonic and carminative properties and the anti-spasmodic virtues of asafoetida. Administered in flatulence, flatulent colic. As a condiment with curries, in batter for frying fish, chicken and vegetables.

In England and Germany it is used for the manufacture of thymol, enormous quantities of which are now made and used as an antiseptic.

CHIRAULI NUT
Botanical Name: Buchanania latifolia
Family: Anacardiaceae
Hindi: *Chironji, Charoli*
The kernel of this fruit is a common substitute for almonds amongst Indians. Largely used in sweetmeats, its flavour is described as between that of the pistachio and the almond and not unlike the pine nut.

CINNAMON
Botanical Name: Cinnamomum zeylanicum
Family: Laurineae
Hindi: *Dalchini kalmi*
Cinnamon is a stimulant which is aromatic and carminative. Used in flatulence, flatulent colic, spasmodic afflictions of the bowels. Flavouring spice in curry. True cinnamon is native to Sri Lanka. Used in Indian

cookery, pulaos with cardamom and cloves; used in garam masala for curries.

Pleasing fragrant odour and astringent sweetish taste.

CLOVES

Botanical Name: Caryophyllus aromaticus
Family: Myrtaceae
Hindi: *Laung*

This is a stimulant which is aromatic and carminative; used in atonic dyspepsia and in gastric irritability. The oil is used externally in rheumatic pains, headache and toothache, strengthening the gums and perfuming the breath. Useful in carious teeth. Used as a spice throughout India. Is one of the ingredients of garam masala. The word is taken from the Latin *Clavus* and the French *clou* both meaning nail, which describes its shape. Used in Indian pulaos, meat dishes and curries. Strong aromatic odour and hot pungent aromatic taste, less astringent than cinnamon.

COCONUT

Botanical Name: Cocos nucifera
Family: Palmae
Hindi: *Narel, Nariyal, Nariel*
Dry kernel, *Copra, Khopra*

Water from the green fruit makes an excellent cool drink. All the parts of the plant of the coconut are used medicinally. The water of the unripe fruit is described as a fine-flavoured, cooling drink, useful in thirst, fever and urinary disorders. By scraping down the ripe kernel of the coconut and adding a little water to it a white fluid is obtained by pressure, which resembles milk in taste and may be used as a substitute for it. Extracted juice of the grated kernel is used extensively in medicine—in debility, incipient phthisis and cachetic afflictions. Used as part of diet in regional curries of South India and Bengal.

CORIANDER

Botanical Name: Coriandrum sativum
Family: Umbelliferae
Hindi: *Dhanya, Dhania*

Carminative, refrigerant, diuretic, tonic and aphrodisiac. Seeds are universally used as a condiment and form one of the ingredients in curry. Used as flavour in meat products, bakery goods, tobacco, gin and in curry powder. All parts of the coriander plant are used in Asian cooking. Coriander, fresh is an aromatic herb of the parsley family. It resembles flat-leaf parsley in appearance. Do not wash the leaves or remove the roots before storing. Fragrant odour in between parsley and mint, the seeds are universally used as a condiment and form a part of the ingredients in curry.

CUMIN
Botanical Name: Cuminum cyminum
Family: Umbelliferae
Hindi: *Zira, Safaid jera*
Aromatic, carminative. In India it is used as a spice. Cumin seeds form an ingredient of some curry powders and pickles. Cumin is, with coriander, the most essential ingredient in prepared curry powders. Cumin and caraway seeds are similar in appearance, but the flavours are completely different. One cannot replace the other in recipes. It is indispensible to most curries with ingredients which make curry taste like . . . well, curry. Seeds boast a very high protein content. Heavy distinctive aroma, stronger than caraway, and a mild after-taste of anise.

CURRY LEAF
Botanical Name: Murraya koenigii
Family: Rutaceae
Hindi: *Kurry patta, Kari patta, Mitha neem*
Prevents the formation of bile. Cultivated in gardens for the leaves, used in making green chutney. Its leaves are used either fresh or dry, to flavour curries. Leaves are fried in oil, until crisp, at the start of preparing a curry.

FENNEL
Botanical Name: Foeniculum vulgare
Family: Umbelliferae
Hindi: *Sonf*
Fennel is grown in Europe, India and Argentina. A liquorice-like flavour resembling anise. Fennel seed is shaped like a miniature watermelon, it has an agreeable smell and a liquorice flavour.

FENUGREEK

Botanical Name: Trigonella foenumgroecum

Family: Leguminosae

Hindi: *Methi, Muthi*

Fenugreek has been known and valued as a medicine from antiquity. Sanskrit writers describe the seeds as carminative. It is the 'Fanum Gracum' of Latin writers, like Discorides and other Greek authors. Leaves when young are used as a vegetable in India. Seeds used as a condiment to flavour curries. Brownish beige seeds are essential in curries. Green leaves are used in Indian cooking when spiced, the bitter taste is quite piquant and acceptable. Fenugreek has a curryish, celery-like bitter taste.

GARLIC

Botanical Name: Allium sativum

Family: Liliaceae

Hindi: *Lasan, Lahsan, Naharu*

Cultivated all over India. Allylic sulphide is the chief constituent of the oil. As a medicine garlic was held in great repute by the ancient physicians. Also used in modern practice. Almost universal in application and is also prized for its health-giving properties. In particular, garlic is claimed to be an agent which can help regulate the body's cholesterol and cholesterol which inhibits hypertension. Strong odour is the gourmets' major complaint.

GINGER

Botanical Name: Zingiber officinale

Family: Scitamineae roscoe

Hindi: *Adrak* (fresh), *Sonth* (dried root)

Sanskrit name *sringavera*. The Greeks derived the name from Sanskrit. It was also known to the Greeks and Romans as a spice. Grown in many parts of India, but the best and the most exported grows on the coast of Malabar. Described as acrid, heating, carminative, rubefacient and useful in dyspepsia, afflictions of the throat, head and chest, hemorrhoids, rheumatism, urticaria and many other diseases. In European medicine highly valued as mild carminative and enters into many official preparations. Agreeably pungent.

Largely employed as a condiment, especially in the preparation of curries. Essential in most Asian dishes. Fresh ginger root should be used. Powdered ginger cannot be substituted for fresh ginger, for the flavour is quite different. Ginger is a hot, sweet, clean-flavoured spice that gives zest to meat. Fastest growing use for ginger is in beverages such as ginger ale, beer and wine. Today India is its largest grower and exporter but it does flourish elsewhere.

MACE
Botanical Name: Myristica fragrans
Family: Myristiceae
Hindi: *Jaivitri*
Mace and nutmeg are two distinctly different spices produced from a single tree. Nutmeg is used in Indian dishes in some curries. Mace is also used to flavour sauces and sweets. Nutmeg is used grated fine and mace coarsely crushed.

Fragrant nutmeg flavour and aroma with a background mild aroma of saffron.

MINT
Botanical Name: Mentha viridis
Family: Labiatae
Hindi: *Podina*
Although there are many varieties, the common, round-leafed mint is the one most often used in cooking. It adds flavour to many curries, and mint chutney is an essential accompaniment to a biryani meal or as a dipping sauce for samosa. Mint is also used in Laotian fish dishes. It has the property of removing flatulence.

MUSTARD (BROWN)
Botanical Name: Brassica Juncea
Family: Cruciferae
Hindi: *Rye, Rie*
Mustard seeds, tiny, round, blackish-reddish-brown are used throughout India for pickling and for seasoning everything from yoghurt to beans. A product of great antiquity and grown in most parts of the world, this variety of mustard seed is smaller and more pungent than the yellow variety. Indeed the word 'mustard' comes from two Latin words *mustum* and

ardere. Mustum is newly fermented grape juice and *ardere* means to burn. Food history was made the day that mustard met the sausage. In India it is used whole for tempering dishes. It is also an important ingredient in certain masala powders. Efficient substitute, especially in the preparation of mustard poultices. Alba or white mustard is not used in Asian cooking.

MUSTARD, BLACK
Botanical Name: Brassica nigra
Family: Cruciferae
Hindi: *Sarson*
Used for culinary purposes. Cultivated abundantly in India; it extends westward to Egypt. The leaves are used as a vegetable. Seeds are small, round, dark, reticulated. Seeds, whole or broken, used to flavour curries, as for example vindaloo. Used for pickles and culinary purposes; the oil-cake is given to cattle. Mustard oil is used for many preparations of fish and vegetables in Bengal and Northern India.

NIGELLA
Botanical Name: Nigella sativa
Family: Ranunculaceae
Small fennel, Wild onion seed (so called)
Hindi: *Kalonji*
Originally exclusively cultivated in many parts of India for its seeds, indigenous to India. Used in loss of appetite, diarrhoea; as a tonic praised by Hippocrates. The seeds used in India in curries and other dishes. Frequently sprinkled over the surface of bread alongwith seasamum seeds. French cooks employ the seeds as *qautre epices* or *toute epices*. Black seeds are similar to onion seeds and are not to be confused with them.

NUTMEG
Botanical Name: Myristica fragrans
Family: Myristiceae
Hindi: *Jayphal, Jaiphal*
Found wild in Moluccas, Singapore and Penang, as well as Brazil and the West Indies; established in India on the Nilgiri hills. The nutmeg was known to Sanskrit writers by the name of *jatiphala*. Medicinal properties were known to India and was famous as one of their most valuable

308

medicines in **dyspeptic** complaints. Prescribed in the low stages of fever, in consumptive complaints and humoral asthma. Used as tonic for stimulating and digestive purposes. Also used for choleraic diarrhoea, obstructions of the liver and spleen. In European medicine it is regarded as a stimulant and carminative, it is also narcotic; used in atonic diarrhoea, flatulence, colic and some forms of dyspepsia. Sometimes used in garam masala. Very acceptable aromatic odour and a slight bitter but agreeable taste.

ONION
Botanical Name: Allium cepa
Family: Liliaceae
Hindi: *Piyaz*

Cultivated all over India. Volatile oil containing sulphur, albumen, much uncrystallizable sugar and mucilage, phosphoric acid. Volatile oil acts as a stimulant, diuretic and expectorant. Hot and pungent, useful in flatulence. Cultivated very extensively all over India. Herodotus mentions that 1600 talents, equal to £428,800 were paid for the onions and garlic eaten by the workmen engaged in the building of the Great Pyramid. Commonly used onions in Asia are red onions. Most basic of foods, infinitely adaptable and containing rich supplies of vitamin C, minerals, sulphur and other trace elements. Used as a flavouring and thickening agent in curries. Onion is, next to salt, the most valuable of all flavouring substances used in cookery.

PEPPER DRY, Black pepper
Bot: Piper nigrum
Fam: Piperaceae
Hindi: *Kali mirch*

Found in forests of Assam and Malabar and cultivated in the hot damp localities of southern India—earliest articles of Indo-European trade. Sanskrit authors describe black pepper as an acrid, pungent, hot, dry, carminative and useful in intermittent fever, haemorrhoids and dyspepsia. Pepper was the earliest spice used in Europe. Dioscorides knew pepper to be a product of India. Trade in pepper is perhaps the oldest. The most important of all spices, indeed it formed the very symbol of the spice trade, to which Venice, Genoa, and the commercial cities of Central Europe were indebted for a large part of their wealth. Tribute was levied on pepper, the ransom demanded from Rome in 408 AD by Alaric, King of the Goths, included 3000 pounds of pepper and after the conquest of Caesarea in 1101 AD by the Genoese each solider received 2 pounds of pepper as part of his booty. Pepper rents were not uncommon, by means of which the wealthier classes secured from their tenants a supply of their favourite condiment. Pungency due to alkaloids, piperine, piperidine and chavicine.

White pepper corns are the berry gathered when fully ripe, while black ones with more aromatic scent and flavour are picked unripe and retain their covering. Quite simply, pepper is the king of spices. The word 'pepper' is from the Sanskrit *pippali* meaning berry.

POPPY SEEDS
Botanical name: Papaver somniferum
Family: Papaveraceae
Hindi: *Khas-Khas*
Used in Indian curries for thickening since cornflour or other starches are never used. The seeds are ground to a powder or paste. The grinding of poppy seed is easier said than done. They require a special grinder common in Austria and Germany. These are used to add a nut-like flavour to curries. Odour slight, pleasant, nutlike; taste agreeable and decidedly nutty. Poppy seeds come from the same plant as opium. In India, the seeds are used in spicy sauces both to contribute their own flavour and add texture.

RATANJOT
Botanical name: Onosma echioides
Family: Boragineae
Hindi: *Ratanjyot, Ratanjot*
Biennial plant, frequent throughout the western Himalaya, from Kashmir to Kumaon. Widely distributed from Siberia and Kabul to France. Imparts a rich red colour to oils and fats.

SAFFRON

Botanical name: Crocus sativus
Family: Irideae
Hindi: *Zafran, Kesar*

Used in fevers, melancholia and enlargement of the liver. It is also a stimulant. Saffron threads are Orange-red dried stigma of a flower of the crocus family.

Saffron is the aristocrat amongst spices. Its aroma is subtle, its colour is gold, and it is expensive. Today its principal areas of cultivation are Iran, Kashmir and, especially, Spain. Saffron is the stigmas, or female sex organs. Used for one of Spain's traditional dishes, paella. Saffron is used widely in up-market Indian cooking and in many festival foods in Iran. Also used more extensively in northern India than anywhere else. Used in the preparation of rice pulao and curries. Do not confuse it with turmeric, which is sometimes sold as 'Indian saffron'.

SESAME

Botanical name: Sesamum indicum
Family: Pedalineae
Hindi: *Til, Gingli*

The seeds are toasted and ground and mixed into the meal. Eaten by the Hindu population of India. Theophrastus and Dioscorides say that the Egyptians cultivated a plant sesame for the oil contained in its seed and Pliny adds that it came from India. Also mentioned in ancient documents of Egyptian, Hebrew, Sanskrit, Greek and Latin literature. Serviceable in piles. Ground to a paste with water and given with butter to treat bleeding piles. Sesamum oil forms the basis of most of fragrant oils used by Indians medicinally and for cooking. In India they are used in curries and other sauces. Sesame seeds, sources of polyunsaturated fat give an interesting taste and texture to various foods and breads. Used to make *tahina* paste, a standard Middle Eastern condiment.

TAMARIND

Botanical name: Tamarindus indica

Family: Leguminosae

Hindi: *Amli, Imli*

Cultivated throughout India. Indigenous to some parts of South India. One of the most beautiful of the common trees of India. Its name is *tamar i Hind* meaning date of India. *Tamar* in Persian is date. Sanskrit writers consider the fruit 'refrigerant, digestive, carminative and laxative' and useful in diseases supposed to be caused by bile. Diffused in water, it forms a thick tremulous, somewhat glutinous, and turbid liquid, owing to the presence of pectin. Tamarind, nearly every part of which is useful, is necessarily of considerable value. It is dried and sold in packets. For curries and other savoury dishes only the unsweetened tamarind must be used. The pulp is valued for its rather acid sweet taste.

TEJPAT

Indian Cassia Lignea

Botanical name: Cinnamomum tamala

Also Cinnamomum

obtusifoliam

Family: Laurineae

Hindi: *Tejpata*

Leaves of the two given trees are known as *tejpat*. Leaves are aromatic and used in curry. Leaves are also used as a spice. In Indian cookery they take the place of Bay leaves in Europe.

TURMERIC

Botanical name; Curcuma longa

Family: Scitamineae

Hindi: *Haldi*

The rubbing of turmeric and oil is an essential part of the Hindu marriage ceremony, as well as some religious festivals. Used as a stimulant in native medicine. Often administered in disorders of the blood. Its use as an external applicant in bruises, leach bites etc., is perhaps its most frequent medicinal application. Dried rhizome of *Curcuma longa,* grown in India; deep yellow colour used both as condiment and (permitted) dyestuff. Turmeric with its orange yellow colour is a main stay of curry powders. Should never be confused with true saffron and the two should not be used interchangeably. Turmeric originated in India but now is cultivated throughout Southeast Asia and Jamaica. On account of aroma and colour the spice is an essential ingredient in curry powders. Turmeric forms one of the indispensable ingredients in curries and in prepared mustard. Imparts a bright yellow colour to any sauce and adds its own unique musty flavour. Characteristic pepper-like odour and slightly aromatic.

Herbs

SACRED BASIL
Botanical name: Ocimum sanctum
Family: Labiatae
Hindi: *Tulsi*

The *tulsi* is the most sacred plant in the Hindu religion; it is consequently found in or near almost every Hindu house throughout India. Hindu poets say that it protects from misfortune and sanctifies and guides to heaven all who cultivate it. The leaves have expectorant properties, and their juice is used by native physicians for catarrh and bronchitis. This preparation also is applied to the skin in ring-worm and other cutaneous diseases. An infusion of the leaves is used as are for gastric disorders of children, and in hepatic afflictions. The dried leaves are powdered and employed as a snuff in ozaena. The infusion of the leaves is extensively used as a carminative and laxative for children. Leaves are said to possess diaphoretic properties. It is a vital herb and is used extensively in the kitchens of South East Asia. Pounded leaves and/or deep fried leaves are used in practically all the pastes which make curry-type dishes in Thailand, Malaysia and Burma.

COMMON SWEET BASIL
Botanical name: Ocimum basilicum
Family: Labiatae
Hindi: *Kali tulsi*

The plant has a strong aromatic flavour like that of cloves and is often used for culinary purposes as a seasoning. The seeds are sometimes soaked in water and eaten. Leaves form the basis of a celebrated nostrum for the cure of ring-worm, and the bruised leaves are applied to parts stung by

313

scorpions to lessen the pain. The powdered dried leaves are said to be an effectual means of dislodging maggots. The plant is also credited with diaphoretic properties. The juice of the leaves mixed with ginger and black pepper is given in the cold stage of intermittent fever.

DILL

Botanical name: Peucedanum graveolens
Family: Umbelliferae
Hindi: *Sowa, Soya, Kurz*

The fruit and the leaves are both employed to impart a flavour to curries and condiments. Both stalks and seeds are used in pickles and the seeds are also used for flavouring salads and vegetables, particularly cabbage and squash. Dill greens are used as a vegetable. The properties of dill-oil, dill-water, and the other preparations like gripe water in which the fruit is administered, are too well known to require detailed description. It is considered a remedy for all and for colic, forms of indigestion and abdominal pains in women. It is also considered a lactagogue.

MINT

Botanical name: Mentha arvensis
Family: Labiatae
Hindi: *Pudinah, Pudince, Pudina*

A herb of the Western Himalayas, found in Kashmir. This variety yields an essential oil similar to that of peppermint. The dried plant is a refrigerant, diuretic and stimulant. The leaves are eaten and a chutney prepared from the fresh herb is in use all over Northern India. Also used in raitas and condiments. It is used in sauces, jellies, vinegar, salads, candy and other desserts, julep and tea.

Nuts

Nuts are valued in cooking for much more that just their high nutrient content. In savoury dishes they make unusual combinations of flavour and texture and nuts have always been a favourite ingredient in desserts, cakes and cookies. Nuts have always been popular raw, cooked, fried, roasted or ground.

314

The following are some of the most used in cooking.

ALMONDS
Botanical name: Prunus amygdalus
Family: Rosaceae
Hindi: *Badam*
Cultivated in Kashmir, Punjab, Afghanistan and Persia. The almond yields two distinct oils—an essential oil and a fixed or fatty oil. The essential oil is obtained from *var* and *amara*, and is well-known under the name of 'oil of bitter almonds'. Dymock discusses its properties at considerable length. Two kinds of sweet almonds are described—a thick-shelled, and a thin-shelled or *kaghazi* (*amandes des dames* or *amandes sultanes*). Burnt shells are made into toothpowder and the unripe fruit (*chugala*) given as an astringent application to the gums and mouth.

The therapeutic properties and uses of both bitter and sweet almonds, as recognized in Europe, are too well-known to require recapitulation. The seed lobes or kernels of the sweet almonds are largely used as a dessert. Considerable quantities are imported into India from Afghanistan. These add texture and flavour in cooking and baking. Almonds taste particularly good with fish, seafood and chicken. Characteristic soft texture and fragrant taste.

CASHEWNUTS
Botanical name: Anacardium occidentale
Family: Anacardiaceae
Hindi: *Kaju*
Established in the coast forests of India, Chittagong and over South India. Called *kaju* as a rendering of the Brazilian name *acajau*. The French, by a similar transliteration called it *cashew*. The acrid oil is used as an anaesthetic in leprosy, and as a balm in warts, corns and ulcers. Anacardic acid possesses powerful rubefacient properties. Cashew nut is, commonly eaten roasted, a process which improves the flavour. Kidney-shaped, creamy white and sweet, the cashews come mainly from India. They add flavour and texture to curries, casserole dishes, salads, desserts and candies.

CHESTNUTS
Botanical name: Cupuliferae

Family: Cupuliferae

Hindi: *Chestnut*

Introduced in the Himalayas and grown in hilly regions especially in Darjeeling and Khasia Hills. When ground into meal they form an important article of food. Chestnut purée is very rich and must be used sparingly.

HAZELNUTS

Botanical name: Corylus Colurna

Family: Cupuliferae

Hindi: *Findak, Chalgoza*

Found in England, France and the Far-East.

GROUNDNUTS

Peanuts

Botanical name: Arachis hypogaea

Family: Leguminosae popilonaceae

Hindi: *Moongphali*

Cultivated throughout India, but chiefly in South India and Bombay. Seeds of this plant afford on extraction a clear straw-coloured, non-drying oil. It resembles olive oil in taste and in India is now being used as a substitute for it in medicinal preparations. Keeps for a longer time without becoming rancid. In Europe it is now extensively used as a substitute for olive or salad oil, both medicinally and for culinary purposes. Has a distinct place in the manufacture of soap. Little more than 40 years ago the oil was unknown to European commerce.

Arachis oil forms a good substitute for olive oil in pharmacy. In the United States is known as the 'peanut'. The most common nut, shelled, roasted and salted, made into peanut butter or peanut oil. Use in cooking is vast, ranging from peanut soup to peanut cookies, cakes and candies.

PINENUTS

Neosia

Botanical name: Pinus gerardiana

Family: Coniferae
Hindi: *Chilgoza, neoza*

Found in the valleys of the North-West Himalaya from Kunawar west-wards. Seeds are considered an anodyne and stimulant. Staple food of the inhabitants of Kunawar. Widely used in Eastern and Italian cooking. They give flavour to meat, rice and vegetable dishes. The chief product of this tree is the almond-like seed, contained in the cones. When the cones ripen, they are plucked before they open, and heated to make the scales expand. The seed is then easily taken out.

PISTACHIO NUTS
Botanical name: Pistacia vera
Family: Anacardiaceae
Hindi: *Pista*

Small tree, forming forests at altitudes of 3000 feet and upwards. Well-known as the pistachio nut, is oval-shaped and varies in size with the amount of cultivation which the tree has. In India the nut is much appreciated by all classes, is a very common article of food with the more well-to-do classes, and a frequent ingredient of confectionery. It is also considerably used in European desserts. By Indians the nuts are generally roasted with their shells in hot sand and then thrown into a hot paste of salt-water, and stirred so as to make the salt adhere to the shell. These nuts are grown in Turkey and Iran. Roasted unsalted pistachio—in ice-creams in cakes and candy are delicious additions to pulaos, stuffings and terrines.

Other Ingredients

SILVER FOIL
Latin: Argentum
Hindi: *Chandi-ka-varaq*

Prepared by beating pure silver into a very thin leaf. It is edible and is used for decoration. It is prescribed by Indian doctors along with different preserves, particularly that of *anvala* fruit. It is used as an amalgam in preventing tooth decay.

EMBLIC BERRIES

Botanical name: Phyllanthus emblica

Family: Euphorbiaceae

Hindi: *Amla, Anvala*

The acidic fruit, which is the size of a small gooseberry is used for foods and preserves. It is made into a sweet-meat with sugar or eaten raw as a condiment and also prepared as a pickle. It is an important ingredient in the *Hindu Materica Medica*. It is an astrigent, refrigerent, good for the heart and a purifier of the humours of the body.

Fresh fruit contains 20 mg vitamin C per 100 g edible portion. Dry fruit is used as a colouring agent and imparts a beautiful brownish yellow shade of colour

KHOYA

Dried fresh whole milk—buffalo's or cow's. It is boiled briskly in a heavy pan (*kadahi*) stirring all the time until it leaves the sides of the pan and has stopped sizzling and is reduced to a thick dry lump, ivory white in colour.

KULCHA

Small leavened bread baked lightly in an oven. Much like a flat large muffin.

QUINCE

Botanical name: Cydonia vulgaris

Family: Rosaceae

Hindi: *Bihi*

Pear-shaped sour fruit of Cydonia species, with flesh similar to that of the apple; rich in pectin and used chiefly in jams and jellies; used to be known as the apple and the vine. Cultivated in the North-west Himalayas up to 5,500 feet and in the Kangra groves. Grows wild in North of Persia near the Capsian Sea and in South Caucasus and Anatolia. The fruit is considered a tonic for the brain and the heart. It is also eaten baked, and used in preserves and relishes.

318

Proximate Principles and Energy*

Name of foodstuff	Edible portion percent	Per 100 g of edible portion						
		Moisture (g)	Protein (g)	Fat (g)	Minerals (g)	Fibre Carbohydrates	Other (g)	Calories
1	2	3	4	5	6	7	8	9
Asafoetida	...	16.0	4.0	1.1	7.0	4.1	67.8	297
Cardamom	...	20.0	10.2	2.2	5.4	20.1	42.1	229
Chillies, green	90	85.7	2.9	0.6	1.0	6.8	3.0	29
Chillies, dry	...	10.0	15.9	6.2	6.1	30.2	31.6	246
Cloves, dry	100	25.2	5.2	8.9	5.2	9.5	46.0	285
Coriander	...	11.2	14.1	16.1	4.4	32.6	21.6	288
Cumin seeds	...	11.9	18.7	15.0	5.8	12.0	36.6	356
Fenugreek seeds	...	13.7	26.2	5.8	3.0	7.2	44.1	333
Garlic, dry	85	62.0	6.3	0.1	1.0	0.8	29.0	142
Ginger, fresh	...	80.9	2.3	0.9	1.2	2.4	12.3	67
Mace	...	15.9	6.5	24.4	1.6	3.8	47.8	437
Nutmeg	...	14.3	7.5	36.4	1.7	11.6	28.5	472
Pepper, dry	...	13.2	11.5	6.8	4.4	14.9	49.5	305
Tamarind pulp	...	20.9	3.1	0.1	2.9	5.6	67.4	283
Turmeric	...	13.1	6.3	5.1	3.5	2.6	69.4	349

* W. R. Aykroyd, *The Nutritive Value of Indian foods and the Planning of Satisfactory Diet*, Indian Council for Medical Research, New Delhi, 1963

319

Table of Food Values

II Minerals (per 100 g edible portion).

Name of FoodStuff	Calcium, mg	Magnesium, mg	Oxalic acid, mg	Phosphorus Total (a), mg	Phosphorus Phytin (b), mg	Phosphorus (b) as per-cent of (a)	Iron Total (c) mg	Iron Ionisable (d), mg	Iron (b) as per-cent of (a)	Sodium, mg	Potassium, mg	Copper, mg	Sulphur, mg	Chlorine, mg	Acid base balance ml. N/10 solution Acid	Acid base balance ml. N/10 solution Base
1	2	3	4	5	6	7	8	9	10	11	12	13	14	15	16	17
Asafoetida	690	:	:	50	:	:	:	22.2	:	:	:	:	:	:	:	:
Cardamom	130	:	:	160	:	:	5.0	0.6	12	:	:	:	:	:	:	:
Chillies, green	30	24	67	80	7	9	1.2	0.4	33	:	:	:	:	:	:	:
Chillies, dry	630	:	:	393	320	81	17.9	2.1	12	6.5	217	1.55	34	15	:	12
Cloves, dry	160	:	:	370	71	19	2.3	1.3	56	32	990-	:	:	:	:	:
Coriander	740	:	:	100	:	:	4.9	0.7	14	:	530	:	:	:	:	:
Cumin seeds	1,080	:	:	511	153	30	31.0	:	:	:	:	:	:	:	:	:
Fenugreek seeds	160	:	:	370	:	:	14.1	:	:	126	980	:	:	:	:	:
Garlic, dry	30	:	:	310	:	:	1.3	0.7	54	19.0	530	:	:	:	:	:
Ginger, fresh	20	:	:	60	:	:	2.6	0.6	23	:	:	:	:	:	:	:
Mace	180	:	:	1.00	:	:	12.6	:	:	:	:	:	:	:	:	:
Nutmeg	120	:	:	240	:	:	4.6	0.7	15	:	:	:	:	:	:	:
Pepper, dry	460	:	:	198	115	58	16.8	3.2	19	:	:	:	:	:	:	:
Tamarind pulp	170	:	:	110	:	:	10.9	2.4	22	:	:	:	:	:	:	:
Turmeric	150	:	:	282	97	34	18.6	1.8	9	25.0	3,300	:	:	:	:	:

Table of Food Values

III Vitamins (per 100 g edible portion)

Name of FoodStuff	Vitamin A value, I.U.	Thiamine, mg.	Riboflavin mg.	Nicotinic acid, mg.	Vitamin C mg.	Biotin, µg.	Folic acid, µg.	Choline, mg.	Inositol, mg.	Pantothenic acid, mg.	Pyridoxine, mg.	Vitamin K, mg.
1	2	3	4	5	6	7	8	9	10	11	12	13
Asafoetida	8	0	0.04	0.3	0	..	..	..	..	..	..	..
Cardamom	0	0.22	0.17	0.8	0	..	1550	..	..	..	..	..
Chillies, green	292	0.19	0.39	0.9	111	..	..	..	..	..	..	..
Chillies, dry	576	0.93	0.43	9.5	50	..	..	..	..	..	..	..
Cloves, dry	422	0.08	0.13	1.1	0	..	..	..	..	..	..	..
Coriander	1570	0.22	0.35	1.1	0	..	1077	..	..	..	..	..
Cumin seeds	870	0.55	0.36	2.6	3	..	1065	..	..	..	..	..
Fenugreek seeds	160	0.34	0.29	1.1	0	..	1161	..	..	..	..	..
Garlic, dry	0	0.16	0.23	0.4	13	..	..	..	..	..	..	..
Ginger, fresh	67	0.06	0.03	0.6	6	2.4	..	..	..	..	..	..
Mace	5045	0.25	0.42	104	0	3.8	..	..	..	..	..	..
Nutmeg	0	0.33	0.01	1.4	0	11.6	..	..	..	..	..	..
Pepper, dry	1800	0.09	0.14	1.4	0	14.9	..	..	..	..	..	..
Tamarind pulp	100	..	0.07	0.7	3	5.6	..	..	..	..	..	..
Turmeric	50	0.03	0	2.3	0	..	..	..	..	..	..	..

Indian and Botanical Names

Name of foodstuff	Indian names	Botanical names
1. *Cereals and grain products*		
Arrowroot flour	Arroroat	Maranta arundinacea
Rice	Chawal	Oryza sativa
Sago	Sagudana, Saboodana	Metroxylon sago
Semolina	Sooji	Triticum aestivum
Vermicelli	Sewian	Triticum aestivum
Wheat flour, whole	Atta	Triticum aestivum
Wheat flour, refined, flour, white floor	Maida	Triticum aestivum
2. *Dry beans, pulses and legumes*		
Bengal gram, chick pea, Garbanzo (American)	Chana	Cicerarietinum
Bengal gram, roasted	Bhuna chana	Cicerarietinum
Bengal gram, split or chick pea split	Chane ki dal	Cicerarietinum
Black gram	urad	Phaseolusmungo
Butter beans	Fras bean, Safed beans	Phaseolus vulgaris
Kidney beans	Rajmah	Phaseolus vulgaris
Green gram	Moong	Phaseolus oureus
Lentil	Masoor	Lens culinaris Medic
Red gram pigeon pea	Arhar, Tuar	Cojonus cajan
3. *Vegetables*		
Banana, raw	Kela	Musa paradisiaca
Beet root	Chukandar	Beta vulgaris
Brinjal,	Baingan	Solanum melon gena
Aubergine (Britain), Eggplant (America)		
Cabbage	Band gobee	Brassica oleracea
Capsicum	Simla mirch	Capsicum grossum
Carrots	Gajar	Daucus carota
Cauliflower	Phool gobee	Brassica oleracea
Courgettes	Ghia tori	Cucurbita pepo
(Britain or France), Zucchini (America)		
Cucumber	Kheera	Cucumis sativus
Drumstick, greens		Moringa Oleifera
Coriander greens	Dhania	Coriandrum

Name of foodstuff	Indian names	Botanical names
		sativum
Dill greens	Soya	Glycine max
Fenugreek greens	Methi	Trigonella foenu-mgraecum
Mustard greens	Sarson	Brassica campestris
Rape greens	Sarson	Brassica napus
Spinach	Palak	Spinacea oleraceae
Gourds		Lagenaria family
Crookneck gourd round gourd	Lowki, Ghia, Kaddu	Lagenaria vulgaris
Jack fruit	Kathal heterophyllus	Artocarpus
Knol khol	Ganth gobi	Brassica caulorpa
Lotus root Bhean	Kamal gato, nelumbo	Nelumbium
Marrow	Hara kaddu, Kaddu safed	Cucurbita pepo
Morel	Gucchi	Morchella esculanta
Mushrooms, champignon	Khumb Button mushroom	Agoricus campestris Agoricus bisporus
Okra, lady's finger	Bhindi	Ambelmoschus
Pearl onions, spring onions	Hara pyaz	Allium cepa
Peas, green	Hara matar	Pisum sativum
Potatoes	Alu	Solanum tuberosum
Pumpkin	Kaddu	Cucurbita pepo
Radish, white	Muli	Raphanus sativus
Shallots	Hara pyaz	Allium ascalonicum
Squashes	Ghia	Trichosonthes
Tomatoes	Tamatar	Lycopersicon esculentum
Turnips	Shalgam	Brassica rapa
Yams:		
ordinary	Ratalu	Thyphonium trilobatum
elephant	Zaminkand	Amorphophallus companulatus

Fish

Common names	Zoological names
Baby sea bass	Bicentrarchus labrox
Beckti	
Betki	
Begti, Bhetki	Lates calcarifer
Carp	Cyrinus carplo
Cod	Gadus morhus
Flounder	
Halibut	Hippoglossus
Herring (Indian),	Poellona brachysoma
Mali	Clupea harengus
	Rasbora daniconius
Monk	Lophius piscotorius
Plaice	Pleuronectes platessa
Pomfret	
White	Stromateus sinensis
Black	Formio niger
Rahu, Rohu	Labeo rohita
Rainbow trout	Salmotrutta
Red mullet	Mullus barbatus
Red snapper	Salman family
Shingara, singala	Arius Dussumieri
	(cat fish/Arius sona
Sole	Cynoglossus semi fasciatus
Dover sole	Ophiocephalus striatus
Surmai	Cybium commersoni

References

Aykroyd, W.R., *The Nutritive Value of Indian Foods & The Planning of Satisfactory Diets*, New Delhi: Indian Council of Medical Research, 1963.

Copeland, Marks, *Varied Kitchens of India*, Harmondsworth: Penguin Books, 1981.

David, Elizabeth, *Spices, Salts & Aromatics in the English Kitchen*, Harmondsworth: Penguin Books, 1981.

Govindarajan, V.S., *Capsicum-production, technology, chemistry -Evaluation of quality - Processed products*, 3 papers (Cardomom, Ginger, Pepper), Florida: Boca, Raton, 1977, 1980, 1981.

Greenberg, Sheldon & Elizabeth, Lambert Ortiz, *The Spice of Life*, London: Mermaid Books Blackrod Ltd., 1984.

Loewenfeld, Claire & Philippa Back, *The Complete Books of Herbs & Spices*, Devon: David & Charles Publishers Ltd., 1985.

Mushran, Sarswati, *Ruchika* (Hindi), New Delhi: Bhavnani & Sons, 1971.

Prakash, Om, *Food & Drinks in Ancient India*, Delhi: Munshiram Manoharlal, 1961.

Pruthi, J.S., *Spices & Condiments*, Delhi: National Book Trust.

Purseglove, J.W., Brown, E.G., Green, C.L. & Robbins, S.R.J., *Spices*, in *Tropical Agricultural Series*, 2 vols., New York: Orient Longman, 1981.

Veeraswamy, E.P., *Indian Cookery*, Bombay: Jaico Publishing House, 1987.

Walker, Jane, *Creative Cooking with Spices*, London: Apple Press Ltd., 1985.

Watt, George, *A Dictionary of the Economic Products of India*, 10 vols., Calcutta: Government Printing Press, 1889.

INDEX